The Making o

THE MAKING OF A PURE POET

Rilke's *Letters to a Young Poet* (1904-1908)
and his life while writing them

Things That Happen When Reading Rilke

Volume One

AUGUSTUS YOUNG

Ashgrove Publishing
London

'Then the poet suddenly found himself transformed'

Søren Kierkegaard (1843)

'Happy are those who know behind all language there stands that which is beyond words…'

Rainer Maria Rilke (1910)

'As for me, poor poet, I've broken my arms embracing clouds'

Charles Baudelaire (1857)

'Rilke was a pure poet even when he washed his hands'

Rudolf Kassner (1927)

Where an asterisk appears in the text, see the following *Note* (to myself):

Contents

•

Preface – 7
Prologue – 9
Introduction – 11

Chapter One: Pawing the Ground: letters one and two (2-4/1903) – 33

Chapter Two: Getting into his Stride: letter three (4/1903) – 39

Chapter Three: 'Black Widow Waves': letter four (7/1903) – 49

Chapter Four: Matters Arising from Letter Four – 57

    1. The Worpswede Monograph – 57
    2. On 'Living an Idea' – 59
    3. 3. *Sehnsucht/Geschlecht*: – 60
    4. 'Sex of the Mind' – 64
    5. Marital musical chairs: – 65
    6. 'Love your solitude' – 66
    7. The Novel – 67
    8. How to Handle the Family – 69
    9. A Repetition Forward: – 70

Chapter Five: Rome and Room Enough: letter five (10/1903) – 71

Chapter Six: A Christmas Greeting: letter six (12/1903) – 77

Chapter Seven: Introduction to the Jobian Tendency – 89

Chapter Eight: 'The World is an Unfinished Work': mentors (Lou and Rodin) – 93

Chapter Nine: 'Love is a sealed parcel': letter seven (5/1904) – 99

Chapter Ten: 'We are alone': letter eight (8/1904) – 113

Chapter Eleven: The New Love – 129

Contents

Chapter Twelve: Gender Politics in a Cold Climate (Ellen Key) – 141

Chapter Thirteen: A Cold Reception in a Hot Climate (Rodin and Rilke) – 155

Chapter Fourteen: A Pause for Thought on the Transmigration of Words – 167

Chapter Fifteen: Eleventh Hour Redemptions – 171

Chapter Sixteen: The Short Goodbye: Letter Nine (11/1904) – 183

Chapter Seventeen: Rilke on a High – 193

Chapter Eighteen: Sympathy by Other Means – 199

Chapter Nineteen: On a Peak: letter ten (12/1908) – 221

Chapter Twenty: 'Requiem for a friend' – 229

Chapter Twenty-One: A Princess Comes to the Rescue – 237

Chapter Twenty-Two: What Happened to Kappus? – 241

Chapter Twenty-Three: What Happened to Rilke – 245

Chapter Twenty-Four: A Boring War and its Aftermath – 253

Chapter Twenty-Five: What's Wrong with America? – 263

Chapter Twenty-Six: Rilke the Inimitable Poet – 269

Chapter Twenty-Seven: A Word from the Author – 277

Epilogue: A Lap of Honor (1925-26) – 285

Post-script: The Last Word to Rilke – 295

Appendix – Guiding Notes to literary and philosophical terms – 299

Chronology of Rilke's Life – 307

Preface

•

Travels into the mysterious interior of Rilke (1875-1926) are not for those in search of the literal. In order to encourage readers to accompany me on this journey, I provide in the appendix a) a short lexicon of literary and philosophic terms that signpost his trajectory, and b) a biographical chronology of two of the three main protagonists, Rilke and Søren Kierkegaard.* The third is the author, who shyly lurks behind Roland Barthes's reader – 'I have no biography… I am the story that happens to me.' Reading Rilke happened to me as a story. This book tells it.

---

*The biographical chronology for Kierkegaard will appear in the second volume.

Prologue

•

When he began writing to the young poet, Rilke was twenty-eight and preoccupied with four salient concerns: his estrangement from his wife, Clara Westhoff, the mother of his eighteen-month child; his love-hate engagement with Paris and Auguste Rodin, the sculptor; starting on a novel; and the modernisation of his poetry.

Inevitably, the quartet interact, and by investigating them (mainly through letters, and memoirs, *i.e.*, primary sources), I seek to weave a patchwork portrait of the poet and man, and his intimates, most particularly Clara, whom he married on the rebound from her friend Paula Becker, and Lou Andreas-Salomé, the friend he corresponded with most openly and regularly during this period of personal and artistic crisis. Through marriage, Rilke had Clara more or less in a vice grip, but he was putty in the hands of Lou, fourteen years older than him a formidable woman of the world made him change his first name from René to Rainer. It sounded more manly).

The titular poet is Franz Xaver Kappus, a cadet in the elite branch of the Military Academy that Rilke attended a decade before. Three years after Rilke's death, Kappus edited *Letters to a Young Poet* (1929). In the preface he says he was inspired to write to Rilke because 'I was on the verge of committing myself to a career which was directly opposed to my natural inclinations', and felt 'if anyone was to understand this dilemma it would be the author of *To Celebrate Myself* [1899]'. His replies to the ten letters were not kept but, as Rilke studiously responded to matters raised, it is possible to get a fair idea of their key content.

Would-be poets approaching established ones with their poems often get short shrift. Max Jacob returned the juvenilia of Edmond Jabès in an ashtray. Ezra Pound scrawled in pencil on the back of a batch of poems a young poet sent him in Rapallo: 'Not hopeless if you are less than twenty-one'. A. S. J. Tessimond was twenty-three. Kappus (nineteen) could not in his wildest dreams have expected such a generous response from Rilke: ten letters amounting to about fifty pages, immaculately scripted in a miniscule hand.

How did Kappus react to receiving a storm of letters from an acclaimed German poet over a period of eighteen months (the tenth letter came four years later)? No doubt he was flattered to be taken into his

PROLOGUE

confidence. But the correspondence was by no means one way. The young poet clearly had a mind of his own. I have attempted to reconstruct how Rilke's letters might have been received by him and, with the help of biographic information, the effect they had on Kappus's life.

Letters, particularly edited ones, are not written on tablets of stone, and inevitably my reading between the lines includes some subjective speculation. Although, having spent thirteen years reading around them, I'd like to think my guess-work is 'educated'. But I'm mindful of a comment Rilke made to Lou Salomé (letter, 1904): 'The recognition of a writer is often based on the sum of misunderstandings that gather around a name'. I would mollify the caution by countering that misunderstandings have not been unknown to lead to the truth by the backdoor.

In reading Rilke, Søren Kierkegaard is always at the back of the mind. The Danish philosopher was his 'spiritual grand-uncle' (unmarried). At the turn of the century Rilke started to learn Danish in order to study him in the original. During his engagement to Clara, they read Kierkegaard together, especially Søren's courtship letters. Inauspiciously, as the pivotal motif in Kierkegaard's work is the rejection of his fiancée. Rilke waited till after his marriage to put Clara on the long finger. But he isn't drawn to Kierkegaard's philosophy for sentimental reasons merely. Kierkegaard saw himself as a poet who couldn't write poems: 'I lack the experience to go with the gifts that God gave me. Nevertheless, through them I've reached an understanding with the truth by way of poetical ideas.'

Poetical ideas abound in *The Letters*, influenced by many hands, not least the writings of Rudolf Kassner, the eugenicist-philosopher. However, as they only met in 1907, and there are no known letters between them in the first decade of the century, his presence in my text is drawn from memoirs and letters to mutual contacts. Their friendship though was one of the most lasting in his life. The eighth *Duino* elegy is dedicated to him. Kassner commented with brilliance on the work and with mocking affection on the life ('Rilke was a pure poet even when he washed his hands'). He felt the need to apply a certain 'ironic logic' to some of Rilke's more unexpected ideas.

Finally, as the letters to Kappus were a prelude to his future as a pure poet, I felt it necessary to look into how his hopes were realized. In 1923, Hugo Von Hofmannsthal (1874-1929) wrote to Rilke on receiving a copy of *The Sonnets for Orpheus*, 'You are a rarity amongst poets in that you transform your style from book to book. Each one is a surprise.' The transformations that lead to *The Sonnets* and the *Duino Elegies* would not come as a complete surprise to anyone who has read *The Letters*.

Introduction

•

Rilke's Dog

Port-Vendres, 11 November 2006

The local cinema has a late-night performance of Rilke's *Letters to a Young Poet*. The actor is Laurent Terzieff. I'm paying homage to the star of Luis Bunuel's *Milky Way*, a road movie set on the pilgrimage from Rome to Santiago de Compostela. I saw it in the Everyman in London eons ago and all I can remember is Christ being dissuaded by the Virgin Mary from shaving off his beard.

There is a suspicion of cheap wine and unwashed clothes in the air. The sparse audience has been augmented by tramps in from the cold (high winds have been blowing from the snow-capped mountains). I sit at the back; not sure I'll be staying. As the lights go down a tramp with a large dog sneaks in and installs himself on the floor behind me. I had noticed him earlier crouching outside in the eaves. I wondered if he was blind as he wore sunglasses in the dark.

Terzieff reads a Rilke poem in silken French between each letter. Something of a respite from the hectoring monologues rolled out with *Parigot* uvular Rs (*grassayer*). Alas, the beautiful young man with the slight strabismus is now a skinny old dear unsteady on his feet. I can't bear to look at him. His movements are exaggerated as though regulated by pulleys. I wonder why he's in Port-Vendres, a nowhere town on the theatrical map. Then I remember that in *Milky Way* Terzieff plays a vagabond who preys on pilgrims, and Port-Vendres is a sacred stop on the route to Santiago De Compostela. He is revisiting his glory days. Perhaps.

The dog has a hunter's raised nose and lowered tail. But, apart from a whimper during the barely audible rendering of 'A Young Girl's Tomb', and a yap when Terzieff's angular form becomes a giant shadow thrown on the screen in 'Blind Man. Paris', his stance is attentive, a retriever waiting for his master to set him off.

'One has to be able at every moment to place one's hand on the earth like the first human being.' Terzieff concludes the Rilke letters, leaving the idea hanging in the air as though it will make sense when it falls to

Introduction

earth. The audience is expecting more, but the dog is on to Rilke's scent and breaks the silence with a single bark. The applause comes belatedly.

I don't wait for Laurent Terzieff's curtain-call. Having heard Rilke's 'Blind Man. Paris', I'm in a hurry to translate it.

After a night of pounding the boards in my attic, I come up with:

> Look, there he goes interrupting the traffic
> like a black crack running through a china cup.
> In his darkness the city doesn't exist for him.
> It traces on his fleeting shadow a graphic
> transparency of sights that he cannot take in.
>
> What he sees in himself causes the hold up.
> His insight illuminates the world, and imbues
> the streets with little waves of feeling, a frisson
> that leaves us dumbstruck as he lifts his hand to choose
> some bystander to lend an arm to help
> him across the boulevard. No one could refuse
> with the almost festive air he offers himself.

But I'm not satisfied. Too literal. John Jordan's comment, 'The crack in the teacup oughtn't only open on the land of the dead but also on the perilous seas', although he is the wisest of critics, is no help. I can't relocate Paris to Le Havre. Maybe the poem, like the blind man, needs a dog.

I turn instead to the blindman's song in *Madame Bovary*. His leering intrusions at embarrassing moments unnerve her. I've been trying to render it into English ever since Joab Comfort, my all-knowing friend and counsellor, told me Flaubert got it from Charles Baudelaire, whose poems of the damned haunted Rilke. In the small hours I drop off and next morning find:

> Sometimes a girl in the heat of the day
> with dreams of love gets carried away.
> Her ardent fingers pluck ears of *blé*
> before they're ripe and make a nosegay.
> And leaning over the garden wall

where all the young men are playing ball,
she throws to the wind her harvest gift,
which blows it back, and her hemlines lift...

The dog would like the doggerel.

•

Invitation to the Voyage

I jump out of bed. 'One has to be able at every moment to place one's hand on the earth like the first human being.' The idea lands badly. But as I no longer know my primal self from Adam, I decide it's time to read *Letters to a Young Poet* properly. Absorbing it years ago as a literary boy in English translation, understanding was the last thing on my mind.

By dusting down my technical German (pre-medical studies required a foreign language), I read the original, though hesitantly. But now I'm more at home with French, I gain confidence with Claude Porcell's superb French translation. Particularly as when I cross-check them on a surprising detail, I invariably find they are in close accord. Still, despite Porcell's generous annotations, Rilke's meanings often evade me. And so, to accompany further readings, I decide to embark on a voyage into his life and work.

It proved to be an odyssey longer than Ulysses', of whom Du Bellay says in his poem '*Heureux qui comme Ulysse*', 'Happy is the man who returns from a voyage overflowing with thoughts and experiences.' I would shyly say that my return after twelve years (Ulysses was away ten) was not without both. But, recalling Homer's hero wasn't exactly welcomed home, I worried what the reception of potential readers would be? At best, I hoped poetry lovers would greet me like the father did the Prodigal Son, and at worst, feared literary critics would be the older brother.

Note (to myself): John Ruskin dismissed the critics as 'beating the air'. They are 'bats amongst the birds', according to Voltaire. But they are a necessary evil, I think. Like talking to Joab Comfort to confirm that I'm less wrong than I fear, or that I had better think again. For instance, 'evil', he would tell me, is an amateur concept invented by the theologians; just say 'necessary'.

Introduction

No voyage is without its setbacks and detours. But when I'm diverted – captured by notional pirates or misguided by delusionary shortcuts – I hope the reader is diverted too. Travelling in the intricate terrain of Rilke's mind calls for interim stops. But it is not a journey into the unknown or the unknowable. He left tracks in poems and sigh-posts in letters and one can expect to arrive at a place where his reality exposes itself. I've logged his itinerary so I can make the return journey and write up a report. That said, tighten your belt, dear reader, and go with his flights and my fancies. Richard Brautigan's dust-jacket blurb for Ed Dorn's *Gunslinger*, 'Thanks for taking me along. It was fine trip with some splendid scenery', be our guide.

•

Context

Letters are written (and read) in solitude, and Rilke cultivated solitude like no other. He wrote so many that it would take a hundred years of solitude to read them all. The letters tended to be long. Ten pages was nothing to him. Despite his impatience to get his thoughts down on paper, the tight-knit handwriting might strain the eyes but was always perfectly legible. What he called his 'letter labour' was less a personal communication than a self-examination of his state of mind and writing. Those written on dove-blue notepaper were billets doux. Letters also served to woo potential patrons.

In 1920 he wrote to Baladine ('Merline') Klossowska, the mother of the painter Balthus, on dove blue: 'Please excuse my tardy response to your letter. But think, this morning alone I wrote a hundred and fifteen.' An exaggeration is a relative truth. Over seventeen thousand letters have been recovered from recipients for the Rilke archive, mostly impassioned meditations on art, poetry, religion, life and love, sent to his support system of friends, fellow poets, patrons, ardent schoolgirl admirers and even housekeepers. They are as much a part of his oeuvre as his published work.

When in August 1902 Rilke leaves his rustic home in Worpswede (in the far north of Germany) for Paris, to stay in student digs in Rue Touillier, he sends Clara, his wife at one-remove, long letters veering between ecstasy and horror at city life. Tranches from them were to become the opening of his autobiographical novel, *The Notebooks of Malte Laurids Brigge*. Everywhere he looked there were hospitals and sick people, and 'the ferocious poverty that shames the grandeur of monuments and conspicuous wealth'. On the streets he notes the faces flying past him, 'hell-bent, without hiding anything. All the nuances of joy, of misery and loneness overlap one another, wave upon wave, each new face perpetuating the memory of the previous one, but stamped with a reality that passes into the next look, faster and faster until the vital flow levitates and takes shape as a falling star of faces lit up by a comet's tail of those yet to come.'

Apart from introducing himself to Rodin, Rilke keeps to himself, a model tenant, not mixing with the students, fearing his French would be misunderstood. He discovers Paris all on his own and it's as intimidatingly brutal as Charles Baudelaire forewarned in his essay 'Counsel to Literary Youths' (1846). He writes to Heinrich Vogeler, the founder of the Worpswede commune and his mentor, 'I'm only staying on in Paris because it's Difficult' (*Schwer* as opposed to *leicht* [easy] meant something special to him having read Nietzsche's *The Gay Science*). Nevertheless, he could wax lyrical to Paula Becker celebrating 'Dusk falling on the purple flowers in the Luxembourg Gardens', and 'Paris's insatiable nights of spices, of life, of music, and dresses'.

His letters to Clara become more perfunctory, like asking for his last letter to be returned. He is burying himself in books at the National Library in order to bone up on French literature, in particular Baudelaire and Flaubert. In a note to Rodin he confides that, 'books in Paris are more discreet. They speak to you slowly and in a low voice. This contrast brings benefits,' and promises himself that when visiting his studio again, he won't be so tongue-tied.

But feeling that he is being transformed by the shock of the new, the letters to friends, apart from Lou, almost dry up: 'What good is it to say to someone that I've changed? I am not who I was, and have nothing in common with the former me. And I can hardly write to strangers, to people that didn't know me' (*The Notebooks of Malte Laurids Brigge*).

But the resolve has two exceptions: Ellen Key, the Swedish educationalist and proto-feminist who wrote to him about his last book *Tales of the Good Lord*, to whom he confides his life story without mentioning his separation from Clara. Secondly, his correspondence with the young poet. It begins after Christmas, and for the next two years it concentrates his mind on the transformation that he thought would have been wasted on familiars (excepting Lou and, to a lesser extent, Clara).

INTRODUCTION

The nine substantial letters to Franz Xaver Kappus were sent between April 1903 and November 1904. At the outset, the young poet is on the verge of twenty and unpublished. Rilke is twenty-eight and the author of ten collections of poems and stories. He is working on two fronts: *The Notebooks of Malte Laurids Brigge*, which begins like a long letter to himself (though it was to Clara); and the 'thing-poems' (*dinggedichte*), his breakthrough to modernism, influenced by Rodin, Cezanne and the shock of city-living.

In the 'thing-poems', the human world is inverted in non-human terms, objectified like toys playing with a child, or tackle with a fisherman. It's very Cartesian (to Descartes, we are all things). But it owes most to Nietzsche's concept of 'reversal': what the landscape thinks of the sightseer, the animal of its master, the knife and fork of the eater, any object of its user.

Rilke uses verbal-sound effects and set-square syntax to solidify the object/subject. Sometimes, as in the poem 'The Carousel', he deploys elided imagery ('the little blue girl'), or repetition of descriptive phrases ('the white elephant comes around again') to catch the rotations of the merry-go-round. Most of his 'thing-poems' were to appear in the two-volume *New Poems* (1907/8) where, nevertheless, his trademark neo-symbolism is still often in evidence, mounting metaphor on metaphor, in line with earlier work. In order to keep his German readers afloat, he hadn't burnt all his boats, but they had to do some unaccustomed baling.

In order to put *Letters to a Young Poet* in context, I supplemented my reading of *The Notebooks of Malte Laurids Brigge* (1910) and the *New Poems* with coterminous letters to Clara, the wife he sent back to her parents, and, of course, to Lou. The content inevitably overlaps between the three, but his different angulation towards each offers a fourth dimension. He may apologise to Lou and Clara for his 'desperate exaggerations that seek to get to the bottom of (my) Sincerity', but not to Franz Xaver Kappus.

Correspondence is a fuelling art, burnt up by the answer and rekindled by the ricochet. As Rilke didn't keep letters, the most direct way of guessing how they were received was to read his next one. He assiduously picks up issues that his interlocutor raises. In order to read his mind, recipients had to be patient, or skip to the ending, as often he gift-wrapped his response in fancy preambles. These served to clear his mind of something he was working on, but also acted as strategic padding to forestall the impact of the final paragraph. The signing off with Clara and Kappus could range from conspicuous impatience to fulsome praise with a bout of self-pity in between. 'The pith is in the postscript' (Hazlitt). He was more circumspect with Lou as he felt a need to justify himself with her.

Note (to myself): I hasten to add that the letters to those he doesn't feel responsible for or to, relaxes him, and he can pursue, without constraint, his 'relationship with the world of things', or how 'consciousness shapes reality… in order to transform oneself'.

Despite the extant correspondence being one-sided (none of my chosen three kept copies of their own), it is possible with his responses, written at speed and without revising, to make a fair guess at what is happening in Rilke's life. The dashed off can be revealing, and he's particularly off-guard with Clara and Kappus, knowing her all too well and him not at all.

Speed can also be concealing by default. The letters to Kappus sometimes contain contradictions and leap-frogging logic. This gives them a certain spontaneity, and may not be mere accidents of the slapdash. Rilke was working on Baudelaire's *lyrique-hystérique* style of the *Petits poèmes en prose* for *The Notebooks*. But when the letters are unified into a book, clarifications and modifications would surely have been made. However, *Letters to a Young Poet* (1929) was published three years after his death, and edited by Kappus. It is not an author authorised text, and there is no record of Kappus's editorial policy. For instance, we don't know what is corrected or excluded.

Inevitably, since the main letters were written at three- or four-month intervals, and were often delayed responses, the breeze-shooting blows hot and cold. Rilke sometimes bumps along chattily about matters raised without needing an explanation between friends. Other times he is so high-flying that readers get lost in the clouds and divining what is meant requires a leap of faith. In other words, it's a free-for-all for readers, and some will no doubt arrive at views different to what was originally intended (as is their prerogative).

Mindful of Rilke much-quoted citation, 'happy are those who know behind all language there stands that which is beyond words,' as I read along, I transcend the text and reinterpret the more obscure or incomplete passages, using hints from Rilke elsewhere and right reason. This

Introduction

led to translations as free as when I adapt poems which can't stand on their own if literarily rendered into English. I needed to do so in order to makes sense of what Rilke is trying to say, or, as I prefer, *nearly* saying. Sometimes I tie up loose threads with additions suggested by them in order to seal what the passage means to me. It could be regarded as a form of arbitration, mediating between the ambiguous and the obvious.

I told the all-knowing Joab Comfort that 'I feel I'm in empathic dialogue with Rilke'.

He questioned this: 'You can't be inside two heads at the same time.'

But I stood up to him: 'You can bang them together. Seeing stars can be illuminating.'

Joab gave me a strange look. 'You've been reading too much Rilke recently!'

I reminded him that Rilke's reputation in the anglophone world is much more firmly established than in German-speaking countries. This is due to translations in the thirties by eminent poets like Spender, Day-Lewis and Auden in England and Robert Lowell, Randell Jarrell and Robert Bly in America. Most of them bypassed literality and felt free to make self-standing poems (in Lowell's case even more *outré* than anything I'd dare). Indeed, his reputation in America accords with what the critic Herbert Gunter claims it is in Germany 'the sum of misunderstandings that gather around a name' (quoting mischievously from the letter Rilke wrote to Lou on fame in 1904)).

Still the image of Rilke, the pure poet, remains intact, true to the man, if not the work. Anniversary compendiums compound this trend. In 2007 a collection by prominent poets in England produced versions mostly true to themselves. Ruth Speirs and Robin Robinson are closest to the originals and Tom Paulin the furthest, with Don Patterson somewhere in between. Jo Shapcott is painfully honest in admitting her Rilke can hardly be called versions of the original; more 'tender and taxing conversations' with a lover and angel who has transformed her through his poetry. They are more her poems to him than his to her.

According to Karen Leeder the tendency with Rilke aficionados is 'to start with veneration, move on to identification and end up with critical exchange'. W. H. Auden is a good example. In his youth he wrote poems modelled on the 'thing-poems', incorporated images from Rilke's poetry and anecdotes from his life as a suffering poet, but got impatient with him. Hannah Arendt, who in her youth was smitten, came like W. H. to prefer Brecht. Her apostasy as a native German speaker is more critical, but it didn't damage his reputation in the anglophone world.

•

Transpositions

Anthony Rudolf wrote a book about reading entitled *Silent Conversations* (2013). I too enjoy a quiet chat with the authors that I meet between the covers. This has not always, though, been my experience when reading Rilke's poetry. He seems to be talking to himself, and himself alone. I am able to appreciate his softening of the rather military metre of the German tradition, the elliptical flourishes and ideas so strange you have to think about them. Clarity isn't helped by his aesthetic play with meanings, for example visual figurations like 'the crack in the cup' ('Blind Man: Paris'). Or stain-glass windows in cathedrals that seize the heart and send it hurtling into God ('The Rose Window'). Choirs of angels crying out in a storm are the guardians of an undivulged mystique. Such voices-off suggest another world. John Jordan's remark that he was more at home 'in the land of the dead' than the 'perilous seas' was certainly true of the man. He voyaged deluxe with Alfred Schuler, the Gnostic philosopher, during the Great War to explore, ancient Teutonic burial practices together, and talked about death as a continuation of life. And yet in photographs of Rilke at the time he looks like someone whom Proust's Aunt Leonie could safely invite to her tea-party. Indeed, in a poem of this period titled 'Death' (1915), the Great Ineffable is domesticated:

> So here stands death, an azure infusion,
> in a cup without visible support,
> poised at the back of the wrist. Look, no hands!
> It doesn't matter that the handle's broken.
> Dust off the faded legend. It reads 'Ho-pe'.

Despairing of ever 'seeing' Rilke 'plain', I resorted to a drastic means of divining where he was at with his *felt* thoughts rather than those explained (*felt* thoughts being ideas that sound right, and so their meaning can be presumed rather than understood; see Guiding Note 8). Reading between the lines of his long poem 'Requiem for a Friend'

INTRODUCTION

(1909), I found myself embellishing it with supplementary words and phrases, suggested by him, but not spelled out. The poem commemorates Paula Modersohn-Becker, an artist friend who died in childbirth, and closet medical details vie with inchoate ideas from philosophers (Schopenhauer, Kierkegaard) to express a bereft refusal to mourn the death of an unrequited love. My presumption was emboldened by Tillie Olsen's concept of 'trespass vision'; that is, in the case of an impasse in understanding, trespassing beyond the received text in order to unriddle what is really going on.

Tillie Olsen was inspired by Virginia Woolf's observation that 'literature is no one's private ground. Literature is common ground. Let us trespass freely and fearlessly and find our own way for ourselves.' And so, you can go against the formal logic of literary theory (then the textually-bound New Criticism) and, by crossing imagination with experience of life, arrive at a view that is clear, at least to oneself. It's a process of translation – in the ontological or existential sense – and not unreasonable. Scholarly criticism presupposes that the text is written on tablets of stone. But writing, as much as reading, is based on remembering, and the memory is selective, subjectively triaged, and so it can be as unreliable as recalling dreams, or a storyteller spinning a yarn. Olsen believed that the writer ought to be held to account for his or her work, and if this is not possible, accounted for by the application of common sense.

Gretchen Malherbe, Joab's German scholar colleague, approved my adaption of 'Requiem' for publication in *Translation Ireland* without realising I had tampered with the text. Rilke's ellipsism was sufficiently suggestive when spelt out to pass as faithful to the original. I have applied translation by trespass to passages of *The Letters* that, out of context, couldn't be fully understood without extensive notes. I'd like to think that the method I've chosen is analogous to musical transcriptions. A composer pays tribute to another with an arrangement of one of his/her works. It's an honourable tradition practised by Bach, Beethoven, Brahms and, above all, Liszt. The composition is reworked so it can be understood and appreciated by a wider or different audience without losing touch with the original. I ask myself, why shouldn't transcriptions be applied to literature? And particularly letters that are the equivalent of musical sketches, improvised on the spur of the moment.

•

Introduction

Hindsight

Reading the letters more than a century after they were written, I have a historical advantage over Kappus. I am able to read other letters sent by Rilke around the same time which allow me to draw conclusions that the young poet might have entertained, if only to dismiss ('It's just me'), or countenance in his reply with a query. Mindful of Rilke's comment on his poems in the first letter ('You respect your masters too much'), he never hesitated to speak out. Indeed, Kappus wasn't to know that the curtailing of the correspondence in 1904 (the last letter four years later was a courtesy) coincided with Rilke starting his novel, *The Notebooks of Malte Laurids Brigge*, in earnest. I take it he decided that this young poet was too sensible and forthright to offer anything to his portrait of the fragile, febrile Malte.

In trying to get a grip on *The Letters*, I found myself sympathising with Kappus when Rilke, like Pascal's Scaramouch, 'goes on for a quarter of an hour after he has said everything'. Although Rilke on the didactic rampage has a certain grandeur, galloping on into the boundless plain with his hunting horn sounding Gustav Mahler tone poems, I can envisage the completely thrown young poet skipping to where the rhetorical thinking returns to a more meaningful trot, and then going back to reread purple patches, marvelling at their poetical force but, to understand them, attempting to read between the lines and to bring the sublime down to earth.

My transcriptions too are sympathetic to interrupting Rilke in mid-flight to ask him where he's going. Truly I admit it's difficult not to distort Rilke's ideas. He frequently refers to them himself as 'desperate exaggerations with which I seek to get to the bottom of (my) Sincerity'. But attempting to bring them down to size can be hazardous. I need to remind myself not to overreach my remit.

Lengthy letters tossed off in the heat of the moment have their peril, as Henry James was painfully aware ('I'm sorry, but I don't have time to shorten this' was his postscript to a long-suffering recipient). Rilke can be excused of the heat, if not the toss-off. In almost all the letters to Kappus he apologises for the delay in replying, and he excuses one tardy response with a facetious exaggeration of his daily output, as he did to Baladine ('Merline') Klossowska, adding, 'Of course, none is as long as

Introduction

General von Sedlakowitz's, but still not one is less than four pages, and many as much as eight or twelve, and written in my tight little hand...' The General's memoir, *Letter to Merline*, was addressed to her.

Locating Rilke was never simply a matter of ideas. Courtesy of his prodigious letter-writing and the variegated postmarks that accompanied these missives, chroniclers can always know where he is, if not what he's at. Stuck in his barracks, Kappus's imagination must have been fired by receiving letters from Paris, Tuscany, Northern Germany, Rome and Sweden.

•

The Poet as a Chameleon

There was nothing fixed about Rilke. Addresses apart, even his appearance seemed to change between book covers, and the young poet must have wondered if he'd recognise him on the street. Rainer Maria had a penchant for disappearing himself, but knew how to make his presence felt, especially with women. By all accounts, he intrigued rather than attracted them. The way he looked deeply into their eyes made them wary or swoon. Men hardly noticed him sitting in a quiet corner. He was happy to be invisible, behind a pen writing letters.
Stephen Spender describes him:

On his slightly built, rather short body, Rilke's head appeared large, almost top-heavy, and the most striking thing about his face was the contrast between its upper and lower halves. All spirituality seemed concentrated in the magnificent vault of the clear forehead and in the wide-open mauve-blue eyes, while the nose ended in broad nostrils and the mouth was excessively large; a drooping, thin moustache made the fleshiness of the lips less noticeable; the chin was receding, a continuation of the curve of the cheeks.

As Spender was only a boy when Rilke died, he must have been drawing from photographs, paintings and hearsay. Portraits of him tend to highlight his hyper-sensitive 'mauve' eyes and Chinaman moustache. Later photographs show he had learned how to pose to advantage: the chin does not recede and the pendulant lips are pursed. He had lost the 'unprepossessing expression' of his youth, Pierre Seghers noted in a compendium of Rilke memorabilia. Rilke at least inverted Leigh Hunt's coyly snide description of Byron 'The lower half of his face was a model of beauty'. Rilke's upper half – where the brain resides – was that of

Introduction

Ralph Waldo Emerson's 'hero' who is 'immovably-centred', a quotation he used as an epigraph for his monograph on Rodin. Contemporaneous portraits tend to flatter him, but not those by Paula Modersohn-Becker, whom he loved and lost in Worpswede. She saw his prickly side. But gave him colour.

Pierre Jean Jouve, the French poet, met him in his last years and saw him as 'a little man with bulging eyes, drooping ill-cut moustache. Folds around the corners of the fleshy mouth. A high forehead which seems like belonging to someone else. Ugly until you caught his look, full of light softened by being only focussed on you. A face serene but sad.'

That look, no longer reserved for women, was also observed by the German poet Rudolf Schroder: 'the most solitary and perhaps impenetrable gaze in the domain of poetry.'

Rilke's poem 'Self-portrait' meets with Schroder's description:

'The steadfastness of an ancient lineage
shows in the curled sureness of the eyebrows.
Blue eyes retain a trace of childhood fears.
A deference, not that of a servant,
more of a dutiful poor relation.
The mouth, generous but pursed, not given
to saying more than is necessary.
The brow is noble, though the head favours
a discreet downward look as with a book.
What it adds up to is less than a whole.
Neither peace nor pain feature, as of yet.
Still the fitful traits are holding their own,
vaguely promising that what is behind
the dead expression will work itself out.'

Paula Becker warned Clara that, 'when Rilke looked deeply into your eyes, he was seeing himself in the reflection.' What she didn't know is that he didn't like what he saw. In a letter to Baroness Sidonie Nadherny von Borutin, (1913) he confides, 'O I would like to be without a face, and roll myself up like a hedgehog that only opens his coat at midnight in some ditch to hold its grey snout up at the stars.' Clara would know that look. In company, Lou observed that he could 'close like a flower'. Rudolf Kessler spoke of his 'polite presence', and Stefan Zweig described him entering a soiree:

Introduction

A frail little man with the air of a boy sneaking in amongst the grownups, little steps as though on tippy-toes, and seats himself in the corner with his hands folded on his knees, and his head lightly inclined so you could see his face, preparing himself to listen... He had learned from his youthful humiliations in Parisian drawing rooms when, with his guttural French, he talked in paragraphs about matters that were probably too heavy for the occasion. Guests walked away and he was left talking to himself... Now his silence was eloquent to those who knew who he was.

•

Neo-Troubadour

The Hapsburg baroness Sidonie Nadherny was probably the most cultivated of his long-distance lovers, requited by a passionate correspondence (from 1906 until his death). She briefly entertained the idea of a ménage a trois with Karl Kraus, her intermittent partner. They wouldn't be short of agreeable conversation at breakfast. Kraus's 'Psychoanalysis is the disease that believes itself to be the cure' would have pleased Rilke. Lou's obsession with Sigmund bored him. However, as the Hapsburg Empire disintegrated, Sidonie opted for strategic marriages. They tended not to last, and Kraus was invariably reinstated, though not as a husband. Rilke counselled against it because of 'an unrepeatable difference'. Kraus was Jewish (Rilke was a nobility snob, not anti-Semitic). In 1913 her beloved brother killed himself and Rilke composed a long letter advising that she play Beethoven on the piano that very evening ('I'll be listening for it on the wind from Janowitz Castle to Gottingen'). As a practical form of mourning, it made good sense as she was an accomplished musician.

At the time Rilke is staying with Lou and, as she talks of nothing except opening a psychiatric centre, he is delighted to receive an invitation from Helene von Nostitz to visit the fashionable spa town of Heilgendamm. Helene thinks she is in love with him. They walk hand in hand into a beech forest bordering the Baltic, and he waxes lyrical about 'the blue sky and the sea, black and unforgiving'. She is between the deep blue eyes of Rilke (which Lou said 'made women forget the rest of his face'), and the devil of a husband, furious with her for inviting this 'strange little poet'. He relaxes on realising Rilke is only interested in seances with a local 'spiritualist', and attends one. But when the medium spirits up a 'presence' advising him to throw a ring or a key into the fire, he chooses the latter and leaves town in high dudgeon, thinking it's was a conspiracy to get him to discard his wedding ring. His wife follows him as she couldn't get into the house.

Hardly has Helene taken herself off than Rilke is wooing the admiration of a young actress resting in the village. She is Ellen Delp, Max Reinhardt's favourite *ingenue* and a prodigy of Lou. The poem he presents her suggests romance is in the air. It begins 'Beyond the beech trees, more sinned against than sinning, her silent face. Moths are drawn to it, birds chirp… and the-soon-to-be-lovers smile at one another', ending with 'a ray of sunshine in a clearing illuminates a bright figure levitating'. Rilke is making Ellen, the diva, feel that she is the limelight. The neo-troubadour is making the lady shine while the poet remains in the shadows.

•

Recipient and Donor

But back to what started the correspondence with the young poet. Franz Xaver Kappus, a cadet at the Military Academy in Weiner Neustadt, Lower Austria, was reading a book of poems by Rilke under an ancient chestnut tree in the garden. 'I was so absorbed that I didn't notice that Herr Horacek, the chaplain, had joined me. Reading the cover, *To Celebrate Myself* (1899), he said, 'I always knew René would make good.' He told me that, ten years before, Rilke had completed his training in the lower school of the Academy; a highly gifted boy, quiet, serious, self-contained and, despite being of a delicate disposition, put up with the discipline, passing on to the upper school with honors. He often wondered what happened to him'. The 'happy intrusion' gave Kappus a pretext to write to Rilke, whose title poem ending 'Let me be a garden at whose fountains/ my swarming dreams could pluck new blooms' made him want to be a poet.

Rilke would have been touched by the chaplain's confidence in him, and chuffed at the imputed military prowess. He despised his father, Josef, for ending the family's proud military history in the self-same Academy. When the boy Rilke had a fit of coughing on parade, the old sergeant had barked, 'No, not another Rilke!' Apparently, a tickle in the throat had put an end to his father's career (you couldn't have a coughing officer on State occasions). Nevertheless, the family disgrace allowed Rilke a left-handed excuse to break with family tradition and become a poet.

Rilke is twenty-seven and the seven-year age difference makes for a generation gap. He has already published thirteen volumes of poems and is married with a child. His poetry doesn't earn enough to support a family. And so, he has returned Clara to her family with baby Ruth and thinks of freelancing as a journalist to supplement the small stipend Josef claims he can no longer afford (a bad investment meant having to live on a railway official's pension). But there is no question, as his father suggested, of buying himself a new suit and getting a proper job. Poetry is his life and he must live by it.

Note (to myself): *The title, *Mir zur Feier*, when translated as *To Celebrate Myself*, though literally correct ('*Mir*' means 'Me'), is misleading. Rilke is not peacocking his feathers to celebrate the self that Pascal hated ('*Le soi est haissable*), but the self in the ontological sense. 'To Celebrate The Self' would be a more accurate reflection of the poems.

Although his reputation as a neo-romantic symbolist poet (See Guiding Note 1) in Germany is high enough to speak down to an aspirant, far from patronising Kappus, Rilke expatiates at epic length and breadth on the relation between the life and work of a poet, letters that would have been awesome to receive but, from the evidence of the refracted replies, he isn't over awed. This is not due to the arrogance of literary youth, but a studious level-headedness. He is eager to learn and asks questions. Rilke's reactions to them veer between empathy and evasiveness. The younger man not only challenges his mentor's amplified thinking, but insists on repeating questions raised and not answered. Rilke's impatience with this may contribute to the falling off in cordiality of the later letters – his pupil is an ingrate – and the cruel-to-be-kind bossy insouciance of the penultimate letter (the last one four years later is a nostalgic wave).

There are more ways than one to read *Letters to A Young Poet*, a complex, sometimes contradictory, text. His opening two letters are written as a poet master to his supplicant pupil. He focuses on Kappus, testing him by being tough on the poems he sent him, while concomitantly conveying a genuine regard for a serious youth setting out on a sacred quest. Once he gets into his stride the letters can be taken as a sounding board for a youngish poet at the crossroads to float ideas for his future poetry. But far from being a manifesto for posterity, they are highly personalised.

This is why, unlike Max Jacob's less complicit *Advice to a Young Poet*, (1941) it has never been out of print, even in translation. Rilke was thinking aloud with a specific reader in mind, a young poet not unlike himself a decade before. Once he gets over the master and pupil stage and the young poet proves resilient to a poetical put-down, he feels free to be himself. The not infrequent obfuscations and excesses retain the fervour of students talking late into the night. However, there is nothing heart-to-heart in them, no clinking of the steins. Rilke's youthful ardour is 'an urgent enquiry into himself, first and foremost' (Ulrich Baer). His initial letter to Kappus is exceptional in that he seems to be giving the young poet *all* his attention, answering blunt questions (am I any good?) with what Kappus retrospectively qualifies as 'warm and tender concern', but which is as forthrightly honest as if he was in the same room, and telling the young poet to start again from scratch if he really wants 'to live and die for poetry'. The self-focus is not lost sight of. He is telling himself that too. Essentially Rilke is establishing terms to register his place in the world as a pure poet.

In general, the communication is dignified by indirectness. Kierkegaard's 'Law of Literary Delicacy' rules. He uses his own experiences but keeps their truth to himself, only detailing them as it suits his purposes. This can be tantalising, but sometimes, as often happens when shooting the breeze about oneself to a friendly stranger, inadvertently indiscrete. It would be possible for Kappus to make a fair guess as at the state of Rilke's soul at the time. The changes in posting addresses alone are revealing. Three of the letters came from Rome and only one from Worpswede, Germany, the family home.

Note (to myself): Max Jacob's *Advice to a Young Poet* according to Louis Guillaume ('R. M. Rilke and Max Jacob', 1952): 'The soupcon of false modesty jars when Jacob says, "I can't open the doors that I design, because the doors exist beyond me... Maybe you can do better."' His generosity does not include opening his mind with the vulnerability of Rilke. His ironical tone backfired tragically. The young poet sloped off to become a collaborator with the Nazis. When Jacob was arrested by the Gestapo, his journal entry 'What remains is the future' is ironic optimism in despair.

Introduction

Polishing the Pebble...

The existential moment with letters is how they are received. The interaction is page to page, not face to face, and so misunderstandings can be expected. The sender is responsible for them. He ought to anticipate them by gauging the recipient's mind and character, and tailor his words accordingly. Thus, creating a complicity that is reciprocated in the response. In 'modern letter-writing', according to Samuel Johnson, as opposed 'to Pauline epistles or the Cicero-driven missives of the Elizabethans, as little as possible is said elegantly'.

Dr Johnson was as likely to have Rilke on his mind as the other way around. But he would have been sympathetic to *Letters to a Young Poet*. He decried 'an epistolary style of ease and simplicity, even flow and an artful arrangement of obvious sentiments when the importance of the subject impresses solitude, and a remote principle is to be investigated. On occasions that are not familiar it's only natural to depart from familiarity of language. The writer is required to try every inlet at which love and pity enter the heart. As the pebble which hopes to be valued as a diamond must be polished with care, the words ought surely to be laboured when they are intended to stand for things.' Rilke's epistolary style would broadly conform to the good doctor's proscription.

•

Due Attention

In his self-effacing preface, Kappus says 'In my first letter, without it being my express intention, I opened my heart, and laid myself bare in a way that I never did before or since.' Rilke's reply came quickly. He is delighted no doubt with the wise old army chaplain's words. Less so, with the verses Kappus had enclosed. But he gives them due attention, without, the young poet will notice, suggesting changes, or an offer to lend his name to place them. Still sharing hortatory cogitations on artistic creation with Rilke is to be at the Poetry Olympics. However, Kappus must have known that he is just a spectator. After the opening two letters, Rilke was performing for himself, with the odd nod to him. But still he could read them closely as an onlooker like Montaigne suggested (*Essays*, 1580):

Our life, said Pythagoras, is like the great and crowded assembly at the Olympic Games. Some exercise their bodies and minds in order to win glory in the contests. Others bring merchandise there to sell for profit. There are some – and these are not the worst – whose only aim is to observe how and why everything is done, and to be spectators of other men's lives, in order to judge and regulate their own.

Chapter One:

Pawing the Ground:

Letters One (17 February 1903) and Two (5 April 1903, Paris)

•

Letter One

Rilke's opening letter is a master class on how to response to an incipient poet who has sent you his work. He does not paw the ground but, setting the bar high, leaps to sanctify his vocation. By way of apologising in advance for the remarks he's about to make on Kappus' writings, Rilke says that 'there is nothing less apt to touch a work of art than criticism. All one ends up with is glib misunderstandings. Things are less graspable and knowable than we are led to believe. Mostly events are facts that are describing themselves, and occupy a space where our words cannot penetrate. Nothing is more ineffable than works of art. Their existence is a mysterious companion to ours, and persist after we've passed away.'

Rilke, however, delivers the devastating judgement, 'Your verses have no identity of their own, though there is a suggestion of something personal struggling to get out. Most emphatically in your last poem, "Soul". The lovely one to Leopardi identifies to some extent with this grand solitaire. Still none come alive enough to stand on their own. However, the fulsomeness of your accompanying letter makes the defaults I detect in your verses explicable, tacitly, as I can't quite put my finger on them. Unless it is you respect your masters too much.

'You ask if you're wasting your time? I can't answer that. Nobody can tell you whether your compositions are any good except yourself. A work of art is good if it has arisen from "the terrible bite of necessity" [Montaigne]. In the quiet of the night pose yourself the question, would you die rather than be denied the right to write them. If the answer is loud and clear, a simple yes, you must build your life around this necessity, making the merest moment important, every movement a cause, in order bear witness to this irrepressible need. Make it your first and second nature!

'Be as though you are the first man, and express what you see and experience as though its nascent. But don't write "love poems" or echo forms that are familiar to you from school and other poets you've read. To measure up to the bountiful past you must gain the strength to seed-bed a future that flourishes poems that can only be yours. Be humble and forego writing about the universals for the ordinary everyday things.

'Comb your sorrows and desires, your fleeting thoughts and what you find beautiful even though others might not. Ardently pursue the images you daydream and the things that memory evokes. If as you say you think that you lack material in your life for poetry, blame yourself, not it. Tell yourself I'm not poet enough to summon up life's riches. Life is no poor thing.

'Constant curiosity ensures inspiration isn't lacking. Even if you were locked up in a "little ease" with no contact with the outside world, the walls are not blank. They will speak to you without "the noise of words". Not least of childhood, a boundless treasure trove. You can make it live again, renewed with words. Turning inwards opens up as large a landscape as looking out. And poems will come. Whether they are considered good or bad poems is not the point.

'Don't bother with outside opinion. It will only disappoint you. Instead, you must go into yourself to examine the depths from which your inspiration springs. A work of art is good when it issues from an urgent, inner need. If you achieve the inevitable, award yourself and don't leave it to others. He who creates makes a world of his own, and within it finds himself.

'Even if in your solitary plunge into yourself nothing comes of it that is worth dying for, it's not the end of the world. The journey as I have sign-posted it will serve you on other paths that you may decide to take. If so, I wish with all my heart that your chosen path be as far-reaching, enriching and goodly as poetry. There is not only one way in life.'

In signing off, Rilke re-iterates his caution against looking outside oneself for answers that only oneself can give, and his delight at what his old spiritual guide in the Academy had said about him. 'Remember me to the aimable scholar who taught me things I will never forget. I'm returning the verses you entrusted to me. Thanks for your confidences and your confidence in me to respond to them. I have endeavoured to do so as empathically as a stranger can.'

•

Note (to myself): it's significant that as the letter goes on that Rilke increasingly refers to Kappus's poems as verses (*vers* rather than *geditch*). In the 1960s, I was amongst some student poets who read with an established poet and the event was advertised in the local paper: 'Desmond O'-Grady will read his poems. Hugh J. Murphy, Augustus Young and Robert Welch will read their verses.'

Kappus must have felt that was that. Rilke had said all he had to say on reading a young man's less than promising juvenilia. His approach is proscriptive (come back to me when you have grown up as a poet). But the advice is a sound basis for the making of a poet. Though young Rimbaud would have laughed at it Having modernised French poetry in his late teens by breaking all the rules, he found more grown-up things to do in darkest Africa.

But the young poet might have wanted some practical encouragement. For instance, James Stephens on approaching Percival Graves, Robert's father, was told all he needed to do to write poems is to read a great one and allow yourself to be carried away with one of your own. Rilke, rightly, would have winced at that. Still Stephens did so with surprising success with children's poems. My own father on his deathbed read my first published poem and picked out a line which he thought was good. I saw how bad the others were, and when I attempted another at least I wasn't starting with a blank page. But still, Kappus was fortunate not to get Horace Walpole's response to the budding poet, Thomas Chatterton: 'Marvellous boy, you are a genius. You ought to be advising me.' Rilke's counsel has the merit of not being too encouraging, and yet more generous than he probably felt. This is possibly because he was thinking of another young poet years back, himself.

•

Letter Two

Kappus's thank you letter evidently impressed Rilke and he is moved to write to him again seven weeks later. He blames the delay and its brevity on his health and the need to recuperate on the coast near Pisa. In a concurrent letter to Ellen Key, the Swedish proto-feminist, he moaned elliptically about money, and his marriage: 'It is as though someone had closed the window into the garden where my songs live.'

No doubt in response to Kappus's letter, he says, 'At bottom, in the important things we are on our own.' Nonetheless, Rilke offers him advice on irony. It is not clear why. I don't think Kappus would have been ironical with him. Perhaps Rilke was reacting to Jules Renard's latest piece in *L'Humanité* on irony as the '*pudeur* of *l'humanité*'. Renard defined pudency 'as a sense of subliminal shame crossed with bashful propriety', and called it 'the good manners of the mind'.

Rilke isn't sure, and of its rival, politesse, considers that 'although not wholly sincere, it's one-remove makes for a tolerable world… Don't, dear Kappus, allow yourself to be ruled by irony. Avoid it when you're lacking in inspiration. Use it in creative moments as one of the many means to get a grasp on life. Deployed purely, for irony too can be pure, it's nothing to be ashamed of. But next to great and serious matters it becomes all small and helpless, and this allows you to turn away from it to plunge into the depths of things where irony daren't follow. Confronting the great and serious, irony either shies off or, if it happens to be an integral part of your nature, it can recover its poise, gain strength, and take its place as a valuable tool in developing ideas. But for ironic logic you'd have to be a Socrates for that'.

Note (to myself): the either/or suggests the Renard prompt was supplemented by a memory of perusing Kierkegaard's doctoral thesis, *On the Concept of Irony*. In sum, Socrates' 'salvation through ignorance', which in pointing out to the Athenians what couldn't be known, was his death warrant. 'The savants who knew not irony, nor what to think, were enraged. And so, this good-natured, garrulous, droll old man, who does neither evil or good, and doesn't stand in the way of anyone, and is kindly disposed to the world as long it's willing to listen to his blather, was given the hemlock.'

Rilke recommends reading the Bible and Jens Peter Jacobsen, the late nineteenth-century Danish writer, very much in vogue in Germany. He specifies his novel *Niels Lyhne* and a short story, 'Mogens'. 'Live in his books, learn what you can from them, but above all love them. This love will sustain you no matter how your life turns out.'

Note (to myself): Could Rilke's invocation to live in J. P. Jacobsen's books be a simpler version of Kierkegaard's life's ambition 'to live an idea'? He had been reading him.

Rilke must have known, but did not mention, that Jacobsen's scientific radicalism and naturalistic ideas were said to have led Kierkegaard's nephew, Poul, away from the Church and into a life of dissipation. Poul inordinately admired his Uncle Søren, but the shock of liberation from an ultra-pious family was too much for the boy and he ended up in a madhouse. Maybe in remorse, Jens Peter wrote two novels transfused from a Kierkegaardian vein, but nevertheless breathing a more accessible life into it. The philosopher's ill-fated mid-century confrontation with the Danish Church reset in a proto-modernist structure anticipates what was to become the existentialist novel.

Finally, Rilke suggests, 'If you want to learn about the nature of artistic creation, apart from Jacobsen, there is 'Auguste Rodin, the greatest artist alive.' His monograph on Rodin has just been published. It is designed to appeal to gallery owners, and also the maître.

Chapter Two

Getting into His Stride:

Letter Three (23 April 1903, Viareggio)

•

This letter comes fast-fire, three weeks after the previous (the mean average interval is ten weeks, excluding the last). Rilke is evidently pleased that Kappus had taken up his recommendation, and insists now he must read Jens Peter Jacobsen's *Marie Grubbe* and his collected non-fiction, specifying the best edition and price. Jacobsen mattered greatly to Rilke, not merely because he read his stories as a child and they were the first works that he had broached with his newly-acquired Danish. Jacobsen (1847 – 85) was a precocious scientist who translated Darwin at a time when evolution was taboo in largely Protestant Denmark. On contracting tuberculosis at twenty-five, he dedicated his remaining ten years to writing with a fury that excluded everything else. He brought the meticulousness of a scientist to his style, which modernised Nordic literature in a manner not dissimilar to Flaubert in France. His output is limited to the two novels and some stories, 'all driven by the struggle of individuals to override the obstacles imposed by society to prevent them living in their own way' (Rilke, unfinished monograph).

•

Pressed Rose Petals

Rilke in a letter to Ellen Key (April 1904) wrote, 'Jacobsen and Rodin have become my masters, an inexhaustible reference point. Both had a profound insight into nature and an ability to transform what they see into a reality that enhances it a thousand-fold. Both make things with sure boundaries, intersections and sidelines that have given me a template.'

Neils Lyhne, the novel that Rilke tells Kappus 'has everything and provides immense pleasure', is a grimly wry account of the perils of being an honest agnostic in an 'unchristian Christian' society, a theme drawn from late Kierkegaard.

Rilke writes excitedly about the joys of re-reading Jacobsen, referring to its 'beautifully woven fabric in which each thread is drawn with infinite delicacy, and held together by hundreds of others'. However, when it came to shaping *The Notebooks*, Jacobsen's tightly knit plotting proved too much trouser, and gave away to Schopenhauer's metaphorical pattern for our lives, 'an embroidery in which the first half is the upside that presents the design, and the second half is the underside that shows how the threads have been worked together' (See Volume Two).

Rilke's nod to Kierkegaard is indirect. It's as though he took his intensive study of him at the turn of the century as some sort of military training with career options once he passed out. His experience of forced barracks comradeship prompted him to attain the solitary life Kierkegaard imposed on himself. The difference was The Doleful Dane preferred to be alone in a crowd. Rilke liked his own space and place. Guarding his peace of mind obliged him to shut out the world. But the Kierkegaardian trademark dread was not for him, except in small doses. Even external threats to his person were treated practically. Kierkegaard and Rilke had pyrophobia in common. The Dane's, founded on the Great Fire in Copenhagen that nearly engulfed his home in childhood, was existential, while Rilke's was a worry that his papers might be destroyed and he took sensible precautions (metal boxes).

Still Rilke was never a one not to turn a phobia to literary purposes. His fable celebrating his family's military past, *The Lay of the Love and Death of Cornet Christoph Rilke* (1906), ends with the hero consumed by fire when he runs at the marauding Turks with a burning flag. Curiously, the climax of Jacobsen's novella *Mogens* is when the hero's fiancée jumps into a fire and perishes. Rilke's settles for a heroic gest. Jacobsen, rather speciously, gives his hero a happy ending. However, Rilke in his last years, when intermittent physical pain introduced him to dread, Kierkegaard's existential and his security fear of fire come together in one of his last poems, 'Christ in Hell'.

Jacobsen's short story of a pilgrimage to Rome, 'There Should Be Roses', however, gives Rilke a form for his meditation on religious art in *The Notebooks*. Veiled lines from it, for instance, 'Love has exchanged the eternal freedom of dreams for a happiness which is measured by hours and which hourly grows older' enter several of his poems, not least the second *Duino* Elegy. The ending of the story imagines 'the roses that should be as a shake of petals falling from the heavy branches and, caught by the wind, whirling after the author to be pressed in the book he is closing'. It quite possibly influenced the epitaph on Rilke's tomb:

> 'Rose, oh pure contradiction, delight
> in being no one's sleep under so many
> lids.'

•

'In Longing I Live'

The lyric freedom of Jacobsen's prose could only be beneficial to a young poet. He unleashes descriptions of nature that work as narrative. The psychology of his characters in *Mogens* veers from the ardent adolescent to the knowing trickster, modelled on Ibsen's *Peer Gynt* (a play, written a decade previously and in Danish). But Jacobsen holds it all together with an authorial voice that is anything but a still centre:

> Mists were drifting down on the meadows touched by the first moonlight. And, everything is sad, all of life, all of life, empty behind him in a dark place. Those who were happy were blind. Through misfortune he had learned that everything in this world is a worm-eaten lie. Justice, Faith, friendship, mercy and hollowest of all is love, smouldering lust takes fire, flames, sparkles and flickers out leaving nothing but dust and ashes. How he wishes he was blind, believed in everything like he did as a child. Ah! a world of beating hearts and the heavens replete with a loving God. Then he hears a voice of a woman singing, 'Flower in dew, dream for me, fill the air, with elfin things, rise up above despair, and give me wings, your fragrance makes me want to dance. In longing I live. In longing I live.' There is something in trees and flowers that the sun and the rain makes them grow, but I know not what.

The young poet would learn how the romantic excess is trained in by precise detail, and how moral despair is the compost that seeds an idea that later could bear fruit. On the other hand, it is the refrain 'in longing I live' that resonates for Rilke. It echoes throughout his life and work.

GETTING INTO HIS STRIDE:

Critical Love and Hate

When Kappus takes issue with the editor's preamble to Jacobsen's story 'There Should Be Roses', which 'explains too much', Rilke reiterates his contempt for critical theory: 'Don't read it. Works of art are created in infinite solitude, and *only love can grasp, and hold, and fairly judge them*. Such things cannot be measured by time or tide. Solitude exists in the dead of night when time has stopped. The surest way to fail it is to put a clock on it, as critics invariably do. Solitude has no time. It is a condition that is making space for you, the writer, frees your spirit. Patience is all… To be an artist means to grow like a tree which doesn't hurry its sap, but stands at ease in the wind and rain of spring, knowing it will have its summer.'

Evidently Rilke (aged twenty-eight) was disputing Baudelaire's 'Counsel to Literary Youth' in seeing love as the pivot of literary judgement. Charles (aged twenty-five) felt hate would be more useful, if manifested as a sort of martial arts without the discipline. The literary youth ought to be violently critical of everything in sight to show he had higher standards than everybody else. The creative blood in his veins must be made to make it flow.

Baudelaire's counsel goes beyond self-promotion through notoriety. It is Wallace Stevens's 'violence without absorbed into the violence within', and invective is the short route to syphon it. However, Rilke did take to heart advice that Baudelaire gave on writing itself: 'Lost time is the least precious thing in the world… Scribbling away without forethought is verbal diarrhoea. You must work all the time in your head. That's what inspiration comes down to.' But he would have baulked at the bad boy of French poetry's counsel against 'honest women, bluestockings and actresses. They have their public to please. The choice is between love or beef stew: the silly young things, fresh pastures, or stupid old girls who cook.'

Around the time of the third letter, Rilke asked Rodin how to live as a poet, and his maître simply said, 'to work hard and exercise patience'. He elaborates on this advice to the young poet with a favourite metaphor of poems as embryos. Kappus had expressed impatience with himself and editors who reject his poems. And in consolation Rilke tells him that the pure poet, if he persists, will get there in the end. 'You must let every impression and germ of feeling complete themselves in your innermost being, which is an entity obscure to our brains and doesn't have a known lexicon. But the true artist has no choice but to wait humbly and patiently for the moment of parturition when the delivery sees the light of day. There is no measuring the terms of time, a year or ten is nothing. The artist does not count or calculate but holds out a tree that is assured that spring storms will pass and that summer will come. It comes for those who rest calm in temporal time knowing eternity lies before them. I know this as I live with it every day. It is hard but I am thankful for it: patience is all. Every poem must be carried to term before it is born.'

•

Hanky-panky

Poems can mean more than one thing, and readers can make of them what they will. Kappus, a lonely young man in an all-male compound, would sing along with Rilke's, 'Love drips like honey from a hive / Constant, sweet, precious, flows into your heart / each and every moment, if you allow it'. The last clause would give him pause. 'Allow' was surely not in Rilke's free-floating lexicon. He knew by heart the early poem, 'If you're the dreamer / I'm the dream you dream. / Wake up and I will / possess your full splendour / like the star-filled silence / over the wondrous city of time'. Rilke would never have asked permission to love.

But Rilke's recommendation of Jacobsen's other novel *Marie Grubbe* excites him. He knows the history: this seventeenth-century Danish noblewoman had a weakness for footmen. Adultery was a capital offence, but neither of her husbands had the heart to recourse to the law. Rereading Jacobsen's 'There Should Be Roses', I come across 'Large, opulent, deserted women, pale as hatred... could one but kill with a thought or open hell with a wish... Ai! women and men! It's always women and men, even these delicate white virginal souls who press against the black latticework like a flock of lost doves and cry out "Take us" to imagined, noble birds of prey.' Strong stuff for a young man to gulp down. But the antidote to dread in the novella is requited love with a good woman, 'clasped in two white arms, two eyes as your temporal heaven and the certain bliss of two lips which exchange dreams for a happiness embedded in the real.'

When Kappus reads Rilke's recent poem 'Orpheus, Eurydice, Hermes', the line 'Her sex is closed like a young flower towards the evening' shocks him into imagining the 'young flower' of the girl befriended back home and whose letters made him daydream. He wasn't to know (nor Rilke either) that the floral metaphor pre-empts Proust's famous bees and pollen analogy for sexual congress, but more explicitly. On second reading, he would have realised the poem is not about a sexual experience (*Geschlecht*), but longing/yearning (*Sehnsucht*):

Eurydice, having regained her virginity in the underworld, is keeping herself for Orpheus, whose plaintive lyre touches Hades, and a bargain is struck for her return to the land of the living. As Hermes guides her in the wake of Orpheus, his 'light touch' makes her feel uncomfortable, and she runs ahead like an adolescent until the messenger of the gods pulls her back. Orpheus is breaking the bargain in turning to see the woman he desires. But his look, as Eurydice sees it, is the blank face of Orpheus's death. Shaken at first, she comes to see the bright side. When both are dead, they will be finally united in consummate love. And so patiently and longingly she waits…

A conspicuous absence in *The Notebooks of Malte Laurids Brigge* is sex. But Rilke makes up for it with *The Letters*. The first stirrings come when in replying to letter two Kappus expresses his admiration for Richard Dehmel, the rising star of Germany poetry, and Rilke's bad-boy rival. Dehmel's *Woman and World* (1898) had been a *succès de scandal*, and Rilke had reason to think that it stole some of his own thunder as the lightning flash of Teutonic Eros. He tells Kappus that Dehmel 'has written some good things but one was never sure when turning the page that he wouldn't spoil the effect, and change the admirable into the unworthy'.

Kappus had epitomised Dehmel as 'living and writing in heat'. Rilke likes the idea and relieved not to be demeaning himself by indulging in denigration (and literary criticism), he warms to it. Common ground can be found with Dehmel. 'Artistic experience is so close to the joys and pains of the sexual instinct that making poems and love share the same desire and felicity. I mean sex pure and simple, the rose without a thorn, without the suspicion of sin and guilt.' He doesn't disapprove of the priapism, only Dehmel's handling of it:

> He could claim his creative power derives from primal instinct, and the poems erupt like streams of lava from a volcano. But it is all rather forced, too willed. The true artist must remain

innocent and unconscious of the source of his salient virtues so that they spring up with virginal purity. The sexuality that courses through Dehmel's veins is nor mature enough to put on its knowledge with its power in order to find the human good and true. Instead of 'in heat' I would say 'rut' is the right word. He ruts with relentless, befuddled drive, weighed down by the usual male prejudices that disfigure love by overriding it. As he indulges himself merely as a rampant male, there is something nasty, brutish and short about it, a panting bestiality that I find repugnant. In short, his love poems are premature ejaculations and will die with his body.

Nevertheless, is possible to take pleasure in the rapacious passion, but make sure not to be carried away by it. His world is a painful one, fraught with anxieties, infidelities and confusions. He is remote from real destinies, which indeed may bring suffering, but of a less transient kind, and that offers us an opportunity to show our true mettle, gives us courage to rise above the painful in order to live and die achieving that rare thing, something that will last.

Rilke's deadly warning against going down Dehmel's way of all flesh, 'the carnal quagmire where women only exist for men, and men only think of themselves', is heart-felt. He pulls out most of the stops, but holds back from warning the young man to distance himself from the brothels and beerhouses that his fellow soldiers no doubt frequent. His love of women is protective rather than predatory, and it is one of the reasons so many of them felt that they were the only one. But now that his own arrangements with the opposite sex are going nowhere, with Clara on the blip, Lou settling for friendship, and Paula Becker marrying the well-off landscape painter and widower, Otto Modersohm, his sex life (*Geschlecht*) is in abeyance while his longing/yearning (*sehnsucht*) must content itself with nostalgia in poems. This bothers him. And he is already planning to elaborate a cosmic schema for sex in the next letter.

Kappus had asked for a signed copy of one of Rilke's books. The letter concludes, 'I am very poor, and as soon as my books appear, they no longer belong to me. I can't afford to buy them myself, let alone give them to those who would value and look after them.' He encloses a precisely detailed list of all those in print. 'I leave it to you, dear sir,

to order one or two, if they take your fancy. I will be glad to know that my books are in good hands,
All good wishes
Rainer Maria Rilke'

•

Sublime Sublimations

Of course, there was a time when Rilke was a sexual innocent like Kappus, and he gently mocks his alter ego, Malte, in *The Notebooks*: the fleshpots of Paris pass him by. Accosted by a prostitute, he is bewildered and asks her, 'Can I help you? Are you in distress?' She disappears into the night with a curse.

He is believed to have lost his innocence with Lou Andreas-Salomé at twenty-two. Hitherto, his sexuality was latent. Not uncommon in young men whose mother didn't like them (Rilke's 'Phia' always wanted a girl. And he pretended to be one to please her. It didn't). He showed himself to be naïve with Lou, more smitten by her intellectual interest in sex than the real thing. Through her, he became a libertine of the mind. Although Lou wasn't above titillation. Not least in changing his first name to the more manly Rainer.

Rilke's relations with women were passionate but, for the most part, teasingly platonic (Kassner, his closest male friend, supports this view). He took a troubadour's leaf from dedicated writers of the previous generation like Turgenev and Flaubert who made sure their lady loves (respectively Pauline Viadot and Georges Sands) had a husband with whom they made friends. Thus, Rilke's first visit to Russia (1899) with Lou was chaperoned by her husband, Carl Andreas, a renowned linguist, who interpreted for him with Tolstoy and the painter Leonid Pasternak, Boris's father.

On their second journey to Russia the following year, Carl Andreas didn't bother to come, saying, 'They all speak German anyway'. This was a not necessarily an insult to Lou, who was Russian born, or Rilke's manhood. Their marriage was never consummated. However, something happened (or didn't) on the second visit that made Rilke decide that he ought to get married to Paula Becker. But still he fared better with Lou than poor, infatuated Nietzsche twenty or so years before (their engagement was broken off when Nietzsche's sister rowed with Lou over a frock). Lou's jealousy when he married Clara (on the rebound when Paula refused him) must have made him almost happy. And they remained best friends for life.

On the visit to Russia without Carl, the second meeting with Tolstoy didn't go well. The young poet, with a dozen books of poems behind him, abased himself before the maître as a 'lazy writer', prone to dreaming about it and getting nothing done. Tolstoy didn't encourage his false modesty, and told the young poet, 'Just write, write, write'. Subsequently, Rodin echoed this advice, but adding 'be patient'.

In a way, Rilke went further than Dehmel as a literary free spirit with his embrace of the idea that writing poetry is as close to making love as makes no difference. A belief that Wallace Stevens may have borrowed from Rilke in the 'Plot Against the Giant'. His female Cupid sings:

> I shall run before him,
> with a curious puffing.
> He will bend his ear then.
> I shall whisper
> Heavenly labials in a world of gutturals.
> I will undo him.

Rilke's embrace of free love (but not free verse) was more tied up with Higher Things than Steven's lyric lightness. His *Sehnsucht* (longing/earning) aimed to find a *Geschlecht* (sexual experience) able to create something everlasting. He arguably achieved literary orgasm with some of the 'thing-poems', and a certain immortality ('The Panther' is sacred to every German schoolboy, it's said). But this new modernist mode, encouraged by Rodin, does not wholly satisfy him. He considers it essentially ephemeral. Such poems would die with him. He seeks to transcend them 'with a heart beating faster to the point when desire is almost requited, giving my spirit space to breathe' (letter to Lou, 1904). Teilhard de Chardin's 'ecstasy of *almost* touching' comes to mind.

In sum, his poetry itched to move on to the bigger and better sublimations of what was to become the *Duino Elegies* with their 'Order of the Angels' and the seductive Lament family. However, two years before this letter, almost to the day, he had a *Geschecht* that created something other than a poem, namely Ruth, his only child. But she, alas, was only too mortal, and he seems to lose interest in her, like the 'Thing-poems' once they were published.

GETTING INTO HIS STRIDE:

At bad times, most notably during the Great War when he was stranded in Germany, encouraged by Lou, he diverted his chagrin by writing a series of poems in praise of the phallus and another poem, 'Himmel' (Heaven), celebrating the female parts. However, in writing about sex he avoids words in German like *begierde* and *begehrlichkiet* that could imply the sex drive or marital rights. Sex in the abstract was sacred to him and its reduction by Catholicism to a reproductive process was anathema. In his last years he accused the Church of 'deforming and repressing a profound and ecstatic event by putting in the wrong a blessed right that the whole of creation engages in. Love is stigmatised and distorted into an intolerable mixture of contempt, concupiscence and prurience.'

Nevertheless, and *thinking* about sex is where his relationship with Lou was at its more passionate, he showed an unhealthy interest in the foreplay of wolves in courtship (the she-wolf rubs noses and then falls back to expose her genital parts in submission). God forbid if I attribute Rilke with a dirty mind.

Chapter Three

Black-Widow Waves:

Letter Four (16 July 1903, Worpswede)

•

A Ray of Sunshine

His fourth letter is headed '*at present at* Worpswede'. He is staying with his Clara's family. The prosperous artistic commune there has commissioned him to write a monograph on their '*Heimat*' (homeland) modernism. Heinrich Vogeler is the leading light. His precocious success in Munich with paintings inspired by folktales and his workshop for handmaking household objects put the commune on the buyer's market. In 1900, Vogeler, a passionate Slavophile, had invited Rilke, just back from Russia, to visit the commune.

Rilke accepts the commission, not merely because he needs the money and to look in on Clara and Ruth. He can't wait to see how Paula Becker is getting on with her new husband, the stolid Otto. But what's most on his mind is finding a model for Malte Laurids Brigge, the young poet adrift in a big city. Vogeler has become something of an older brother to him. Sensitive to Rilke's dithering with the novel, he tells him about Sigbjorn Obstfelder, a young, demented Nordic poet who failed to make his way in Paris and died of tuberculosis in his early thirties but left an unfinished novel, A Priest's Diary, recently published.

Rilke works on the monograph, something he could do with his eyes closed. The Worpswede commune's polite primitivism accords well with his muted vitalism (Schopenhauer filtered by Lou through Nietzsche though tempered by Rodin). He thinks of Kappus, picks up his last letter and, with his cosmic schema on sex in mind, begins what is his longest reply so far. The letter starts with a damp squib: 'I left Paris ten days ago for my health, but I'm still exhausted. Although the height of summer, it has rained interminably. But this morning a ray of sunshine appeared, and I felt I must write to you.'

His apology for sitting on Kappus's letter for two and half months is ingenious. 'It's the kind of letter I read over and over, feeling as though you are in the room and we are talking. I re-read it now and, in the calm of the boundless plains, I am moved by your fine concern for life, even more so in the confines of Paris where so much is lost in the infernal din which sets things rattling. However, here where the winds blow across the vast expanses from the North Sea with its black-widow waves, I can't help wondering if your questions and feelings are no more than rhetorical. Even the best minds are at a loss to find the words to grasp such intangible, almost unsayable, things.

'But I believe the answers reside in refreshing your eyes, as I do now, looking out of the window, beholden to nature, to the simple little things that people scarcely notice and, if you love them sufficiently for their insignificance, and bow to them like a servant, giving yourself, they can spontaneously generate into something huge, tumescent and, what was almost nothing, becomes everything to you. You can't will this transformation. You let yourself go and it comes. Your intellect doesn't know what is happening and stands back, but deep down in your consciousness, you feel something that makes everything simple, astonishing, and consummates with the blessed release of a knowledge dormant in your depths.

'You are young. Be patient with what is not clear to your heart, and try to love *the questions themselves* like books written in a language you don't know. Suspend the search for answers. They cannot be given to you as you have not been able to live them. Live the questions for now, and imperceptibly you will begin to live your way into the answers. The serious things in life are heavy (*das schwierig*). Don't fight them and they'll lighten up. But above all, don't lose the idea of yourself, but live the idea to the full.'

Note (to myself): Rilke came by the concept of 'living an idea' two years before during his readings of Kierkegaard with his wife Clara – who was pregnant and must have wondered who was living what. The borrowing wasn't a straight lift, or a crooked one (acknowledgement is only necessary in a scholarly work). Søren would have understood perfectly that an unattributed quote saves starting a good idea all over again, while avoiding tangling the thread of thought with someone else's, and evading the scrutiny of the savants. Such 'borrowing' can lead to twisting and turning of the original for one's purposes. Kierkegaard wasn't averse to deliberate misquotes. But never with Socrates, who for him stood alone above all thinkers, 'simple and wise, a reformer by default'. He developed his questioning method '*to counter ascetic solitude*' (in contrast to Rilke's espousal). Socrates needed 'people in order to love the questions'. They were his 'salvation through ignorance'. And the answers gave him 'more questions to love… and so his life was to end with a question mark'.

'You may not yet know how you want to live. Not to worry. It will grow on you gradually, without you noticing. You contain within you the possibility of forming a happy and pure way of living. Groom yourself to take what comes. As long as you have the will for it, and a deep-felt inner necessity, accept it without shame. Sex is Difficult (*Schwer*). But Difficult things are what we were set out to do. Almost everything serious is Difficult, and everything is serious.'

The sudden transition, I take it, is due to Kappus's response to Rilke's paradoxical homily on Dehmel and sex. The letter continues with a veritable hymnal to primal sex, fertility and 'the great maternity overlying all' (Clara would be amused, but Lou would approve despite being nulliparous). This is less surprising as the young poet clearly expressed his inadequacy in dealing with girls. He is given some serious advice: 'Let your sensual resources, drawn from your innate nature, and strengthened by the experience of growing up, establish a relationship with sex that is wholly your own, uninfluenced by convention and custom. Then you have no need to fear of losing yourself by becoming unworthy of your best possession.'

Rilke tells the young man that *Geschlecht* (sexual experience) is 'the exquisite juice of the ripest fruit from the tree of knowledge. It is tasted on the tongue. The knowledge it imparts is everything to be known on this earth in its splendour. Sadly, most people abuse and squander it. They use it as a diversion.'

•

The Quiet Life

Ulrich Baer paraphrases Rilke's recurrent counterblasts against the modern world: 'The fragmentation of modern life lacks stimulus despite being subject to constant distractions, diversions and interruptions. We are alienated from the true life because of our inability to rest our eyes and minds on one thing at a time.' To counter that, Rilke chose the hermetic option, isolating himself. Solitude is the poet's salvation from a disintegrating world.'

Pascal is not mentioned, but clearly Rilke espoused his *pensée*, 'The unhappiness of men arises from not being able to staying quietly in one's room.' In Rilke's case the stay is to write letters and poems, or looking out the window, contemplating the horizon 'where landscape and man meet and find one another in solitude'. According to Pascal, people feel that they must 'get out of themselves' and kill time 'chasing a hawk or a hare or a servant maid'. It is the sport of kings. Such diversions bring out Baudelaire's prince of *Spleen* in Rilke for the young poet's digestion: 'The necessary quiet moment is interrupted by a pointless compulsion. It's like eating in order to vomit in order to eat again. Natural appetite is replaced by gluttony. Hunger becomes surplus to requirements, and thus *Sehnsucht* (yearning/longing) becomes as impossible as satiation. The simple necessities by which life renews itself are in trouble. You end up with a bad stomach.' Kappus might be tempted to forgo the communal meal, but he's a hungry boy.

Rilke goes on to idealise plants and animals: 'The beauty of their kingdom derives from a mute, enduring form of love and longing... They increase and multiply, quietly and patiently, from a necessity that is greater than pleasure and pain, and is more powerful than wanting or withstanding' (rather ignoring that the basic life of beasts and vegetation is rumination and terrestrial nourishment, the young poet might think as he digs into a sauerkraut). 'If only humans could embrace this mystery which penetrates nature down to its merest element, humbly bearing the weight of responsibility, which is not to be taken lightly, and respecting its fertility and fruitfulness, whether it be of the mind or body, for all the creations of the spirit spring from the corporal. Ideas are embodied, and indeed the body acts on them. However, the pure fruits of the mind, such as the poetry of love, compared to the elective *affinities* of carnal sex, are more delicate, concentrated and lasting' (see Guiding Note 4).

•

The Mind and Body of Sex

Rilke is implying that all love poems are essentially *Sehnsucht* (longing/yearning). *Sehnsucht* signifies the sex of the mind and *Geschlecht* is its bodily function. He sees no difference in kind between 'the desire to engender' a work of art and sexual desire. He evokes the mystery of nature as the seedbed of the pure poet: creativity is ballasted by 'the assent' coming from the animal and plant kingdom through their respective fertility and fruitfulness since time began. Thus, poetry and nature share the same mystery. He now broadens the argument to include all thinkers in this inheritance: 'In one creative thought, a thousand unremembered nights of love revive and lend it sublime majesty. Those who come together in the dark, entwined and united in the cradle of desire, are carrying out serious work in amassing the honeyed sweetness, dark savours, and other enrichments that will nourish some poet-to-come in order to rise up and chant of unspeakable delights.'

Note (to myself): indulge me. Trotting through my head is a jingle:

> I caught a little raindrop,
> and gave it to a flower.
> And a little bee
> put it in a tree,
> and made a little honey
> for you and me
> (Claude King, 1966)

'They summon up the future, and no matter what happens between them afterwards, the future will come in the form of a new creature, for based on a chance act the process comes into being in which *the bursting seed is received by a leaping egg.** It is not on the amorous surface, two people making love, but in their depths that it happens. And no matter if the lovers play this mystery false and are unfaithful to it, and many do and they are the losers, what materialises is passed on like a sealed package. Don't be distracted by love stories and Freudian case histories.'

Rilke's ellipsis between *Sehnsucht* (longing/yearning) and conception and birth fulfilled itself when the offspring is a poem. Kierkegaard found the key to unlock the mystery of creating a work of art in the score of Mozart's opera Don Giovanni, and he named it the 'musical erotic' (*Either/Or*). Both saw this realisation in terms of the libido. Interestingly, given their respective reputations, the springboard for Kierkegaard, the absent lover, is voluptuous, and for Rilke, the absent father, reproductive. The Dane sees the leap as an 'immediate' live performance. Rilke prefers to hold back and 'in solitude divine the essence of *Sehnsucht/Geschlecht* in order to come to know the beauty of their purpose, the purpose of their beauty', and so, in the fourth letter, he envisages a triptych of the three ages of women: the wonder of a young girl as a presentiment of motherhood; the glory of the young woman surrounded by her children; and the dignity of the old woman alone with her nostalgia (letters and photograph album).

'Mother earth and her fruits thereof are longed for, but in men there is a sort of maternity, both spiritual and physical, which brings them closer to women than is generally thought. They too are giving birth. And so, homage must be paid – ever so humbly – to man's carnal desires and their acceptance by woman. It is the man's *Sehnsucht* that makes the *Geschlecht* possible (in the act of possession, *the seed tracking to the open yoke*). Perhaps men and women are two sides of the same coin, and the regeneration of the world will consist in their joint liberation from all sentimental errors and disappointments, to find one another, not as opposites but as brothers and sisters, or at least good neighbors. They will be united, equal human beings, to carry together the heavy responsibility that sexuality has imposed on them, thus simplifying the usual problems with serious intent and mutual patience. But the mother and father of the issue is *Geschlecht*, and our deepest bow must always be to sex's mystery.'

In a letter to Lou, he adds, rather tactlessly given her reservations about motherhood, 'The mystery is like a poem written for us in invisible ink. The words appear on the page of their own accord, and cry out to us – ecstatically, eternally – when we hold the baby in our arms for the first time.' 'Holding the baby' is a *memory* sacred to Rilke, commemorated in the poem 'Great Night' (circa 1912-16), and in a letter (December 1906) responding to Clara who wasn't happy with him (Note 5, Chapter Four). On the other hand, Lou would have been sympathetic to his regeneration theory. Asked what she saw in Rilke, Lou said, unlike most men, he wasn't afraid to show his feminine side.

Note (to myself): *Rilke's '*the bursting seed is received by a leaping egg*' curiously reverses Lou's 'Homeric' theory that 'it is the restless movement of the sperm, and the inertia of the egg, produces the masculine need to wander out into the world, and the feminine need to stay at home and wait'. He is concerned with the making of poetry rather than *Geschlecht*, love-making (*'the seed tracking to the open yoke'*). For him, the egg is the seed-bed of poems, which the poet's *Sehnsucht*, longing/yearning, explodes into words. In that sense, Lou's diagnosis of his feminine side could reside in his status as pure poet: Rilke was a 'she' in his poetry and a 'he' in his life.

•

Sound Advice

The letter continues:

> 'One day this gender regeneration will be possible for the many. Meanwhile the solitary person must prepare the way, building bridges with hands less likely to be distracted. And to that end, my dear Kappus, learn to love your solitude. I know at present you find it hard, but profit from the pain it causes you by humming to yourself a lament. You tell me that those that you feel close to are far away, and that means you are beginning to expand the world around you. If what is close is far away the space created has no boundaries and you are already amongst the stars. Embrace your solitude. Take pleasure in your growth in a place nobody can accompany you.
>
> 'Be gentle but firm with those who you leave behind, and don't trouble them with your doubts or frighten them by confiding other-worldly experiences, whose joys and pains they cannot hope to understand. Look to find a level with them that is basic and affectionate, that does not allow them to interfere with the changes within you. Love in them a life that you are a stranger to, and be understanding with the older ones who distrust the very solitude your life relies on.'

Evidently Kappus has mentioned family tensions, and the penultimate paragraph concludes with how he should handle them. 'Avoid anything that will stir up the disputes that tend to occur between parents and children, exhausting and draining events which can kill the natural warmth. Nevertheless, it will survive a lack of comprehension if you accept deep down their love is unconditional, and when family quarrels can't be avoided, you find ways of putting up with the unpleasantness. Be a hypocrite, if necessary. Don't expect to be understood, and avoid asking for advice; you might have to take it. But remember, parental love has to be taken on trust. It comes from a long way off. It was there many aeons before you were born. It is part of your inheritance, and will outlive you. Believe in it, and it will bless and sustain you, no matter where life's journey takes you.'

The letter ends with Kappus's choice of profession given qualified approval, an expert one. 'As a trainee officer in a barracks in the middle of nowhere you have a lot of time on your hands, and that gives you independence. How you use it is up to yourself. The discipline of army routine is not confining if you are able to submit to it without sacrificing your inner life. Army life is not easy for anyone. The demands made are based on ancient conventions, and interpreting your duties leaves no room for swaying them. But, despite the other recruits, your solitude gives you a hold and a home for yourself, and all paths lead from it. You have all the time in the world to decide which one to take. My best wishes accompany you,

'Yours,
Rainer Maria Rilke'

Kappus would have been thoughtful about the concluding sentiment. 'He is not taking me seriously as a poet, knowing I'm more likely to die for my country than to write poems? But, sharing his most intimate thoughts, he doesn't think I'm stupid, I suppose. Though when he quotes back something I confided, I'm ashamed. It sounds so juvenile. His advice veers between the highfalutin and the practical, and the latter is what a kindly uncle might offer. I'm grateful for it. But his higher ideas are not always clear to me. They are more like soundings that cross the border into a county I'm excluded from, the limitless land where his poetry comes from. I wonder why he continues writing to me. Perhaps the kindly uncle wants a son and an ear. That said, it's all rather thrilling. When he floats high-flown ideas, I feel I'm rising up in an air balloon and the gods are pulling the strings. Still, I was happy when I knew, like Socrates, what I didn't understand. Now I know, I understand only too well and it doesn't make me happy…'

Chapter Four

Matters Arising from Letter Four

•

1. The Worpswede Monograph:

It wasn't that Rilke was writing the monograph with his eyes closed. His eye for art was ever open, particularly when it came to landscapes. Here the sun is often stifled behind the mists but, when they clear, the boundless plains are revealed: to the south an alp or two, to the north the sea which has to be imagined with its white cliffs and 'black-widow waves'. The bleak beauty of Worpswede's horizon inspired Heinrich Vogeler, who believed it was a proxy part of Russia.

The aesthetic that united the commune was a rapport between nature and man, with a value-added penchant for rural myths. The monograph was intended as a commercial venture for all the artists. Rilke abided by the letter if not the spirit of the protocol that Otto Modersohn drafted. Paula Becker and Clara, as wives, are not mentioned. Heinrich Vogeler, with his established reputation, dominates. Otto fares worst, faint praised as an illustrator of fairy tales. But Rilke himself is the presiding spirit, a distant figure looking seawards like Casper David Friedrich's incarnation of German Romanticism, engaged but not at home with what he sees, finding in the landscape 'a life which is not our life, without compassion for us, and as ineffable as the mystery of death'.

Otto got more than he bargained for. A solidly successful landscape painter, I doubt if he felt estranged from his subject matter. Moreover, Rilke is breaking with the commune's aesthetic: 'Landscapes are alien to us. One is terribly alone with a budding grove or a babbling brook. It is easier to feel closer to a dead body than a tree.' But he makes a concession, claiming 'in childhood this is not so. This oneness with nature is lost by growing up. Recapturing this unity is the artist's task so man and landscape, figure and its environs, find one another.' Rodin had been working on his highly subjective neo-romantic symbolism, and seeing beyond the self is his object. 'A portrait is not the representation of a person but a figure as a landscape.' Rilke sees a simulacrum in art of the 'thing-poems' he has begun to write.

In the monograph, he elevates his celebrated friend so far above the other artists that reissues of the monograph are entitled *Rilke's Heinrich Vogeler*. Interest in Vogeler has been sustained anecdotally by his subsequent about-turn. During the Great War, the successful businessman-artist discovered communism, and in 1931 immigrated to Russia, where he briefly thrived as an architectural artist but did not escape the purges and, deported to a workcamp, died of malnutrition (1942).

Rilke composed a sequence of poems in response to Vogeler paintings. They conform more than the monograph to the ethos of the commune, limiting the influence of Baudelaire that led him to write to Lou around this time that beauty could be created from the ugly and the alien: 'It will become paltry and insignificant when looked for only in the pleasing. Beauty is everywhere to be discovered, even in what some people find repulsive.' Rather, the poems show the affinity with Keats that Kassner, noted ('They both have a marvellous Narcissus-like lyricism'). The pictorial preciseness does not have Keats's visual voluptuousness but they share his *negative capability* (See Guiding Note 2). He soaks up impressions without imposing his personality and takes them as they come, allowing himself to be surprised.

Rilke in his last year (1926) wrote to Marina Tsvetayeva, regretting that poetry can only emerge from 'a purely anonymous centre', echoing to the end Keats's view that the true poet lacks 'character', and 'self-passion', and is therefore able to identify with 'any one particular beauteous star'. Keats entered the soul of his poetry in his youth and never really left him, even during his modernist phase with the 'thing-poems'. Although he came to baulk (thanks to Baudelaire) at Keats's 'beauty is truth, truth beauty', and variously asserted that the sublime and the sordid cohabit this dialectical world and the synthesis is poetry (the Hegelian triad is mine).

The Worpswede poems though are on the sublime side ('A girl, white and before the evening hour'), but deceptively so. An apparently anodyne line, 'The roses were never so red', although descriptively apt after a rainy morning, it is a sly reprise of a line in Verlaine's 'Spleen', a poem expressing disenchantment with natural beauty (when his muse-wife became a disaffected siren). The Verlaine is in turn a homage to Baudelaire's more famous 'Spleen' poems. When Rilke seems simple, watch out.

•

2. On 'Living an idea':

This unattributed tribute to Kierkegaard is a left-handed one. He skims over the concept so lightly that Søren would probably not have recognised it either. True to say, Rilke liked the idea more than its practical application. While Kierkegaard left nothing to the imagination, studiously seeing through what he argued, Rilke left everything to it. And so, the original idea of an idealised life tends to be lost. He is telling Kappus to accept that the big questions are unanswerable and soldier on composing poems and/or preparing for war.

Why Rilke took to Kierkegaard is a moot question. At the time he was an all but forgotten philosopher. There are certain similarities between them. They were both little men who considered themselves physically challenged. Their relations to women seemed always at a cross-roads. But Kierkegaard was more inclined to turn back, and Rilke to move on. Both were elusive. They spend an inordinate amount of time certifying their uncertainties, yet made time to socialise, for opposite reasons: the Dane didn't want to be taken seriously, Rilke did.

Both had father complexes, but Rilke's troubled relations with his low-achieving father were small-time in comparison to Kierkegaard's with his, who at forty was rich enough to sell his business and retire to a life of contemplation, prayer and generating children. Michael Pederson Kierkegaard believed that as a shepherd boy in the barren moorlands of Jutland, he had struck a pact with the devil when caught in a storm. This eventually harvested him a fortune in war bonds during the year of Napoleon's defeat by Wellington in Vitoria and Søren's birth.

In return for the 'Devil's Midas' he was convinced that all seven of his children would suffer a 'quiet despair' and die before him. This would be necessary so God could forgive him. Søren suffered the 'quiet despair' but, as it turned out, three children, including the delicate Søren, outlived Michael Pederson. The 'sins of his father' marked Kierkegaard's writing indelibly, most notably in *Fear and Trembling*, a meditation on Abraham and Isaac. He had to believe in the mercy of his father's God because despite everything he loved him.

Kierkegaard's self-imposed celibacy, which Rilke shared in his fashion, would at least prevent his father's legacy of dread being passed on to future generations. He lived in a no-woman's-land but was tortured by *Sehnsucht* longings he sublimated by writing about them. And so, the last thing he wanted was the 'burden' of his sexuality shared with anyone, let alone a Lou Salomé or a community of free spirits who made love mainly by letters. He courted solitude, but not isolated in a little room faced by the boundless plains. Even when correcting galley-proofs he chose to do so riding through Copenhagen in a coach. He only confided to his journal what he felt about his Regine, his unfortunate fiancée. Otherwise, he feigned indifference to her to save her from himself by putting a more worthy suitor in her way, and she lived happily ever after.

But the fruits of Kierkegaard's rejection of Regine for a solitary existence proved rich pickings; 'Write, write, write' carried to a rare extreme. Upwards of sixty manuscripts, a third of them self-published with pen-names in his life, a variegated commentary on living with an idea that could only succeed with failure. Not that he felt fulfilled. His heart wished that poetry would come from his writings, but his head told him that Jules Renard's '*L'ironie est le pudeur de l'humanitéé*' would prevent that. And he had to settle for a dual carriageway: the inner lane was chalked by the experimental psychology that he applied to his *Sehnsucht* and inspired Freud and others to investigate human sexual response, and the outer lane a philosophy of living an idea which anticipated existentialism. Rilke, on the other hand, was on a one-way street to poems, and poems alone. But the roadmap of the pure poet and the impure philosopher was paved with suffering, borne by seeing themselves, respectively, as an 'immovably-centred' hero and anti-hero.

•

3. *Sehnsucht/Geschlecht*:

Reading other people's letters is like eavesdropping on a one-sided conversation in a bus. You miss elided references, the presumed unsaid and the look of the silent interlocutor that bespeaks volumes. Rilke is the one that does all the talking, often getting carried away with an idea. He doesn't pause to explain and often uses different words for the same thing within paragraphs. It isn't tidy but the general drift can be guessed. Still, an eavesdropper can get it horribly wrong.

Full third-party understanding requires a consistency of terms congenial enough to be shared without hesitation, and thus the facts under description become a narrative event. In *Letters*, I'm stuck for a phrase in my transcription to encapsulate the essence of '*Geschlecht*'. 'Ur-sex', with a nod to *Urgeschichte*, (primitive), would be open to mimic mockery. And 'essential sex' could be from a primer for low-achievers. I consult a range of English and French translations of *The Letters*. They all, including Claude Porcell, strictly adhere to Rilke's variations. I, myself, have used 'sexual experience' most often, but elsewhere 'sex life' and 'love-making'.

In order to establish a single term that would help the reader, I looked with Gretchen Malherbe (Joab's German scholar) for a pattern in Rilke's usage. The adjectives he most frequently qualifies *Geschlecht* with are *Schwer* (heavy, difficult) and *Leicht* (light, easy). It's a delicate balance that meets sometimes in the compound *Schwerleicht*, heavy-light (possibly a see-saw coinage for *Schwerpunkt*, centre of gravity, a word that figures in the letter about Richard Dehmel on the theme of sex). In short, the light-hearted *Leicht* and the heavy breathing *Schwer* are what, respectively, lightens and weighs us down in sexual affairs in order to keep heads above the parapet and feet on the ground. Something Rilke doesn't find easy:

> I'm heavier than gravity.
> I fall, I fall without end
> to get to the bottom of myself.
> ('Man of Depths', circa 1903)

His *Geschlecht-Leicht* evidently is losing out. And despite the 'honeyed-sweetness' of his celebration of *Geschlecht* in the middle of the letter ('the exquisite juice of the ripest fruit from the tree of knowledge'), he prefaces it with a warning: 'In truth, sex is Difficult'. Even though the light/heavy nexus derives from Nietzsche's *The Gay Science*, Dionysian joy (*bejahung*) is an afterthought. Who is he trying to help, I ask?

•

I need a break.

Joab tells me that the 'essence' in '*Geschlecht*' is an 'amateur concept', lacking measurable content.

'Why not? It's just like poetry: only as good as its words, prehistoric before logic became man's criteria for good sense.'

'Yes, Augustus, pre-rationalism is lurking in there. But Rilke's use of the word 'essence' is philosophic – the 'what it is' of man's nature (Aristotle). In sum, what exists, or is made to exist by refining it to its calculus, its dy/dx. Gretchen says that Rilke uses *Wesen* for 'essence', rather than *Essenz*, so the manufacture of an aphrodisiac (or petroleum, essence in French) can be discounted. He has man's primordial nature in mind, our primeval beginnings.'

'Rudolf Kassner has been talking to him?'

'No, Lou Salomé. Rilke essentially idealises *Geschlecht* in its most primitive state, stripped of contemporary conventions and customs, where desire is love, and nature ordains that 'its impulse and purpose have dual consequences: a reflex satisfied, and the perpetuation of the species' (presumably when the moon is right). It's her version of vitalism.'

'The second consequence is his own, I presume, not Lou's.'

'No, Nietzsche is the source for his quasi vitalism. Lou suggested, in the wake of Nietzsche's death (1900), that he write something about the philosopher's unfortunate connection with Richard and Cosima Wagner. He read Fred and got what he wanted for his own purposes. The unpublished essay concludes with a bathos that denotes his heart wasn't in it:

> Nietzsche attached his insights and hopes to what was happening in Bayreuth, not because they had anything in common with Richard Wagner's chauvinism, but because the Wagners were close, far too close, to where he lived in Switzerland and Rome.

'Then Rilke adds something Nietzsche confided to Lou in a letter:

> Wagner says (my headaches) are due to onanism, and I must get married or write an opera. Cosima asked me to buy undergarments for him in Rumpf's in Basle to take to Rome where we meet up, and I will as usual offer them a paw without a claw.'

'In sum, he was naughty boy to Richard, and a convenience to Cosima.

'Gretchen opines that Nietzsche would have introduced Rilke to the idea of the "primordial being", *Urwesen*. "For fleeting moments, we are truly primitive beings, and abandon ourselves to an overwhelming desire for the pleasure in existence. The conventional miseries disappear, and we are no longer individuals, but subside into our primal beginnings to experience the joys of life and procreation."'

'I can't find mention of *Urwesen* in his letters to Kappus'.
'Rainer Maria wasn't encouraging the fun that he wasn't having himself.'

We had arrived at where I left off, and with a conclusion. Rilke's submerging himself in a quest to get to the bottom of *Geschlecht* and its 'essence' could be a desperate attempt to revive his sentimental life. Getting back to a primordial state where sex is just itself, pure and simple, clearly has it difficulties. But the objective is not simply to return to the caveman's 'rutting', which was designed to make his females productive in a world where there is safety in numbers. He is contemplating a repetition forward (See, Guiding Note 5) of Nietzsche's *Urwesen* (primordial being) into primal sex, the sophistication of the caveman's impulse offering a future for sexual relations where nature and nurture meet. Thus renewed, man and woman will advance hand in hand into a horizon of Dionysian reoccurrences.

And so, I arrive at 'primal sex' as my defining phrase for *Geschlecht*. Inserting the prefix 'neo' would be apt, but it sounds like a mouthful of gravel and makes me lisp. It would be premature anyway. Rilke's idea in *The Letters* is only notional as yet, and he is probably not the one to realise it in the early twentieth century. Far from being an advocate of sexual liberation for men, let alone women, Rilke, in merging the dual consequences of primal sex, subsumes the satisfaction of the reflex into the proud father holding the baby. He could be said to be backtracking to traditional Catholic dogma. Although the argument can be made that this is not inconsistent with caveman sex, where the act of possession and procreation are the natural law's cycle for population growth. Whichever, sealing them with dewy-eyed fatherly affections conforms to bourgeois conventions of infant adoration and, given the conduct of his own life, might be seen to be a mite hypocritical.

The happy event of Ruth's birth may have had its joyous Nietzschean moment, but it soon passed. He feels responsible for, but not to, the consequences, and Clara is left holding the baby. In his favour, it could be said, his *recollection backwards* (See Guiding Note 5) on how he felt holding baby Ruth, became the stuff of heart-felt poetry that still lives on, no doubt making German fatherhood more sensitive. In the relatively late poem 'Great Night' a baby cries and her mother can't quieten her. The poet father feels helpless, like a boy, an outsider, not allowed to join in the game. Until suddenly, he realises 'I'm grown up' and can make a game of it. He throws the baby in the air and fields her safely, like a ball. She recognises him with a smile that takes his breath away, and that smile will be lodged within him for ever. But Clara, for one, might well have hoped for a more practical *repetition forward*. An immortal poet doesn't make up for an absent father.

When Rilke thinks like a Janus-faced sphinx, Kappus had good reason to boggle. After riddling that 'creativity' (of the mind) 'has its origins in physical fertility. They spring from the same loins. Except that the creative spirit is more subtle, ecstatic, and less fleeting than the carnal', he celebrates sex's emergence through pre-history and the animal world, and the pleasure and/or pains it brings through the visceral memory (or conditioned reflexes?) of autochthonal in-dwellers, thinking backwards to project it into the present. It is science like Goethe's, poetical rather than based on any form of research except into his imagination, poet to poet. Only the flattery of the confidence would have tempted Kappus to give him the benefit of the doubt.

•

4.'Sex of the Mind':

Rilke was never deterred from ignoring the obvious and waxing world-historical wonders. While closing down his marriage he was carrying the flesh of the world on his shoulders, amplifying it by taking on all sexual activity since time began. In his renewed correspondence with Lou Salomé, such rapturous sublimations signaled a higher plain of epistolary intimacy, and it suited them both.

I doubt if the anthropology of sex was in the forefront of the young poet's mind. Like Malte in *The Notebooks*, he was reading Baudelaire's 'A *une passante*'. The poem is about a sprightly veiled young widow who passed him by in a Paris street, and catches his eye with a look that bespeaks a whirlwind romance with a sweet consummation. But alas, '*Un éclair... puis le nuit*', 'A lightning flash... and then night'. She's off. Their eyes won't meet again. Except in regret. It is a poem that might well encourage a lonely, frustrated young man to romanticise widow women in black.

And then he would be annoyed by Rilke uxoriously going on about making babies, misunderstanding his remark that virgins 'had not achieved anything'. Perhaps he wasn't quite sure what he meant himself. Was he expressing weariness with mooning young girls he had met during the holidays and was too embarrassed and well-brought-up to say that *he* hadn't achieved anything yet, and remained a male virgin? However, on reflection, the triptych's homage to maternity doubling with making poems saves Rilke by the bell. Poetry, like parental love, comes a long way and the poet carries with him the progeny of his ancestors (from Homer to Novalis and Goethe). I doubt that he realised that Rilke, in his life, had lost sight of the analogy. At the time he was still recovering from becoming a father.

•

5. Marital musical chairs:

Kierkegaard was in the same situation as Rilke in turning his back on married love. The difference being that, by cutting the nuptial knot at the engagement stage, he remained a virgin (at least as far as he knew. In his student days friends got him drunk in a brothel). A year before his death at forty-two, he confided to his journal, 'Though sexual relations have long lost their immediacy for me, I'm not ready to become a saint and embrace abstinence unconditionally.' Hitherto, the either/or of sex for him was 'satisfying an instinct or abstaining on reflection.' He admits to 'a certain intellectual embarrassment... marooned between virtue's vice-grip and vice's shame-face', while 'respectable people simply get married to satisfy the instinct and hide the fact behind social conventions'. He quotes Oliver Goldsmith's *Vicar of Wakefield* on 'the service to humanity of begetting a large family', and calls it hypocrisy. 'Still', he continues, 'producing children to serve the commonweal, though transparently bogus, is as good a reason as the next,' and he proposes that 'the State should set up a stable for sex and make the King the Master of the Stud'.

Rilke was not prone to be ironical with himself like the self-lacerating Kierkegaard. Writing letters by the dozen was a release from everyday concerns. Moreover, getting carried away on a tidal wave of spontaneous self-expression loosened him up for poems. Kassner in his posthumous memoir wrote, 'The work and the letters are as a coat to its lining, and sometimes I feel the coat should have been inside out,' conceding that 'clothes worn inside out can still fit'. And, indeed, there's material in his letters that is uncomfortably close to being worn the wrong way around. But his lining has wings to soar beyond almost anything that can be found in his poems. However, not being grounded in prosody, the flight can be strangely unsubstantial, like a kite that has broken from its string. True, it can get caught in a tree and be recovered for poems.

•

6. 'Love Your Solitude':

Although Rilke rhapsodises on solitude to the young poet, his relation to it was not the pleasure of his own company. It is a working condition while waiting for poetry to declare itself. Sometimes, when his muse was not talking to him, he lost patience and cried out to see if he was being heard. Mostly there is a search party of letters to send out, and reading to catch up with. However, his constant companion is the horizon. Chronic wanderlust keeps his eyes on it. Writing the fourth letter, it's probably not on the North Sea with its 'black-widow waves', but the faint outline of an Alp, for Rome, his next interim stop, beckons.

The *tour d'horizon* makes him restless, and restlessness he sees as the poet's condition, a St Vitus dance of the spirits. Half-staying, half-leaving, his mind running on the spot, spins. When it begins to wobble, he takes off. Berlin, Paris, Vienna steady him. But such cultural Meccas seem too 'finite, too definite'. The poet needs 'the measureless, the unobtainable, the impossible'. He only feels at home when alone with the 'spiritual presences' that possess him. It doesn't matter where. It's not a place, it's a space. And there is no room for other people. He repeats, 'I know those close to you are far away, but that means in your solitude you are creating a wider space around you. Soon you will be amongst the stars. Profit from it.' Meanwhile, Rome, the eternal city, will have to do.

During his perpetual peregrinations, Rilke maintained a still centre, confiding to Lou, 'Although I can't escape the fates that entwine me, it is necessary to find the strength to lift life in its entirety and draw it into calm open spaces to pass quiet, deep days of fruitful labor.'

Note (to myself): making a virtue of isolation once again brings to mind Teilhard de Chardin's, 'Do not limit yourselves to the selfishness of corporal contact, but together, side by side, without touching, open yourself to the spaces between the flesh, the royal road, along which there is no satiety, no end or return.' (*The Phenomenon of Man*)

Rilke, in letters to Lou, puzzles over how he himself can profit from this exultant state of mind, born of solitude. She says nothing, thinking perhaps that he should get out more, and/or accept analysis. Kappus would have simply assumed that for Rilke elevated spirits were a prelude to composing poems. But, mindful that despite publishing so many books of poetry to critical acclaim in Germany, his mentor was feeling the financial pinch (no complimentary copies). Maybe he ought to take a leaf out of Jacobsen's book and write a poet's novel. Which of course is what Rilke was doing.

•

7. The Novel:

Writing the letters to the young poet and *The Notebooks of Malte Laurids Brigge* are two sides of the same creative coin. It is in the modelling of Malte that they coincide, at least by refraction. Their most obvious likeness is in their tripod names, which have the ring of blank verse. Malte Laurids Brigge, the lost poet on the brink of madness, Franz Xaver Kappus, the ambitious but naïve poetical soldier with a 'secret sorrow'* (every young poet worth their Basho banana has one. As they get older it becomes a 'secret shame'). Rainer Maria Rilke, the Coleridgean chameleon (see Guiding Note 2), had been all these things a few years before as a callow youth. Malte is desperately seeking to find poetry, like Kappus, while Rilke is fearful of losing it. He needs Malte to be distanced from himself in order 'to stand back and see clearly into his own being' (letter to Lou), and to do so he is putting the young poet between him and the soul lost in Paris that he was not so long ago. Lou, observing his restless movements, both in travel and towards others, remarked that a visit to Freud might unblock the *id* he was searching for.

* *Note* (to myself): when I asked Sorley Maclean, Scotland's iconic poet, what is behind the sorrow in his poetry, he laughed, and said, 'It's no secret. Sorrow is sorrow.' Lord Byron is a prime exemplar of 'secret shame', but for him it was more secret than shame (guilt was absent).

Above all, Rilke wants to write a novel that will sell, and so the notion of Malte as a distinct character that readers can identify with is still on the cards. It was to be an arbour to keep the wolf of responsibilities from the door. But he always has something more important to do as a poet. Clara tries to be understanding and reads extracts sent in letters with enthusiasm, as does Lou (without the enthusiasm). The letters to Kappus allow him to relax and think freely without the constraints of judgement or unfinished business while feeling he is researching.

The novel is more at the crossroads between the beaten track that he wants to put behind him and the intimidating boulevard of experience. They meet where his life in poetry has reached with its uncertainties. In the letters, Rilke is free to think about where he's going or wants to go. His can reroute the pot-holed past into the novel and take a royal road to saunter with a proxy younger self. Or, when he wants to be alone, to levitate an overview of his own future. He has hopes that the dark side of Malte's mooning will surge into the light, 'spiritual presences' having entered and worked on him, releasing him for poetry. The novel is starting out –in Kierkegaardian terms – as a *recollection*, a *repetition backwards*. It is not a happy beginning, but he has tasked himself to evolve it into a *repetition forward* which will bring it back to life.

Note (to myself): Kierkegaard on *repetition* could be simplified as follows: a photograph offers a recollection or *repetition backwards*, whereas, a memory is a new event, a repetition forward. Although a photo can trigger a recollection, it is of the past, and remains so, subject to nostalgia, related to the present by comparison. A memory is less predictable and, more often than not, renews the past to give it a future.

Joab mocks me 'And so *déjà vu* become *deja* new, or is it *nu*?' The simplification of a philosophic idea does not necessarily make it clearer. I'll try again with outside support. Maurice Blanchot says that in Proust events 'can be brought back from the receding tide of time, not as memories but as reoccurrences in real time'. Gilbert Sorrentino comments on Ralph Cusack's novel *Cadenza*: 'The author remembers a night of love as he would wish it to be, and therefore can endlessly repeat it in his mind. It is of the moment, ever present, like something to look forward to.' William Carlos Williams says in his epic poem Paterson, 'Anywhere is everywhere'. Cusack says, 'Anytime is every time. Nothing disappears'.

Maybe, dear reader, you should go to the *Appendix*, Guiding Note 5.

•

8. How to Handle the Family:

Rilke in effect is telling Kappus, 'Such is life. No rose without a thorn, but many a thorn without a rose,' more or less quoting Schopenhauer and anticipating Goebbels' 'there-there' to his fiancée Little Else, discarded as she was 'clinging'. But his advice is common sense: keep your distance. Easy enough in the young poet's circumstances. Nevertheless, he would be relieved, and maybe think, rather than go home for Christmas, I should make a surprise visit to the family. He might reasonably wonder if Rilke was condescending to him or, rather revealingly, advising himself.

When Kappus confesses in his first letter to an unhappy childhood, Rilke reverses its import ('Childhood. You still have got it. Dig deep into that jewel beyond a price, that treasure trove of memories.') and continues on mounting o *altitudinal* without visible means of support. The recipient's revolt is to turn the tables; Rilke's childhood was quite possibly worse than his. He is writing to himself. And, indeed, the 'treasure trove' of Malte's childhood memories, mostly unhappy, embellished his novel in progress.

The revolt is half-hearted. Kappus is thankful to Rilke for his 'tender concern'. But his flights of fancy bemused him. Mercifully they were capable of changing tack when the kite was evidently not going to return to earth. He would have also wondered about the more vatic utterances on primal sex. When Rilke says sex, primal or otherwise, is not a personal phenomenon, but 'universal, communal, planted there by nature' – in short, it is for everybody and nobody – can he be wholly serious?

When Rilke's didacticism becomes tempered with advanced ideas, this would have helped to allay the young poet's doubts and fears. The phallicist and bourgeois sentiments around motherhood dissipate, and he moves on to an assertion of equality between men and women. Rilke claims that once primal sex is universally embraced 'it will break down the differences between genders. Men and women will no longer be in opposition to one another. The difficulties and indifferences between them will disappear.' This happy state echoes what Rilke says in a letter to Lou around the same time: 'Men and women will reach out towards the same objective like brothers and sisters in order to carry together the burden of their sexuality.' Kappus would be cheered up by the thought.

9. A Repetition Forward:

Rilke's optimistic view of the future of primal sex foresees a time when 'a responsible Eros will nourish the Tree of Life, and man will reclaim what he lost with the Fall'. Does he sense 'spiritual presences' in the air that auger this Utopia? Kierkegaard once more could be one. In Either/*Or*, the 'Seducer', in order to get under the skin of Mozart's Don Giovanni, tells the tale of the 'musical erotic':

> There once was a primordial paradise on a mountain called Venus, where wild pleasures could be experienced in their natural state. Dance rather than language was its music. There was no place for reflection. You didn't think twice before you leaped. This is where Don Giovanni was born, and grew up at home with his sensuality. He existed for it. His downfall came when Christendom arrived to establish sin and the flesh lost its independence. Mind over body imperatives brought hesitation into this paradise of sensuality. The delights of the flesh were invaded by the snake of doubt and dread. And so, began the descent into the human, and all hell was let loose.

Rilke turns upside-down the doomed trajectory of Kierkegaard's 'musical erotic', starting with the human and ascending to its apotheosis with a neo-romantic symbolist version of what now would be called a 'New Man'. He acknowledges that this state of grace is for future generations, and offers counsel to the young poet as to how to prepare oneself for the resurrection of primal sex in equity. However, it's more like passing an exam than a spiritual exercise. It progresses by putting what happens into words: 'The solitary man senses with his own hands and eyes, putting what happens into words, making mistakes, but correcting them as he reads back, or is read by a sympathetic friend or another self.' Of course, Rilke is thinking more of Lou, and 'write, write, write' echoes in his head courtesy of Tolstoy and Rodin. Meanwhile, with the fourth letter he was scribbling a billet-doux to primal sex and the young poet recruit loved it.

Chapter Five

Rome and Room Enough:

Letter Five (29 October 1903, Rome)

•

The next letter, his fifth, is short and friendly. Rilke tells Kappus that the two-month delay in replying to his last was because being in transit wasn't conducive to the necessary peace and quiet. He is wintering in Rome. Clara has come with him. This is signalled by the use of 'we'. Her education in art is what they most share now, and Rodin had pointedly remarked that 'all roads for a student sculptor would lead to Rome and the glories of Bernini'. At present, they are staying at a hotel near 'the finest equestrian statue in Roman – that of Marcus Aurelius'. But they don't feel at home, and he looks forward in a few weeks 'alone in a simple, old summerhouse in the depths of a great park, away from the noise and inconsequentiality'. He doesn't think much of the Eternal City. 'Oppressively sad, the stifling museum atmosphere… with the aleatory vestiges of another age, that has nothing to do with our own and, of course, it wasn't meant to.'

The letter can be passed over as a vehicle of advice. It's Rilke's rather jaundiced Roman holiday. 'There is no more beauty here than elsewhere but, despite the restorations, the past is rendered meaningless, heartless and valueless. I admire the lively waterways, and the flights of steps designed by Michelangelo cascading down to where the tourists disturb the peace with their idle chatter…It is always possible with patience to find a few things in which everlasting value can be felt, something you can love, something solitary to part take in silence, away from the maddening crowds. But, in the main, Rome is no different from anywhere else. There is beauty to found everywhere.'

He promises a longer letter to discuss Kappus's writing. 'The parcel containing your work hasn't arrived. Maybe you sent it to Germany where forwarding abroad is complicated. And the Italian postal service is less than reliable. I'm sorry not to have it, but feel free to send me any verses you've written recently. I will read and reread them to get to their heart as best I can, my salutations.
Yours, Rainer Maria Rilke

Rome and Room Enough:

The Schoenberg Deception

The background noises to Rilke's air of dissatisfaction with Rome (and Clara's presence) are musical. The *enfant terrible* of German composers, Arnold Schoenberg, had chosen Richard Dehmel's poems for settings rather than his. Schoenberg's compositions were causing riots, and the leading artists of expressionism (Kandinsky and friends) had adopted him as a rallying cry.

Hitherto, music as an art didn't play much of a part in his life, other than him paying lip-service to the Orphic in poems. As far as he was concerned, Dehmel was adding scandal to flagrant dissonance. But he was galled at seeing an opportunity let slip for a modernist alignment with Germany's particular area of eminence, music. And so, once again Dehmel had stolen a march. Lou, though not unsympathetic, teasingly reminded him her poem, 'The Hymn to Life', had inspired Nietzsche to set it to music ('If you have no more joy to give me/ there still remains your pain').

In the first decade of the twentieth century, Schoenberg was bursting the bond of a bygone aesthetic and changing the face of music. He dismantled traditional tonality, and composed directly from the subconscious ('the inborn, instinctive, primal'). Rilke ought to have recognized that this was an analogous approach to what Rodin had been encouraging for him. And the fruits thereof, the publication of his 'thing-poems' in *New Poems* (1907/8), was to coincide with Schoenberg's atonal breakthrough in his Opus 15. But the text for it, *Der Buch der hangenden Garten* ('The Book of the Hanging Gardens'), was a poem by of all German poets, the venerable Stefan George, an eccentric symbolist with the right French connections (a habitué at Mallarmé's Tuesday evenings). The composer's choice of poets still rankled when ten years later Rilke wrote, 'Music: Breathing of Statues', which puts the art outside human habitation in the silence of his 'solitude':

'Music, the end of language, the pathway towards the heart's extinction, transforming feeling into audible landscapes... A sacred goodbye to melody's other side, pure ether, boundless. We can't possibly live in this space growing around us.'

It is the most ambiguous of revenges, a poem that only Schoenberg could have set.

•

The Domestication of Poetry

Though Rilke had chosen Rodin as his main maître, it didn't exclude the ghost of Mallarmé. Even more than Baudelaire, Mallarmé haunted him. Not least because composers everywhere were setting his poems to music, most notably Maurice Ravel, Rilke's exact contemporary (and four inches smaller than him!). Rodin had warned Rilke against Mallarmé. Not for the poetry, but he scorned the twinning of bourgeois respectability with bohemian slumming. The continuation of Mallarmé's Tuesday evenings after his death would have been of keen interest to Rilke, as all the big names of the avant-garde would be there. More pressingly, given his present circumstances, he must have wondered how Mallarmé had managed to support his wife and daughters in their expected comfort, while filling the pipes and glasses of half the artists and writers in Paris, and yet his poetry didn't seem to suffer.

Mallarmé was the ultimate exemplar of Jean de La Bruyère's 'sensible writer'. He accepted the divide between high art and paid work, learning to put up with the drudgery. His compromise permitted the poetry to flourish in its shade. The job was not so challenging or well-paid that it made Stéphane too comfortable. *Au contraire*, it irritated him often enough into disappearing into himself, and poems obeyed his call, though the mechanical routine was a blessing when his creative batteries ran down. In Vladimir Nabokov's phrase it afforded him 'periods of perfect blankness' to recharge them.

His paid work was three-part: teaching, writing educational textbooks and fashion notes for newspapers and brochures. By varying them he was able to combine a *recherché* literary life with keeping up the family income. Madame Mallarmé, hardly a soul companion in his avant-garde endeavours, was appeased, and in time was persuaded to preside over his Tuesday salon, though she can't have been thrilled with this ragbag of decadent sprites and spongers invading her conjugal home. She kept expenditure down – cheap tobacco and unmatured rum – and this generated an atmosphere of tipsy politeness and genteel coughing that lent artistic excitement through incongruity. It was unmissable for Verlaine, the lost old boy, who was like a living statue (children would give him pennies). Hailed as the prince of poets, he wandered in and out in a silent haze. Baudelaire had seen him coming, 'the king of a rainy country with the green water of Lethe running through his veins.' James Joyce dreamed he went there once but felt excluded by his rather Edwardian poems and nobody asked him to sing. Rilke's French would not have been good enough to make the impression he wanted. But both arrived in Paris in 1902, too late to attend other than the memorial salons that Paul Valéry presided over.

Mallarmé was an uninspiring teacher, and so he gave himself over to the dogged compilation of textbooks, though not with the zest that he edited fashion copy. Indeed, the Impressionist poet of almost Nothingness took ladies' modes very seriously for money up front. Yet his poetry survived forty years of pedagogic and other plodding, relieved by his Tuesdays, and by occasional sojourns in his humble houseboat on the Seine in the company of a lady with long red hair who lived two doors down.

His extended all-female family needed their mittens and ruffs. The wolves at his door were real enough, but he tamed them. While the poets and artists smoked and drank liquor out of his hands, he stoked the furnace to keep the 'Great Work' sparking, 'The Book which would contain the Orphic unraveling of the Earth.' He learned to steal time from sleep through insomnia with his Muse, 'dreadful nights faced by the candid blankness of a white page protecting its innocence'.

Mallarmé died suddenly aged fifty-six in 1898. Auguste Renoir was amongst the many that were sorely affected. His son Jean said that the great colourist only painted in black and white that day. At the commemorative dinner that the Tuesday habitués organised, he uncharacteristically overindulged in food and wine, declaring, '*On n'enterre pas Mallarmé tous les jours*' (It's not every day one buries Mallarmé)). He wasn't bothered when Rodin bitched that the poet didn't like the portrait he did of him, saying 'you gave him the air of a rich banker. *A tout fashion*'. Auguste replied, 'That would not have displeased him. He who struggled all his life to keep his family in the middle class.'

Nowadays, Mallarmé's strategies for financing family, and other distractions, would be under pressure from a literary agent with a well-shod foot in the door demanding marketable copy for a celebrity niche. He would probably have revelled in all this (after all he promoted himself effectively), but it is doubtful that his mind could have remained clear enough to confuse – and this is his achievement – the literary world for over a century with poems like 'A Dice Thrown Never Will Annul Chance'. As Derrida said, 'If it is "about" anything, it's about the need to stop thinking about its aboutness.' Rilke would have sung with that, and once he broke with the 'thing-poems' and Rodin's proscriptions, his efforts to translate Mallarmé were to prove inspirational in approaching his 'Great Work', the *Duino Elegies* and *The Sonnets to Orpheus*.

.

Chapter Six

A Christmas Greeting:

Letter Six (23 December 1903, Rome)

•

The sixth letter came two months later, written on Christmas Eve. Snugly settled in his cottage in the park with no distractions except his own, Rilke thinks of Kappus, all alone, too serious to join in the 'he-festivals, blackguard gibes, ironical licence, bull dances, drinking, laughter' (Walt Whitman) of barracks life. His seasonal greetings are more a commiseration. 'You must be finding your chosen life harder than usual to bear... But it is possible to find solitude anywhere. In a *biergarten* or the side of a mountain. Be overwhelmed by your solitude's creation of a widening space around you until you are amongst the stars. I know those close to you are far away and at this time of year the temptation to seek out company, no matter how inappropriate, is pressing. It is precisely at such difficult moments that, if you guard your solitude, it becomes a solace that grips you, as natural as the sadness that early spring brings or the growing pains of a boy. Don't give up on it. It's what you have to do, going into yourself, and not meeting anyone for hours.'

Note (to myself): the difference between loneliness and solitude would have troubled the young man. 'All alone' means being sad and lonely. You're suspended between boredom and self-pity, and lifting yourself by writing poetry can make it seem bearable. But, like many a youth before him, he finds out that such poems are pastiche, the lonely only hear their own echo and it sounds hollow. He can't read and, rather than submitting to despair, goes against Rilke's injunction and writes an essay about books that mean something special to him. Dare he send it to his maître?

On the other hand, Rilke is too full of his poetry to be lonely. In the background of his solitude he hears other people's echoes, like the brouhaha of traffic you get used to in any city. It fills him with a quiet satisfaction to know he can't hear what they're saying. His solitude is an opportunity to turn himself inside out so he can vibrate with nature, and at a stretch reach out to the horizon and almost touch it. He takes in the landscape in more ways than one, and the sky is not the limit. It can be exhaled. He has cosmic company, 'spiritual presences' that, when they inhabit him, can make him 'go beyond words' to know his feelings and hopefully return to earth to make poems with *felt* thoughts.

•

Be as a Child

'It's not easy, but stay away from people as much as possible, and you can return to the solitariness you knew as a child when the adults about you busied themselves with matters that seemed important because you didn't understand what they were up to. In time, you came to realise that it wasn't much, "all vain tumult and salary". But you must not be hard on them. They too have their solitary moments, only you don't notice because it's usually in a crowd. Draw on the magnitude and direction of your own solitude to recapture the innocence of a child who doesn't comprehend and is happy to leave it at that. Knowingness means you become party to the rejection and contempt that you want to distance yourself from. Don't waste your time and energy bothering to explain your position vis-à-vis other people.

'At first, in your solitude, dear Mr Kappus, think of anything you like. Childhood memories or your future. But be attentive to what's rising up within you, and place it above the immediate. Chart your relationship with it (there is no harm in keeping notes). Work on the heights of your solitude, your own personal world, always with love and you will be well on the way to making a vocation for yourself.'

•

Mixing

I assume the 'vocation' is the exercise of meditation, but it is not specified. Kappus would have hoped for 'as a poet'. But he had been complaining about army life. Rilke, as a product of the system, is impatient: 'I knew it was coming and can't help you. Only to say, all professions require sacrifices, full of demands, full of hostility to the individual. However, those who look down on the innately boring duties in the one they have settled for are subject to collective resentment and contempt:

A Christmas Greeting:

'Yours is no more burdened with inane conventions, prejudices and nonsense than any other occupation. And if there are paid jobs that like to think that they are above all that, you have to go to the moon. The important thing in this life is keeping in touch with the world within yourself. If you make a space for that you can put up with anything – saying, that's how it is – and then can cherish being alive. Go out at reveille and listen to the dawn chorus, or at bugle-call take in a lively sunset, and all the chagrins of routine will fall away like the body in death and you'll find yourself in eternal life itself, at the mid-point of timelessness.'

Note (to myself): Schopenhauer's essay 'On the Indestructibility of our Essential Being in Death' is on Rilke's mind in the final clause. Georges Poulet summarises his reading of the essay: 'The point about time is that it runs out. But space is a constant. Time disperses and decomposes humans, and comes with the body's death. But time, though a force of destruction, lingers on and redeems itself. Once the soul leaves the body, it makes space in space for the *will* (to live), that element of being which is timeless. The *will* survives in the mid-point of timelessness until it finds its time, or time finds it, and the being is reborn again in, or as, another. Schopenhauer gives Rilke the confidence to live without being in continual dread of death. The presence of his identity in endless time is assured.'

Rilke's advice once more gives way to the practical. Kappus had difficulty in making friends amongst his fellow cadets. 'Don't concern yourself. It's the same for everybody. It's only a formation you all have to go through. And non-committal contact with your peers frees you from the oppression of meaningless comradeship. If, as you say, there is no communal feeling between you and the other men, see them as friendly aliens, and try to keep near to what's happening to you elsewhere. Things that won't let you down. The night and the stars will always be there for you, the wind in the trees and the falling of the leaves. Then there is the animal kingdom. It is full of events which you can be a part of. You can answer back the howling of a wolf or low with the cows when they want to tell the peasants they are impatient to be milked. And don't forget children. They are still as you were when you were little, sad and yet happy, and when you think of them you can live amongst them again. Remember, your aloneness then was the wellspring of your solitude now. Adults are a waste of time and their pomposity is just a front.'

Note (to myself): Rilke in the Worpswede monograph cites the artist's task as recapturing 'children's oneness with nature which is lost by growing up'. This might suggest that he hasn't given up on Kappus as a poet? But what follows is a child's possible oneness with God rather than nature.

•

Divine Possession

When Rilke sends the young poet back to his childhood, it's not with the Freudian intention of finding out where it all went wrong but, rather, where it all went right. Kappus had confided that his lonely childhood was filled with thoughts of God, and Rilke asks, 'Maybe you don't like to think about your childhood because you no longer believe in Him? On the other hand, could it be that you have been dispossessed of what you never really possessed? Why do you suppose a child could contain what grown men find it hard to bear, and old men are weighed down by? Could a child's belief in God be based on wishful thinking?'

Concern for the uncertain state of Kappus's soul merges into his own in a concurrent letter to Lou, where Rilke plays with the idea that 'belief is the child of wishful thinking' and speculates that the 'spiritual presences' that inhabit him are manifestations of 'the God he has lost, or the God who has lost him'. Adding rather coyly (Lou is an agnostic), 'Isn't to lose, or be lost by, a Being who may, or may not, exist, a rather beautiful sentiment?'

Rilke can be more forthright to a young poet who knows nobody he knows bar his former army chaplain. And so, it ought to be possible to get closer to what he really thinks and/or hopes with regard to a God that 'grown men find it hard to bear'. His queries on God are the Socratic mode favoured by Kierkegaard, rhetorical questions. The suggestion of irony chimes with Kierkegaard's tartly lyrical *Journals*, which had just come out in a German translation. However, the late entries, tortured with doubt, would have given him pause, and he took his own advice on the limits of irony (letter two) when it came to the big questions.

His tone changes as the letter progresses. Irony is not completely rejected in searching for a model for his novel. He had given up on Flaubert's

A Christmas Greeting:

Education Sentimental for its extreme ironies and then Tolstoy's *The Death of Ivan Ilyich* for their total absence, but had since been engaging with Kierkegaard's *Repetition*, where a balance is struck, recognising that writing about a (f)ailing poet in Paris could not do without an element of it. But, in this letter, he is getting into the spirit of Christmas, where irony has no place. Particularly for a young man missing, and not missing, his family (something they probably had in common).

Kierkegaard needed a God so he, Isaac, could forgive his father, Abraham. Rilke needs God or something like him, feeling the apotheosis of his poetry will depend on the 'spiritual presences' that come to him in solitude. He is not yet ready to submit himself to them. The lure of modernism still holds him back. Rodin, having only time for the spirit of art and the cancans of the ancient Greek gods, might say these 'presences' are merely imaginary models posing for his poems. Lou would regard them as fantasies that haunt his subconscious. *The Notebooks of Malte Laurids Brigge* ignores Freud, and broadly toes the Rodin line of passive resistance to God, until towards the end when a supreme being makes a late entry. The 'thing-poems' might have been a break with the early work, but their *objective correlatives* (see, Guiding Note 3) were only to be an interim stop. He is champing at the bit of his winged horse to find its Mount Helicon. Yet the last few pages of *The Notebooks* are dedicated to an edifying discourse on God's love, and his alter ego's feeling that he is unworthy of it.

In effect, Rilke was saying to Kappus, 'Could your childhood God have only existed as an imaginary friend, one you hoped would hold off the adult world? And when that was no longer possible, you mislaid Him like a toy you had outgrown? If so, you might as well send out a search party for a lost marble. Decide then that Christ was betrayed by his longing (to save mankind), and Mohammed by his pride (in being a chosen messenger). And yet you miss this God you imaged as a child, and strive to recapture what you day dreamed…' But Rilke changes tack:

> 'Possessed by the dread that God doesn't exist, do not despair. His absence is not because he's lost but because he does not yet exist for you. Think of him as the "coming God", who since eternity has laid in wait to give mankind a future, the God who "keeps no man waiting", at least forever. He is not leaving it to you to find him. See him as the eventual fruit of

a tree whose leaves we are. What's preventing you from launching his gestation out into time and space, and living your life as though it is a painful and beautiful day in the confinement of an almighty pregnancy? In delivering himself, God will be your world's deliverance.

'Don't you see how everything that happens is always a beginning again (Nietzsche), and so it is with God. And as beginnings are in themselves beautiful, should not the most beautiful beginning be his? If he is the most perfect being, must not lesser beings come in advance, so he can arrive in the fullness of his abundance, the ultimate entrance that draw into himself all things. What significance would our life have if the one that we thirst for (*verlangen*) had already been?

'And so, to prepare, humbly as a bee gathers pollen, we collect what is sweetest in life to build the hive of *Him*. We begin with the smallest, seemingly insignificant, things, what is almost imperceptible, and, as long as it's a labour of love, work on until, *voila*, in a moment of silence or exquisite solitary joy, without any outside help or external influence, we are beginning *Him*, whom we may never live to know, as our ancestors never lived to know us, and yet they are in us, these people long gone, leaving a legacy that weighs on our destiny, a murmur in the blood or as a gesture rising up out of the depths of time. Likewise, is there anything that can deny the hope of one day dwelling in *Him*, the furthest of the far, the extreme of extremes?'

Note (to myself): Bertolt Brecht's *Stories of Mister K* (1930): 'A man asked Mr. K where there is a God, and he replied, "The answer depends on whether it would change your life if he is proven to exist. If not, the matter can be quietly dropped. If it would change your life, then there is no question to ask, you would have already decided that you need a God."' There is no question with Rilke. He needed a God.

•

Rilke's God and Angels

The idea of becoming part of the godhead is clearly influenced by the Upanishads, courtesy again of Schopenhauer. Invoking 'the coming God' derives from a 'lost' poem of Hölderlin, 'Hyperion's Song':

A Christmas Greeting:

> The fateless gods like a sleeping baby,
> breathing easily, chaste as unopened buds,
> minds always in flower. Their soulful eyes
> gaze calmly, eternally, in simple silence.
> Blissful above our sorry fate.
> We have no place to rest our head,
> and blindly stumble downwards
> like a waterfall splattering from rock to rock,
> year in year out, to no certain end.

Rilke had been moving from his self-conscious neo-symbolism to non-conscious objects with the 'thing-poems' and now craved the materialisation of his 'spiritual presences'. The all-conscious spirits of Hölderlin's 'fateless gods' (precursors of his Order of the Angels) offered a settled overview to rise above a world changing politically and culturally so fast it seemed to be spinning out of control. Hölderlin had asked what can a poet do in 'destitute times'? And answered it himself by imagining a better world where the 'fateless gods' in their infant innocence, without responsibilities and therefore without guilt, dwell in a state of bliss. Hölderlin, maddened by seeing his fellow man going down the plug, is swept up to live in the heaven of his poem.

Meanwhile, Rilke, between the well-wrought 'thing-poems' and the quest for something more, was at the theological crossroads, veering between devil's advocacy and studied piousness in his letter to Kappus. It would have been a good moment to dip into Kierkegaard's *Journal* and vibrate with his double-edged skepticism in talking of and to God: 'If it wasn't mad, it would be funny, were a man to say to God, 'Although I was strictly brought up as a Christian, as you know, I'm a creature of the nineteenth century and have my fair share of its superstitions, for instance, a belief in reason.' Kierkegaard's ironical 'as you know' compounds the stand-back before the straddle high-jump of faith or the long-jump of right reason. Above all, Kierkegaard's crisis of 'faith within faith' would have struck a bell for Rilke: 'Christianity is as good as done away with. But first a poet's heart must break, or a poet must be torn in two in such a way as to close the way to all deception. That is the check; and in our limited sphere my task.' Rilke was always that poet.

The letter concludes, 'My dear Mr. Kappus, despite the existential anxieties that are inevitable during a period of transition, it is a good

A CHRISTMAS GREETING:

time to begin the work that God requires of you and, to that end, celebrate Christmas with the breathless devotion you once did as a child. But be patient and remember not to make his becoming (human?) as Difficult as the earth makes it for the spring to arrive. I wish you the joys of the season and a confident new year,
yours,
Rainer Maria Rilke.'

It was not for nothing that W. H. Auden called Rilke 'The Santa Claus of loneliness'. However, Kappus would be thoughtful about Rilke's ratiocinations and raptures, particularly the final flourish. The leap from hard questions around belief-being-the-child-of-wishful-thinking to the holier-than-thou godliness, topped by metaphorical mountings and tailed by a sanctimonious endorsement of faith-in-hope, would give him pause.

•

God, the Supreme Fact

But the young poet would have been less puzzled had he been able to read the second part of Rilke's *Tales of the Good Lord* (published the following year and dedicated to Ellen Key). The message of these orientalist fables is that God has been made to exist for us through poetry and legend. It is not God as the 'supreme fiction' (what Wallace Stevens called poetry, in response to Manley Hopkins damning it as an obstruction to his faith). The underlying idea is basically spiritual, coming from Schopenhauer's engagement with the Upanishads.

These Hindu's scriptures, comprising a hundred or so ancient texts passed on by word of mouth, are not dictates. They are open to personal interpretation. It is promised that, through engaging with their knowledge, the self (*atman*) perfects itself, and has a chance to be united with the Brahman, the Spirit of Truth, and merge its identity with God's. Thus, *nirvana* is attained, bringing peace, amen. In sum, you have to think about the Upanishads, and think again, until the Brahman gives you the nod.

The Judaic and Christian religions are more unthinking. Revelation is a bolt from heaven that delivers dogmas that make peremptory demands on believers. That's how it is. Faith before reason. On the other hand, all that Hindus have to do is try to think the Upanishads through and if your ideas accord with the Brahman's, *nirvana* is yours. Should you fail, you are still allowed eternal life and another chance to attain Perfection. But since nobody knows 'the hymn the Brahman sings' (Ralph Waldo Emerson), what you come up with is a game of chance without a die. The appeal to reason is an appeal to reason as a gamble. You might as well daydream, let your mind drift with no object except feeling good. In other words, God comes as a *felt* thought (See Guiding Notes 9).

Note (to myself): Aquinas's 'reason without reason' meets Pascal's wager? More anon. Meanwhile, trotting through my head is George Santanya's riddle of faith, 'God is dead, but Mary is his mother.

•

We must be as little Children

In the Christmas letter, Rilke is effectively advising Kappus not to grow up. Daydream alone in a world where doubting God does not exist, and so He is everywhere like poetry. See adults from the perspective of a bewildered child who has no choice but to accept them as they are, and so doesn't waste time and energy on agonising about other people. The motif that poets must be as little children to enter the kingdom of solitude and commune with 'spiritual presences' is recurrent in Rilke's writings (but not in letters to Lou or Clara). When in 1915 he wrote seven poems celebrating the penis, Rudolf Kassner remarked to Anton Kippenberg, Rilke's faithful publisher (Insel-Verlag), 'Sometimes I wonder if our friend has ever grown up.'

In fact, he couldn't wait to. The 'jewel beyond all price and treasure trove of memories' was a dark place for him. In a letter to a college teacher (1897), he wrote 'everyday (of my childhood) resembled walking into a lightless, cold street and a holiday was hiding away in a grey inner court. It made me diffident by nature. It worsened in the military academy with the bullying of the boys and the mockery of the teachers. My escape came through a pathetic disposition towards excessive piety. It grew into a kind of madness under the influence of spiritual loneliness and the coercion of odious duty. I took the blows of comrades with a violent joy, an ecstatic sense of false martyrdom.'

Against this grim background, the divagation of his advice would make sense to Lou as an emotional seesaw between transferred repression and its spiritual liberation. I wonder could Kappus have picked up an inkling of his torment from the chaplain, and be moved not to disagree? Maybe not. One way or another, there was a lapse of five months, the longest interval by far, before he received another letter from Rilke.

I, too, must pause to reflect on another sufferer for poetry who posterity has proved was no martyr.

•

The Poetry of Life and the Life in Poetry

Johann Christian Friedrich Hölderlin's life was a concatenation of contradictions. A man who made a Greek tragedy of his poverty, though he was filthy rich and didn't know it. A poet loser who won out in the end, but was too dead to enjoy it. He lost his father before he could walk and talk, a stepfather before he could read and write, and his religion just as it was to become his occupation. So, he tutored a banker's son, but lost his heart to Suzette, his boss's wife, and then lost his job as a tutor because of his revolutionary politics. Although, like Pushkin with the Decembrist Uprising, he wasn't taken seriously by the authorities (in spite of giving Hegel the idea for the philosophic basis of Marxism, dialectical thinking). And thus, lost the confidence of both his political friends and their enemies, aristocratic patrons of the arts. He worried incessantly about the next bill, and, though in robust health, prepared himself for his imminent demise by borrowing money for his funeral arrangements. His mother chipped in.

He was a coeval of Hegel at college. Their names followed one another in the roll-call (Hegel, Hölderlin ...). Recalling his friend's 'Concept of Hesitation', the Friedrich in him said to the Johann Christian, 'Sod it,' and he jettisoned melancholy to join the blissful *fateless gods*. He needed be mad to believe in them. His family had him committed. The doctor in the asylum fitted him with a mask without a mouth to stop him screaming 'I'm sane' and gave him up as a hopeless case, not long for this world (three years at most), believing that madness poisoned the brain.

A metallurgist, Ernst Zimmer, took him into his family, and Hölderlin was given to scribbling quatrains on pieces of copper left lying around and selling them to ghouls who came to gawk at this holy fool. He lived thirty-six more years, skimping quite unnecessarily as Zimmer would give him anything he wanted. That included improvising the first Zimmer frame when his mobility was impaired (Zimmer Holdings should be called Zimmer Hölderlin). When he died of old age, only the Zimmer family attended his funeral. The poor man was never to know that his mother had kept his father's legacy to him a secret. She had invested it and the dividends were beyond the wildest dreams.

The contradictions in his life went into the poems. Hölderlin left behind what he meant to destroy. In 'Fragments from Pindar', he wrote what good is poetry in times of destitution? In his youth he believed that happiness and misfortunes are the two sides of fate, and poetry is an attempt to reconcile them. But Greek mythology told him that fate is one-sided, and dread is its ministering god. His life was doomed to a dead-end, without redemption. Poetry was like recollecting the good old days. It makes you sad and can only end in tears. 'Such is life, many blossoms, many thorns, and the dark grave.' His poems were to die with him.

Hölderlin's scraps of manuscripts were discovered in the late nineteenth century. His reputation revived as the sublime apologist for sentimental verse. This was a gross misunderstanding, as German poets, including Rilke, soon realised. In the quatrains he had recovered his primal innocence. They are a happy form of forgetting. You do not know what went before them. The cutting off of continuity purifies their joy. It is not so much 'a clear expression of ambiguity' (Kafka) as an ambiguous expression of clarity. We know where we are. We are beyond despair. In these fragments shorn from the ruins, 'the poetry of life' and 'the life in poetry' are at one.

Rilke didn't think that Hölderlin ever went mad. In joining the blissful gods, he ascended in a spiral, 'words sticking to the side like honey to a bear'. We know from letters that in 1912, the year Rilke got started in earnest on the *Duino Elegies*, he was re-reading the extant poems of Hölderlin. The final elegy, started that year and completed in 1922, reflects the influence in an inverted form. Bliss has been replaced by sorrow, and 'the kingdom of light' by an eerie Underworld. After the Great War, he couldn't find solitude. His 'spiritual presences' had long become 'The Order of the Angels', capricious arbiters who could judge him by not listening. But in the seventh *Duino* elegy they hear him out, as he acknowledges them as the preservers of man's creative heritage in uncertain times (according with Hölderlin's answer to his own rhetorical question). The Angels allow the poet the almost bewildering joy of 'the rise and fall of a happy thing'.

Chapter Seven

An Introduction to the Jobian Tendency

•

Having dispatched the Worpswede monograph for his purposes rather than the commune's, Rilke works more discreetly on a revised Rodin monograph. Though this time it is designed to disconcert the art critics by establishing that he is not one of them. Promptly published, it doesn't seem to bother the notoriously contentious maître and does himself no harm with avant-garde art world. Rilke is in effect working for himself, making his way. Allies introduce him to potential patrons and he wields his mystique. His youthful flirtation with the theatre and Ibsen had ended ignominiously in Berlin the year of his marriage. *The Ordinary Everyday Life*, a revamp of Chekhov's *The Seagull*, closed after a few nights. He could now put all that behind him, and was free to roll out the 'Thing-poems' and ponder his future in letters to Lou and others, not excluding Kappus (It's good to have youth on your side). Still, the modest royalties from *The Book of Images* published that year reminded him he had better get on with the novel. After asking back the letters he sent Clara in the early days in Paris to recycle for it, she and Lou began to receive morsels of what was to become *The Notebooks of Malte Laurids Brigge*.

Ever since meeting Tolstoy at the turn of the century, he had been thinking of a novel. It must have been well-mapped since he was sketching out endings. One of them survives. It draws more from Schopenhauer than Kierkegaard. Malte, confronting death, 'fears his soul is so rudimentary that in the afterlife he would languish like a premature baby in intensive care'. In short, he ends up in the limbo that Schopenhauer postulated in his essay 'On the Indestructibility of our Essential Being in Death'. He rejected the ending in advance before Lou could induce him to say, 'Leave my mother out of it.'

Note (to myself): the lack of natural affection between Rilke and his mother Sophia ('Phia') Entz-Kinzelbergers-Rilke dogged his life. If there was any love lost, that was a long time ago, before his birth. She wanted a girl (having lost one in a previous confinement) but, no, this hairy impetuous male child arrives prematurely. Phia's continuing existence had to be faced by him, especially when she gets it into her head to search him out or pretends to be at death's door. Lou wanted him to lay the living ghost in analysis with Freud. But he found other ways. The occasional poem helped:

> Stone by stone upon myself I lay.
> I'm a little shack that nobody lives in.
> Now my mother is coming to demolish me.

His mother isn't the only reason to put a dampener on Schopenhauer's notion of an eternity in the womb. Seeing the light of day is a beginning, and, as he told Kappus, 'everything that happens is a beginning again and beautiful'. Reading Kierkegaard's *Journals*, it is evident from the start that 'to live an idea' isn't just an abstraction. The Dane believed no idea is worth anything which isn't based on personal experience. Objectivity to what was happening to him in life is the basis of his philosophy. Sometimes he deals analogically with experience, but in the *Journals*, he treats it as a confession with himself being both the sinner and priest. In his late thirties – the same age as Rilke when he began his letters to Kappus – he fictionalised the results so far in *Repetition*. Between the Christmas and the seventh letter, Rilke, mulling over his novel, says that he must dust down his Danish to read Kierkegaard again. Although he doesn't say which book, it could only be *Repetition*.

Repetition is an epistolary novel about a young poet who on the advice of his psychologist abandons his fiancée for poetry, and loses his muse and therefore his capacity to write poems. Through study of the *Book of Job*, he eschews suicide, finding there is more to life than *amour propre*. In identifying with Job, he becomes a simulacrum of him, accepting all that's thrown at him and hoping for the best. The 'sincerities' underlying the ironies in *Repetition* would not have escaped Rilke as he embarked on a novel about a dislocated young poet, a 'wounded narcissist' (Andre Gide), at a time he had abandoned his wife and child for poetry.

Subtitled 'An Essay in Experimental Psychology', it is arguably Kierkegaard's most personal work. Rilke in *The Notebooks* flirts with the ironies but pays court to the 'sincerities', almost to the point of embracing Kierkegaard's Jobian tendency (in the last few pages another biblical parable, the Prodigal Son, takes its place. Not wholly surprisingly, as the parable and the *Book* both revolve around the withholding of love, and the Prodigal is a young man like Malte). Rilke never acknowledges* the influence of *Repetition* on the development of the novel, but since it's structural as well as thematic it could hardly have been a coincidence.

Rilke doesn't mention Kierkegaard and *Repetition* to Kappus, and maybe just as well. The young man is troubled enough by his own family and alienation from fellow students. And, recalling the psychologist's anxieties about 'advice that could kill', it may have contributed to the periodic softening of Rilke's tone, particularly in the latter parts of the Christmas letter. Likewise, in *The Notebooks of Malte Laurids Brigge*, when the narrative surges upwards towards a crypto-theological finale, Rilke chooses to reinterpret the parable of the Prodigal Son in a manner not dissimilar to *The Book of Job*. It, too, has a happy ending of sorts. Old Job was forgiven by God but he didn't undo the damage done to his family, property, etc. The Prodigal Son reluctantly accepts his father's forgiveness but, being a man who 'didn't want to be loved', felt he should leave home again.

Note (to myself): *does it matter that Rilke does not reveal his sources? It's a perfectly honourable literary device, particularly for a modernist (Joyce or Beckett are outstanding examples). Robert Vilain, in an essay on Rilke's use of his reading, concludes it's 'rarely possible (and even more rarely is it important) to identify a clear source, an influence or a precise stimulus'. And justifies it with, 'Reading a given work sometimes presupposes a knowledge of its predecessors.' True, but his parenthesis on unimportance goes against my attempt to get to the bottom of Rilke's more mysterious writings. It helps understanding to know from which source his Sincerity has been scraping.

Chapter Eight:

The World is an Unfinished Work: Mentors

•

Is the title of Lou's book on Rilke, *You Alone Are Real to Me* (1928), something he said to her, or her to him? Either/or, the sentiment seems worthy of a fortune cookie. I'm being unfair to Lou. Gretchen Malherbe found the line in *To Celebrate Myself,* his tribute to her. But if it means 'you are the only one' it can't have been true for Lou. Her penchant for *amour fou* with famous men was notorious, and included letters exchanged with the great such as Tolstoy, Ibsen and Nietzsche (the least one-sided). When she moved on to toy with younger poets and artists, the venerables remained on post-card terms with her, probably from relief. Older men cherish a quiet life (Ibsen and Tolstoy gave Lou thirty-three years, the celibate Nietzsche sweet sixteen). She was clever and cultured, but I wonder had Lou Salomé been called Hilda Bellamy would all these great men have paid her their attention?

Names mattered to Lou. It was she after all who proposed that Rilke change his first name from René to Rainer. The Teutonic version had more sunshine than René which rhymed with benèt (dull); and Prague, at the time, was a Bohemian outpost. Rilke accepted it, despite reservations. The French connection was dear to him, and there were enough loud-mouthed Rainers in the beer halls of his youth. But Lou got it right. René Rilke, the poet, would sound silly. The Germanic Rainer served him well as the author of the patriotic fable, *The Lay of the Love and Death of Cornet Christoph Rilke*: 'Riding, riding, riding through the day, through the night... Only when it is dark, do we sometimes think we know the way.' The echo of the Erlking darkens its dedication to his father (Goethe's '*mein Vater*' doesn't even notice that his son is dying in his arms). Lou could do nothing about the Maria. Although it was handed down from his unloved mother's sixth name, he insisted on keeping it out of respect for Victor Maria Hugo (not one of Lou's amorous obsessions. Possibly because he was sixty years her senior).

Lou's professional friendship with Freud was now one of the few remaining embarrassments between her and Rilke. She was retraining herself as a psychoanalyst, and had reasons to believe that Rilke needed help.

But he resisted it with heroic justifications. 'I'm afraid if all my devils leave me, my angels will take flight as well.' Perhaps a subconscious reason was jealousy. Since he tolerated and even welcomed her many infatuations with famous men, this is surprising, and perhaps he sensed there was more to Lou and Sigmund than a mutual interest in erotic theory. Indeed, it was rumoured that she offered him her virginity at forty, but had to settle for picking his brains. Rodin would have been a better bet. The Great God Pan, as Isadore Duncan called him, would have been only too happy to oblige.

Note (to myself): café gossip can be cruel as well as wrong. Evidence is hearsay. Lou had been molested as an adolescent by her music teacher, and swore sexual abstinence in order to concentrate on the life of the mind. She kept that resolve, even bringing it into her marriage. At thirty-five she first met the twenty-one-year-old Réne Maria Rilke (he presented this rather hard-faced blue stocking with a bunch of roses). His opening remark 'Only you are real' disarmed her (hearsay based on a poem in *To Celebrate Myself*). Legend has it that they lost their virginity with one another. Lou fuelled this in a memoir, by writing, 'With Rilke, man and body were indistinguishable from one another for me, but we were as brother and sister, though it could be sacrilegious.' Kassner quoted Freud as saying that Lou was 'Rilke's muse and attentive mother'. And, indeed, they were faithful to one another as best friends. Her abstinence resolve dwindled with the years. One-night stands with impressive younger men were her forte… What did I say about café gossip?

Rilke furiously fended off any foraging by mind doctors into his unhappy childhood (Lou would call it 'dysfunctional'). The Bohemian proverb 'Take the hump away from the cripple and you remove his livelihood' could serve his argument that writing is often an afterthought to childhood, and to knock it into a case history would be to kill the goose that laid the golden eggs. In short, the last thing he wanted was a 'cure' (the word for treatment, not necessarily making you better). Moreover, turning his sub- and un-conscious inside out could, he feared, tranquillise him into leading a respectable bourgeois life, observing the conventions, and that would no doubt discourage the 'spiritual presences' which were the future of his poetry. After all, working with the unresolved is the writer's lot. Once the daemons have been exorcised, you might as well find yourself another job, is more or less what he told Lou, and she kept her counsel. Their friendship survived into an ersatz Oedipal relationship that kept him above board in stormy weather when he couldn't get his poor self together.

As Rilke gets closer to defining the 'spiritual presences' that possess him, *Verlangen* ('I thirst') sometimes replaces *Sehnsucht* (longing/yearning) in his letters. Kappus, on hearing the third-last words of Christ on the Cross describe his desire to reach the 'spirits', would not have been bothered by the near-blasphemous context. After a religious upbringing, he had revolted. And it provided a reference point in common. Though neither would have likely been the soldier who offered Christ the vinegar sponge (which he refused), Rilke might have put honey on it. He had, however, to be more circumspect with his sophisticated Paris friends. In particular Rodin, at whose down-to-earth feet he was still tying the bootlaces. Even with Kappus, Christ is only mentioned once (in the Xmas letter) and in tandem with Mohammed. Formal Christianity was anathema to him. 'Spiritual presences', and God (at a pinch), are as far as he'd go.

Although Rodin liked to sculpt angels, he discourages Rilke's communion with things that lack visible support. 'Art is squeezing blood from stone. The spiritual can be left to look after itself. Objective observation is enough to be going along with.' Michelangelo's unfinished sculptures, and the proudly incomplete cathedral in Narbonne, had inspired Rodin in his middle years to stop leaving no stone unturned to please his clients. After a trip to Italy in the 1870s, Rodin's style changed from the classically smooth to roughened surfaces that gave off disquieting light and shade. In his non-commissioned work, he transformed himself into a self-styled gothic 'craftsman'. Figures emerge out of half-buried boulders, disembodied hands and feet appear, and you have to imagine the rest of the body in the mausoleum or quarry.

More and more, Rodin's legitimisation of 'unfinished work' attracts Rilke. This innovation (or renovation) in sculpture reached its anorexic apotheosis in Giacometti a half century later. Bodies trapped in marble that the maître hadn't the time or inclination to release. Rilke called this 'a bubbling up of their bubbling spiritual essences'. In contrast, Rodin, a spiritual agnostic, stressed the emotional effect of this semi-burial in his own 'unfinished' work, 'like Dante's damned struggling to find their humanity again in Hell' (Rilke used this idea for a late poem, 'Christ in Hell'). Jules Renard ('I'd like to write like Rodin sculpted'), saw 'the blocks of marble' in the backyard of Rodin's studio as 'rocks estranged from their mountain, waiting to come alive, as though they had a desire to live'. He echoes Rodin's doubts about squeezing spiritual blood from earthly stone: 'I don't know if God exists but it would be better for his reputation if he didn't. The world is an unfinished work.'

Rilke was beholden to Rodin in his approach to ideas. Although what they came up with couldn't be more different. Rodin made meaningful jokes, clear as daylight. Rilke floated them so they could be best seen against the night sky and with their loose threads creating 'celestial pantomimes' (Wallace Stevens's poem 'Landscape with a Boat', in which the 'anti-master floribund ascetic' could only be Rilke).

Rodin was more interested in the job at hand rather than belief, religious or otherwise. His art was simply *thoughts* molded in clay, and cast in bronze to illuminate them. Late in life in a unique interview (Paul Gsell, *l'Art* 1911), Rodin hammered home, 'After you see a work of art what you retain is its idea. If the subject happens to have a religious theme, say, the artist is very probably paying homage to the forces of ignorance rather than praying. When things in life don't reveal themselves rationally, the imagination goes beyond the learned to improvise ideas from the hidden depths of experience. Visual ideas are more easily understood than intellectual ones and, once perceived, have the merit of a good ghost story. You don't know quite why you believe them. Yet you do. The imaging isn't subject to the artist's imagination, but supplements it. Still, viewers are becoming too knowing when, for instance, the subject is nature. Science is lessening what it does not divulge, making pantheism a dying idea. Art is the operative in bringing the inexplicable into focus, and so, as the mystery of things diminishes, giving what remains a vital spark is left in the artist's hands to conceal enough so there is something to reveal.' Later in the interview, Rodin remarked, with Voltairean weariness, 'If the mysteries that religion deals with didn't exist, we artists to survive would have to invent them.'

Rilke did not see it as a losing battle. Rodin's semi-burials reinforced the *negative capability* in his own work, and for the 'purely anonymous centre' to hold, he needed to absorb himself in a more ambitious work than the 'Thing-poems' (see Guiding Note 2). But 'personal identity, preconceptions, and the certainties' kept intervening. *Letters to a Young Poet* expresses this struggle, raising more rhetorical questions 'to love' than answers that Kappus badly needed. His paeons to solitude and 'spiritual presences' seemed like lip-service to a spirituality that's longed for but hadn't been attained. Late Rodin would have under- stood. But in the first decade of the twentieth century was discouraging. Nevertheless, Rilke's *Verlangen* (thirst) is reaching out for a more positive 'capability', not one that was sitting in his mind, but that comes from outside himself. It was a long time coming. In 1911 a voice carried in a howling gale gave him the opening line of the *Duino Elegies*: 'Who, if I cried out, would hear me amongst the 'Order of the Angels.'

Note (to myself): it happened when staying with Princess Marie von Thurn und Taxis at her castle in Duino, near Trieste on the Adriatic coast. When the world and Paris was too much with him his favourite sojourn was always there. As a retreat it was a retreat *forwards*. On his first stay, he wrote to Lou, saying he felt inspired 'at though it was offering him the future', a premonition perhaps of the stormy morning a year later when on the castle's parapet the opening line came carried in the bitter northeast local Bora wind, although it could have been the seagulls. But does that matter. The *Duino Elegies* took off.

In *The Notebooks*, the voice is echoed in Malte's daydream of a writerly apocalypse when 'glorious words' that were not his appear on the page. 'I'm in the presence of greatness. Henceforth, I won't write. I'll be written. One word upon another, given meaning like a cloud that breaks into rain. I'm the template they "impress" themselves on. All I have to do is to accept this gift from above, and my torment would turn to joy. Just one step, but I can't take it. It's too late. I fear as a writer I've fallen and broken something. I can't pick myself up.' This was not always true for Rilke.

Once in Rodin's studio, contemplating the torso of a girl before it was cast in bronze, Rilke told Clara that he felt the 'spiritual bubbles released from the clay' enter his bloodstream. 'Something reminiscent of El Greco, and leavened by Venetian ceilings by Tiepolo' …The 'Order of the Angels' beckoned. Ultimately Rodin's influence on him was almost the opposite of what the maître intended. He wanted his young German neo-romantic to learn to write upside down with his feet in the air (as in the 'Thing-poems'), and not in full flight with his head in the clouds. But Rilke saw Keats as a beacon amongst 'visually oriented poets', and carrying his *negative capability* into what was to become the subterranean cosmology of the *Duino Elegies*, with its expressionist bent, was one of the stumbling blocks that contributed to his procrastination. In the last year of his life, he expressed heartfelt regret to Marina Tsvetayeva that the 'purely anonymous centre' of his work had, in effect, dehumanised him. Although he wasn't relenting ('That's how it had to be').

Reflecting on the truly great to Clara after he fled to Paris in 1902, he wrote, 'The unedifying household of Tolstoy (tensions noted on the second visit) and Rodin's uncomfortable domestic arrangements all point to their need to choose between happiness and art. The great men let their lives become overgrown like an old road and carry everything into their work. Their lives are stunted like an organ they don't need.'

Chapter Nine

'Love is a Sealed Package...':

Letter Seven (14 May 1904, Rome)

•

Getting the Malte Ball Rolling

The interval between Rilke's letters is usually three months. The exceptions are the three weeks between the second and third when he was much animated by Kappus express liking for Dehmel, and five months between the Christmas sixth and seventh letter. His Roman sojourn had been disrupted. Apparently, there were money problems with the landlord and this affected his health. But now he has resettled in a 'cozily convenient little house near the center of town' (Letter to Lou). Kippenberg had stumped up an advance.

In Rilke's apology for the delayed response, he mentions 'spring fever' and, indeed, he had sprung the feverish first steps of his novel. The letter of his that Clara returned is a detailed description of the early days in his flight to Paris. He needed it in order to recapture for Malte 'the sights and smells of a poor quarter where unhealthy people got on with their deaths'. Still, in the opening pages of *The Notebooks* he finds redeeming features: 'A pregnant woman heavily inching along a high sun-warmed wall, touching it occasionally as though to reassure herself it was still there. And it was.' And 'a baby abandoned in a pram, covered in rash with its mouth open breathing in the smell of fry-ups and disinfectant. But at least it is sleeping.'

At night when stifled in his bed-sit, Malte can't sleep and opens the window and listens to the jarring, jangling nightlife outside. A window smashes. He hears 'the laughter of the broken pane and the sniggering of the splinters. Someone mounts the stairs and a girl's voice cries out, 'Stop. I don't want to.' At dawn, he hears distant barking. 'What a relief. A dog.' And so Malte dozes off'.

The start of *The Notebooks* answers the opening paragraph of Baudelaire's 'At one o'clock in the morning' (*Petits Poèmes en prose*), which begins, 'I'm alone at last. Nothing can be heard, apart from the clatter of a few belated, clapped out trams. I will have a few hours silence, but I won't sleep.' And ends, 'Still, at least the tyranny of *la face humaine* has disappeared. And I'll suffer only from my own presence.' But the differences are marked. Malte, unlike Baudelaire, gets to sleep, and next day sees the Parisian faces 'flying past him all the nuances of joy, of misery and of isolation overlapping one another... until the vital flow levitates and takes shape as a falling star of faces lit up by a comet's tail of those yet to come'. Rilke's Malte sees them in a brighter light than Baudelaire, who only wants to double-lock his apartment, plunge himself in darkness on the off-chance of getting a bit of work done. And so, to get away from the literary life in which, like Malte, he is on the bottom rung, and Malte, innocent of worldly ambition, lightens up to dance with shooting stars.

Baudelaire, as the poet of the city, is on Malte's mind when he settles down to write. Rilke, also, but more as a buffer to measure himself up against. For example, his poem 'Blind man. Paris' is a 'corrective' to Baudelaire's '*Les Aveugles*. ('The Blindmen'). Rilke is projecting his own experience on to Malte, who is still just a fiction for him. Stuck for a beginning, he is starting with what already exists on paper. He hasn't yet thought about Kierkegaard's 'Law of Literary Delicacy': 'The author has the right to use what he has experienced, but must keep the truth to himself and only let it be refracted.' Which is probably why he would take six years before a final manuscript is delivered. Protecting his reputation as poet and being true to himself with Malte were in conflict. Hitherto with prose he broke the speed record (a reputed night or two for *The Lay of the Love and Death of Cornet Christoph Rilke* and a week for the second part of *Tales of the Good Lord*). The *Notebooks* was to be the long ball, thrall and haul.

Note (to myself): Albert Camus's theory that books written slowly are quick reads is the other way around for Rilke. His rapidly dispatched poems and fables are speedboats, while later slow-boils are Flying Dutchmen (*The Notebooks* drifted between the first and final letters to the young poet, and the *Duino Elegies* for what seemed like an eternity).

As Rilke labored on with *The Notebooks*, he made a troubled distinction between prose and poetry (letter to Rodin): 'Poems are carried along by the rhythm of external things. The lyric cadence comes from nature: the waters, the wind and the night. But to find the rhythm of prose you must plunge into the profound depths of one's being to find in the blood the pulse that makes itself felt at one-remove from the self and it is unpredictable. Prose must be built like a cathedral and its construction is a matter of scaffolding. You are not helped by what came before. You are only conscious of planks. And yet, as I continue to build, men, women, children and old people take form, particularly woman with their needles and thread as they embroider the world around them, leaving a whiteness like a christening gown, enriched with a tenderness and fulness. Such characters become vibrant and luminous on the void of a black page, emerging almost like figures from your marble.'

The bricolage of prose exhilarates Rilke, and there is no question of including samples of poor Malte's attempt to write poems (the diary entries will have to suffice to suggest them). Early on in the novel (section eighteen) he conjures up the famous writerly apocalypse, with its concluding 'but not yet'. Still, he hasn't abandoned hope and supposes 'help might be at hand', and copies out the last lines of the prose poem, 'At One O'Clock in the Morning', in which Baudelaire begs God 'to grant him a few lines of poetry'. Malte has just seen a demolished building across from his lodgings with an inside wall still standing. It shows the inverted remains of lives lived. For instance, the truncated pipes of former toilets sluicing out, he imagines, disease-bearing excrement. Fear of going to pieces is refracted in the dissolution of everything around him. The public hell opens on his private one. Only the words that are *not his* which appear on the page can save him, and they are Baudelaire's, a rather forced *repetition forwards* of them that, nevertheless, encourages him. Should the prayer for poetry be answered, says Baudelaire, 'it would prove I am not the least of men, and not beneath the contempt of those I despise.'

•

Critical Copy

As Rilke gets his excuses out of the way, the seventh letter (the second longest) proceeds, 'Now I'm most happy to say two or three things about your poems.' Firstly, he responds by copying out one of them, saying, 'It's easier to judge one's own work when it's written in another's hand. Read it as though it's by someone else. And you'll find how much it is your own.' Thanks to Rilke, a poem of the young poet survives.

The untitled sonnet begins with the poet trembling on the brink of an ineffable anguish. Only in dreams are things clear and that brings him peace of a sort. But on waking, the great questions rise up before him, and tantalising recede... The poem concludes:

> The stars flicker through a clouding night sky.
> And a sadness settles in the grey air.
> Love is what my hands try to grasp, in prayer.
> But in the darkening gloom the words won't come.
> My mouth is burning, and my lips are dry,
> And instead of giving praise, I'm struck dumb.

As juvenilia it has the merit of a certain logic, but Rilke's gest is generous and avoids appearing as a put down. The apparition of his verses in his poet master's hand would have awed him, but not sufficiently to frame them. Reading the poem as though by someone else was chastening. It was a poem with nothing to say except there's nothing to say. Time to start again with another one and to fail better.

Kappus must have mentioned that finding time and space for solitude is a problem as Rilke moves on to warn him against being diverted from it. Proust said that, 'before we know solitude, we wonder how is it possible to fit it in with our other pleasures, but once we have found it, the other pleasures drift away.' Rilke would have guessed it wasn't like that for the soldier boy. Fellow recruits keep knocking at the door, inviting him out to the mess to meet some local girls, and of course he is tempted ('spiritual presences' be damned). Even if he puts a 'do not disturb' sign on the door, his mind would be distracted by what he thinks he's missing.

Rilke tells him that if temptations to escape from his solitude are overcome, it will strengthen him. 'Barracks conventions are always on the slippery slope to the path of least resistance. But anything worthwhile is uphill. This is the incline that nature and all living things face. Your desire to go out makes staying in with your solitude harder. All to the good. Hold on to the Difficult, its weight will give your solitude ballast.'

Rilke is feeling kindly towards him, remembering no doubt his adolescent self, the apparent abyss between him and others, particularly girls, and solitary hours, enforced by shyness or pimples or whatever makes a growing lad unsure of himself. This sorry state was hardly conducive to conjuring up a 'spiritual presence'. Still, he can't quite bring himself to suggest that the young man should stop brooding and climb out the window to enjoy himself now and then with his peers. However, no doubt prompted by the copied poem, he makes a concession, introducing for the first time the word Kappus is no doubt longing to hear, '*Liebe*'.

•

The Sexual Politics in Rodin's Hotbed

Liebe in the sentimental sense is a word Rilke tends to use more sparingly since he sent Clara back to her family. He only deploys it without reservations in flirtatious correspondence with women who were strangers to his personal life. He uses it in negative retrospect with Paula, clinically with Lou as a burden shared, as a Christian duty with Ellen Key, and about art to Clara. Her troubled younger brother receives a long lesson in love and its vagaries, some weeks before writing to Kappus (there are inevitably overlaps). The novel mainly occupies itself with the Great Ineffables: death, God, (im)mortality (See Guiding Note 6). Meanwhile, Rodin is encouraging him to identify with the non-human for his 'thing-poems'. But still in the atelier of the Great God Pan he could scarcely avoid the Lesser Ineffables: happiness, grief, pain, music, and, of course, love and its by-blow, sex.

Kassner had diagnosed that Rodin's libido was driven by a deeper force than the affections or conquests *a la ronde*. As a eugenicist, he claimed that the sex-urge is embodied in a *repetition forwards* of hereditary factors. In short, desire arouses the genes that carry the amatory experiences of our ancestors. Thus, folk memory fortifies the pleasure or pain. Rilke had already touched on this in his response to the young poet's Dehmel fixation.

In Rodin's case, being Parisian working class, nothing is known of his antecedents, other than that his father was a policeman and his mother a seamstress. When Rilke observes to Kassner that 'Rodin's first mistress and long-suffering wife, Rose Beuret, had been a dressmaker too', Rudolph retorts that 'Auguste's sculpture of the *Man with the Broken Nose* was his father and this suggests either a desire to bash the male Rodin lineage, or that his father was a boxer.' Rilke, slightly Lou-like, opined that 'Rose, his mother substitute, modelled for *The Kiss*. Wouldn't Freud say he has an Oedipal complex?' Rudolf, who hated her, snorted, 'Not at all. Rodin loves all women equal and opposite. Not any particular one.'

When Rilke consults Lou on his own lineage burden, he has to

'LOVE IS A SEALED PACKAGE...':

struggle not to wallow in self-pity or resentment. She stops him short: 'No, it's all about immediate family. Rudolf, hating Sigmund, is evading the obvious.' Rilke returns to solitude and reflects on his childhood. He was only ten when his parents separated, but still old enough to guess why. His father didn't want to be responsible for a demanding wife, her down-at-heel family and a clinging child. And so, if Freud was right, it was possible to see in Josef a precursor of his own failures in love, which began with his mother and continued with Paula, Clara and Ruth (though Lou was not a complete failure). Still, it was harsh to blame all that on his father, or even himself. He prefers to entertain Kassner's theory: 'My destiny as a man and a poet was ordained rather than the result of personal weaknesses.' His forefathers, with their zigzag marital and martial history, whispered debauchery and excessive dutifulness to authority, gives him a moral let-off. He could make his autochthonal in-dwellers responsible for spoiling his pitch.

But his Comforters are knocking at the door. Lou discourages his taking on the burden of generations: 'Rest with what your own heart has to offer.' Kassner stands his ground, scorning her advice as '*an idée recue* on *d'amour* with the emphasis on the "damn", the bane of the bourgeois sentimental life. "*D'amour*" is an amateur concept which is difficult for marriages to live with. The heart offers itself in amorous tachycardia, but after the first fine careless rapture the beat slows down and, despite good will and what the neighbours think, love ends with a mercy killing that leaves behind mutual regrets and children who don't know their parents.'

Rilke is ill-at-ease with a subject so close to his 'Sincerity'. Lou boiling it down to failed marriages is to paddle in the shallows that he felt himself drowning in with Clara. Yet Kassner, by putting the blame on bad seed, could be no more than manly aplomb between a confirmed bachelor and a vagrant husband. Rilke despairs: 'Lou likes to talk about my feminine side... Am I on the brink of becoming some sort of eunuch?' In truth, Rilke badly needs a break, or a hug, and so hugging himself is in order. Maybe by treating the young poet with a love lay and lesson, he could come up with something beyond a eugenic theory and a ritual killing. Something akin to Rodin's *l'Amour* showing at this year's salon: a tortured young man burying his head in the lap of a motherly woman.

Note (to myself): Jules Renard tells how it came to be named *l'Amour*.

'Love is a Sealed Package...':

Rodin asked Alfonse Daudet what he should call this secular *pieta*, and he replied '*la douleur de la volupté*', 'the pain of pleasure'. His brother Ernest disagreed, and quoted Madame Victorine de Chatenay's response, 'It's the soul encountering the body, and doing what it can.' Rodin split the difference with '*La douleur de l'amour*', but due to a mistake by his secretary 'the pain' was dropped.

Rilke's distancing himself from his youthful reputation as a neo-romantic – the symbolism he keeps on hold – has been achieved with the Rodin monograph (second edition in press). As a modernist fellow- traveler, he must have felt sufficiently liberated from his past to let himself go as he had when naming the female parts, and intimating their function, in the recent poem 'Orpheus, Eurydice, Hermes'. Kappus would have learned something about the mechanism of sex, but *Liebe* would still remain a mystery.

•

Marital Law versus Readiness

In the seventh letter, *Liebe* with a capital A is given its wings. Their span is wide and the swoops are rather forbidding, more the release of a falcon than a dove. It's a difficult flight, and so passages in my transcription (by way of Olsen's 'trespass vision') are given more airspace (to include the bats and hummingbirds in the background), and to get a wider perspective on Rilke's 'Sincerity' and the young poet's understanding of it. I'm being faithful to both in my fashion: empathy by association, especially with the boy (I was once one in a boarding school). My speculation on his behalf is prompted by hints of his reply in Rilke's subsequent letter:

'The most Difficult task entrusted to us is for one human being to love another. It's the ultimate test, and everything we do in life is a preparation for it. Since it's not an acquired characteristic, nobody can be educated to love. It has to be picked up on your own with a beating heart, a difficult lesson only learnable in the school of solitude. And since there is no book of love with answers at the back, there's no guarantee you'll come to know how to love before you die.

'Contrary to the common view, love does not have its origins in a mutual osmosis, an abandonment of oneself to merge with another. What

'LOVE IS A SEALED PACKAGE...':

would be the point of such a union between two organisms so unprepared for symbiosis? Love mustn't be shared with its object until it's ready. You have to make excessive demands on yourself, working on this passion on your own, heightening and deepening it in solitude, until you have matured sufficiently to become a world in yourself for the loved one's sake. Merging, surrendering, being at one, will have to wait. It is just as well that most young people have to scrimp and save to afford a home together, and circumstances, as well as parents, counsel patience, for if love is to be achieved the apprenticeship is likely to be long and, for some, life may prove to be too short. But in the learning, there is fulfilment. As you know from the history of poetry, the ripening of the grain of love is more a wonder than the harvesting of the crop.

'Of course, you have to turn your back on fleshly temptations that will damage your health, and infatuations that flatter your vanity, the head-spinning romance, with its dizzying denouement, or the casual affair when one or the other becomes a casualty. So many young people go wrong by believing that togetherness in itself means love and happiness. Instead of standing back and making each other worthy of carrying forward their separate solitudes into a shared burden, they entwine themselves in the knot of passion which has to unravel so the loose threads can be knitted into a white wedding. Although the families may rejoice at seeing them settling down, marriage is not a vessel of a sanctity if the preparation has been bypassed. And, once the rapturous embraces begin to tire, dutifulness insidiously leaks a profane drip of half-broken promises, held together by the hypocrisy of keeping up appearances, or a vague hope of a second coming. Each loses themselves for the other's sake and, if there are children, they lose out too. Everybody loses, and a sterile helplessness leads to a downward spiral from disappointment to a barely disguised disgust, mitigated by the bourgeois conventions that prop up marriage, giving shelter to a sub-species of love that does not go beyond security and formal occasions (births, Xmas and deaths). But what's sanctified by the outside world is a cracked vessel, even before the couple drink from it. How can you be expected to unconditionally surrender your uniqueness, your solitude, your *raison d'etre*?

'Society's patch-up of the marriage is a camouflage designed to provide a stable bedrock to propagate itself. That was natural enough in pastoral times when marriage was land- and property-based. But the gentry have been dispossessed by the middle-class, the bedrock is a deadlock. It abandons the unprepared to a mediocre fate, and a lifelong feeling of failure, shared fatalism, and a warring line drawn under expectations.

'Something more had been promised. And should the couple decide to separate, the agreement, even when amiable, goes with demands that knot again what it was supposed to unravel. Divorce brings in the law, and whether contested or not is tied up with compromises that act as a sort of buoyancy device to keep the sinking ship sinking indefinitely, so one can't start again and sail on. Even if that is avoided, the wreckage of failed love is not so easily disposed of. Its remains are towed behind you, a drag on free movement. The prospect of plain sailing is remote.

'However, it doesn't have to be like this. Patiently preparing for love in solitude, cultivating it in your inner self, before you take the plunge, may be the long way around but it will not let you down. Even if it does not achieve lasting togetherness, love at one remove can preserve the bond. You both live and die with it.

'If you want to hold on to love when you find it, you have to share your solitude with it. What readies one, sustains it. An immense effort is needed with your loved one. Not least because of the risk of alienating family and friends who see your solitude as an empty space that needs to be filled by conventional congeniality. But without it you have nothing of your own to bring to love. Surrender it, and you have nothing except a list of dutiful attributes that ticked-off force-march a convention. Solitude, diverted from its course, means that when the meandering river of life swells into a torrent, love has nowhere to cling to and will be swept away.

'Nonetheless, the common run of marriages, with their short-lived satisfactions and accommodations, are not to be despised. Cracks are cemented over, but it's also a trial of compassion. Don't underestimate the exceptional courage needed to keep afloat the leaking boat. It weakens you, but humanity lingers. While cowards and bullies strengthen their hand and rule the roost tyrannically.

'Whether by braving or brutalising it, things continue because they began. Domestic accidents mount, petty disasters, and wounds open. Where residual affection survives through compassion, people learn to salve and dress them and live with the scars. But there is no space for solitude in the recovery room. It's too crowded. When the children grow up and move on and the grandparents die, a second chance to grow together in isolation offers itself. But, I fear, with the backlog of failure, love can only hope to enter as the ultimate solitude beckons. Love and death coincide and die in one another's arms ...'

•

Pass the Parcel

'You're lonely, and finding your solitude hard-going. That is good news. You're on the right track. Nature knows all about Difficulty, respects it, and evolves by making things hard for itself. It's the mountain of life that makes the man and, if it appears to be an easy climb, beware of the volcanoes and avalanches. You must stand up to all the hazards the mountain presents. And don't wait for them to come to you. Don't listen to those who say you can't be too careful. Avoid thorny paths on the foothills of course, but don't be afraid to tackle the thrill of its treacherous upper slopes. Once you know the ropes you will surmount them.

'Death is Difficult, having no address for its delivery. Love is no less Difficult, lacking a postbox. There are no directions to consign them. Both are Ineffables we carry around with us like a sealed package to pass on to one another without opening. And so, it's impossible to reach a consensus on what it contains. We are free to venture a guess. It's an educated one if entertained in solitude. But since opening the package is not in our gift, nothing can be confirmed. No matter how purposely we work on love and its development, larger-than-life demands are always a step ahead. As beginners on the foothills, we are hardly up to challenging the peaks. However, if we remain staunch and learn to get used to carrying the burden of this package instead of losing ourselves in the long grass of frivolous pursuits, behind which people hide from the high seriousness of life's ascent, then perhaps we can establish a base camp to ease the way to the dizzy heights, if only for those who come after us. And that would not be nothing.

'There are signs that things are changing. In the north of Europe particularly, with experiments in how individuals relate to one another across the gender divide. Women are leading the way. Not only by imitating men's behaviour and misbehaviour, and taking on jobs hitherto a male preserve. But that is merely a stage. Once the shock of the new is absorbed, and woman can dispense with aggressive, sometimes comic, tactics, they can assert their true nature without the distortions imposed on them by men. Women are innately trusting, direct and through generations of experience, riper, more complete, as human beings than men.

'LOVE IS A SEALED PACKAGE...':

Men, who are too up in the air, never having been pulled down to earth by childbearing, and who, in their arrogance, impatience and ignorance of embodying life, grossly underestimate what they think they love.

Note (to myself): introduced to Ellen Key, the woman's activist, in Viareggio in the spring of the previous year, their friendship led to an extensive correspondence, which found her in Bremen, Rome, Paris, Pisa. They had wanderlust in common.

'Women, once they have shaken off the trappings they have been subjected to, will no longer be considered the opposite sex. They will be recognised as they are, free to be the more human of human beings. And with the strength they are endowed with through fruitfulness, women will take the initiative in transforming love from an error-strewn quagmire into one with a solid foundation. There it will be transformed into a relation between two human beings, and no longer between a man and woman. Thus, preparing the way for a love between *two solitudes protecting, circumscribing and acknowledging each other.*'

Kappus had confided in his last letter that he had only loved once, in childhood and hopelessly, and fears he'll never get over it and love again. This little confession could be his sole tangible contribution to the shaping of the character of Malte in *The Notebooks*. He enters by the backdoor into the puppy love of the boy Malte for Abelone, his mother's half-sister, who tries not to notice. Rilke in a postscript tells Kappus that he is half right. He will never get over it, and all to the good. 'As it was your first bud of solitude's inner workings, the memory will repeat itself forwards, and it will bloom again, stronger and riper, and love will bear fruit.

'All good wishes accompany you on life's path, my dear Mr Kappus, Yours Rainer Maria Rilke
P.S. I attach my copy of your sonnet.'

•

Afterthoughts

Despite the encouraging final flourish, I can only sympathise with Kappus. A well-brought-up young man of a melancholy disposition, not sure where he stands with anything or anyone, submitting to military and literary discipline, would find disheartening the idea of *Liebe* as a thorny path with a mountain to climb and the upper slopes possibly leading nowhere other than a mere legacy for the next generation. News of the New Woman wouldn't have reached his bivouac at Weiner Neustadt, and the notion of a race of unisex Brunhildas bestriding the bedrooms of the world would frighten the life out of him. Things being difficult enough, he might have preferred to hear Garance's 'Love is easy' (*Les Enfants du Paradis*, 1946). But Rilke's rundown on how love kills itself when trapped in a conventional marriage is brutal, given the young poet's intimations that his family's life wasn't exactly a bed of roses. Still, he spared Kappus further details on autochthonal in-dwellers determining the course of love.

As it is, Rilke's up-and-down didacticism on love must have given Kappus pause. His experience, so far, has been more level-pegging. Could the great poet be exaggerating a-wee? He regrets the premature disclosure of the sent poems, and feels that 'revealing himself unreservedly more than to anyone before or since' (preface to *Letters*) on the first love of his childhood was spoiled by the self-pitying rider. His sonnet had simply said that he hadn't the words for love. Now trying to find the words is the reason he tries to write poetry. 'Rilke is right about my juvenilia, and gracious not to say that there was too much of the callow youth in them. He is right too about my first love, but for the wrong reason, 'I will love again but not on the rebound. Born to such a love it does not die.'

The context for this first love is childhood, and the most likely object suggests itself. It's rare for any sensitive child not to love his mother, and Kappus (or Rilke in his infancy) are no exceptions. Indeed, without making a Greek tragedy of it, his childhood sweetheart could have been her. It is hinted in Rilke's response, 'a love without complexities, as natural as it was spontaneous'. In other words, a given for mother and child. That they drifted apart as he grew up was the young poet's 'secret sorrow' and Rilke must have felt it shared elements of his own.

The 'silent quarrels' with his poet master would cease once it dawned on Kappus that Rilke was talking about himself and his own 'burden'. He wouldn't have known about his unloving mother Phia, but is aware of Rilke's marriage and guesses from the polyglot postmarks on the envelopes that he is rarely at home. One thread that reverberates throughout the letters is that Rilke wants to be alone. That it is for poetry's sake, he sings for Kappus. In the military camp, getting away from fellow recruits to write has proved painful, managed only at the expense of being considered a snotty loner, possibly even a nutcase. He looks out on the parade ground, encroached by prefabricated buildings only fit for the solitary confinement of prisoners to duty, on to the barren wastes beyond and envies the 'glorious isolation' of Rilke in Paris, Rome and Viareggio, where Shelley's drowned body was brought ashore.

His life so far had taught him that thinking about love and practising it are a different matter for most people. Rilke is an exception. He does what he thinks, and thinks what does. It's the pure poet's licence. But Kappus wonders about the wife and child. Rilke, though a latter-day hermit-saint of poetry, is capable of sinning against his 'dear ones' like everybody else but, from the evidence of the letters, without any qualms. He simply has to get away from others like Simon Stylites. And his pillar is his sacred 'solitude'. Rilke's destiny is to suffer other sufferings. That is the 'burden' he carries on their behalf. Although he shows willingness to share it, particularly with enlightened women, but *not yet*. He's waiting for tomorrow's petticoat revolution, when they will become human beings in their own right. Meanwhile, this 'burden' is something his family have to put up with.

Note (to myself): I doubt that the young poet considered the practice of love that excludes others as either desirable or justifiable. Poetry is a way of life, true, but human life is surely not about withholding love, even for Job's God, or the Prodigal Son. Surely, Rilke knew that.

A portrait of Kappus emerges by refraction from *The Letters*. A very proper young man with his eye on the horizon, which he distrusts. Rilke could well see him stepping out of a Casper David Friedrich painting, and be touched. But his romanticism is modest with a touch of auto-derision and irony. He is pure of heart, but not unaware of the main chance (writing to Rilke in this case), and solitary in order to keep himself for something better. He would have vibrated with Rilke's dictate, 'You have to become a world in yourself by yourself for the sake of what's to come.' But wince at, 'Love is a lonely passion that excludes everything else and 'There is more to life than love, particularly of the "lonely" kind.'

This renews his 'silent quarrel' with the master. He is a trifle disappointed that Rilke didn't privilege him with a more concrete statement on love in the universal sense. True, the futurist fantasy at the tail-end, with women taking men in hand and leading them to the promised land, addresses the larger picture, but it is so wide-sweeping, and could be mistaken for old earth-mother stuff warmed up. Kappus knows something about real mothers! You can't help loving them despite. But mother-love doesn't help with the sort of preparation Rilke was mooting for him in order to deal with girls.

I have been reading around Freud, and gathers that Oedipal love can only be put in a safe place by improving your relationship with your father. And since it is too late for that, what's on offer is either homosexuality or resigning oneself to being beyond 'cure'. He prefers not to think about the former, and even though Rilke says that it's a good thing for a poet to be a hopeless case, does he really want to be one? In sum, the young man is sorry he mentioned his first love. In effect, it isn't anything as grand as 'a secret sorrow', just a vague fear that he won't get a second chance. But fear, he knows from his training, can be faced down.

His sport's master always says that when things are not going well 'expand your game'. And though he hasn't had any luck with girls, he knows that love goes beyond the personal, and had hoped for a word from Rilke on the world-historical love, which has conspicuously failed humanity, proving no match for the hate of other people and peoples. At present, the Turks were inciting one another to wipe out the Armenians, Russia and Japan were at one another's throats, and there are reports of tribal slaughter in the Congo. Where will it all end?

Nevertheless, Kappus, on reflection, might well concede that returning love to 'solitude' to rethink itself isn't as self-centred a notion as it first seemed. If everybody in the world did likewise there wouldn't be any wars. However, he wasn't to know that politics had been of little interest to Rilke (other than in Russia chez Lou). For instance, during the Dreyfus scandal there isn't a single reference to it in his voluminous correspondences. I'm tempted to invoke Herbert Marcuse's 'repressive desublimation', 'an Eros-driven egocentricity sapping the psychic energies that would give you a thirst for politico-social transformations' (*The One-Dimensional Man*, 1964). But that has already beginning to change on meeting Ellen Key, the Swedish proto-feminist and learning about her struggle against gender stereotyping and women's education. And so, the seventh letter trumpeted the opening of the seal on Rilke's political conscience…

Chapter Ten

We Are Alone:

Letter Eight (12 August 1904, Borgeby Castle, Fladie, Sweden)

•

Other Packages

Rilke mentions the young poet in a letter to Clara for the first and only time (27/8). She had forwarded a package Kappus sent to him at Worpswede. It containing poems that he feared lost, and with good reason, what with Rilke's ever-changing addresses: apart from Germany, various Italian locations, five different locations in Paris over the two years, and now Sweden with Denmark to come.

Rilke tells her 'the poet-cadet is going through a hard time', and complaining of being 'worn out'. As Clara was (and said so in a coterminous postcard to Paula Modersohn-Becker, putting it down to delayed post-natal depression, Ruth being now a noisy toddler). She confides this to Rilke less jokingly, and he, with his optimism in the face of other people's troubles, sees the bright side:

> 'He has in his childhood been too beholden to adults and the strength needed for that has weakened him. I suppose it happens to everyone and, although what has been given up to others may drain us, it strengthens us. We bounce back older and wiser. It is like offering up a prayer. If we suffer on our knees long enough, it renews us. And, as you know, everything we do is a form of prayer.'

As the 'burden' of *Geschlecht* weighs heavily on Kappus's mind, procreation and its consequences, rather than religious observation, is on Rilke's, and Clara might well think he's suggesting that devoting herself to the maternal hum-drum as a sacrifice to his poetry, and at the expense of her career as a sculptor, will be rewarded in the next world. Moreover, packaging her exhaustion with the unhappy young poet's wasn't sensitive.

•

We are Alone:

The Longest Letter

The eighth letter to Kappus from Sweden is the longest, and the most open to the young poet's present circumstances. Rilke is staying in Castle Borgeby as a guest of Ellen Key's friend Hanna Larsson. High season in Fadie, a fashionable resort, ought to have lightened his spirits, but the Nordic summer can't have agreed with him. His mood music at first is sombre, bordering on the petulant. In his last letter Kappus had shyly confessed to bouts of 'ineffable sadness', and must have been taken aback to be told, more or less, that having a bad time will do you good if you learn to suffer in silence.

It's doubtful if the letter was written at one sitting. Rilke repeats himself more often than usual, and there are several abrupt changes of tone. Usually prefaced by an intertextual 'My dear Mr Kappus' (five in all). The tinkering with dark thoughts improves his mood, giving way to the conciliatory. At one point he even goes as far as advising the young poet to get out more: 'It will make your solitude all the more precious when you return to it.' I take it that this softening is a sop to Kappus's plaints rather than a change of mind, a mark perhaps of wearying with the correspondence, and, indeed, it was to be the last substantial letter. At the outset he refers to the length of the young poet's letter, and the recurrent 'My dear Mr Kappus' might suggest he had to remind himself to whom he is writing.

It's necessary sometimes to read between the lines to sustain the thread of his argument. Neo-Gnostic epigrams like 'The future is fixed, and it's we who revolve around in infinite space' suggest he's brushing up on his Pascal, or Schopenhauer's 'On the Indestructibility of our Essential Being in Death', in anticipation of writing to Lou or Kassner. Indeed, some ideas expressed in the eighth letter are developed in missives to them.

Rilke is crystal clear about two things. He is looking to the future to amplify his 'solitude' as a springboard to more ambitious poetry. The planks have to be made to support him, and Schopenhauer's death-defying philosophy offers a visible means. Immortal works beckon! And secondly, the young poet, although a bit of a disappointment, still remains an available shield against just talking to himself (which Schopenhauer thought was 'a bad habit'*). If the parrying is sometimes more like prodding, he still plays to Kappus's downbeat sentiments. This last-ditch attempt 'to get to the bottom' of their mutual 'Sincerity' is not without its 'desperate exaggerations' but, once he gets over the techy beginning, shows Rilke at his kindest, if not most incisive.

Note (to myself): as the novel-in-progress shows, Rilke in his late twenties was experiencing the first tremors of *timor mortis*. And Schopenhauer's 'On the Indestructibility of Our Essential Being in Death' is arguably the closest a philosopher ever got to make the case for calming it. He takes, as his point of departure, Plato's 'Vision of Er' (*The Republic*) which treats with the transmigration of souls. Plato made it a myth that defied philosophic discourse. Not so Schopenhauer. He anticipates Nabokov's 'tender ego' disappearing into the vegetation as not the end of life, saying that the flower that dies leaves rotting stalks, petals and roots, and these are used to fertilise a new flower. This I know simplifies Schopenhauer, but personally I find it gratifying that at least my flesh and bones will nourish the earth, and some life or other comes of it. I live on… I'm talking to the voice in my head! Schopenhauer says, 'Talking to yourself establishes thought on such friendly terms with speech that the gulf between what we say and feel is narrowed.' Not such a bad habit for a poet, I suppose?

•

Stop-press

Tracking the scintillating, snipe-like flights for my transcription, I felt the need to change the order of the ideas when I sensed the flow suffered from interrupted composition. When hesitating on a meaning, wherever it was possible, I supplied it from more developed versions of the idea in letters to other correspondents at the time. Conscious that I risked misrepresenting Rilke, I plea an Olsen dispensation ('trespass vision'). Understanding Rilke is my object, as it would have been the young poet's. In effect, my transcription is tripartite, a medley of Rilke (dominant author), and Kappus and myself (recessive interpreters).

•

Read on

'I want to give you a moment again, dear Mr Kappus, although I fear that there is practically nothing I can say that will make a difference… So, now you tell me your great sadnesses have passed. Passed? Think, again. The only sorrows that are bad for us are those treated like the symptoms of a disease rather than the cause. They abate but come back with a vengeance. You can't kill them but they can kill you. You say you have suffered and are glad to get back to normal. Normal? While you were unhappy did not something change within? Something new happened. Something that will endure, for like honey in a sieve what sticks enters the innermost chamber of the heart and is ever-present in the blood.

'This presence is like a visitor whose arrival has not been announced, but who, nevertheless, changes all the arrangements in the household. Nobody knows where it came from, and perhaps never will. But there are many signs that tell us that the presence has been here before. It interacts with what's already there as though it's a close relation, making its presence felt until it's indispensable. In short, it is here to stay. But what is it doing? What is its cause, or because? Could it be that it has made itself at home in order to transform from within our future? That by entering into a relationship with the new old presence, one metamorphoses what is to come?

'When the future eventually comes upon us, it happens before we realise it. Indeed, in life it's a constant struggle to catch up with things that have already occurred. We are taken by surprise by the future, and the excitements that it brings make it seem like an invasion from outside. But if you stand apart from the hullabaloo and keep your head, you will recognise that what's happening is nothing strange or new. It has long been a part of you. And now you're repeating it forwards. It's not an interruption in your solitude for, in effect, what is called your fate; your future, resides in yourself.'

Note (to myself): Kappus would recognise this notional collaboration with the future (chez Kierkegaard). Daydreaming is something he often enjoys. It helps him to rise above his present circumstances. Far from being a waste of time, it is an instinctual form of forward planning. You might, for instance, imagine being a hot-air balloonist and, encouraged by many hours of happy reverie at the prospect, become one. Released into the air, you are born again.

'These presences that inhabit us carry their terrors, like the stories of our childhood that come to us from time immemorial. Bear with them, and the fearful dragon at the last moment turns out to be a princess. Perhaps all the dragons in our lives are princesses, merely waiting for the day when the frog becomes a prince. Maybe deep down everything terrifying is just a timorous thing, waiting to be pleasantly surprised. The terrors and abysses are ours too and we must learn to love them. Only then will the spell be broken, and we can go out to mingle with the world and realise our princely mission. But we must make sure we're not carrying anything weighing heavily on our nature which could lead to a false step that trips us up and plunges us back into uncertainty. We have to be single-minded and turn our back on any distractions demanding help met on the way.'

Note (to myself): Kappus could no doubt fill in the details of the Greek myth that Rilke alludes to (it features prominently in Kierkegaard's *Journals*). The final quest set Psyche by Venus is to fetch Proserpine's beauty potion, and she takes what the Greeks call 'the divine risk', blinkering herself against any roadside diversions, particularly the traps of compassion Eros puts in her way.

'Human beings have paid dearly for believing that their future comes from outside themselves. History has shown that external forces serve only to use and empty us. The caveman was self-sufficient but, once men began to depend on potters and blacksmiths, that changed. In no time they were looking to the sky and the gods for help. It came with a vengeance. Until Christianity returned man to individual responsibility. Mankind was not ready for that. The Dark Ages descended into hell on earth for heaven's sake.'

Note (to myself): my transcription here expands what is suggested more than usual. But I'm holding Rilke's line with him. Together, his kite won't quite fly off. When he slips away to do something else, I keep it afloat. Where this happens, I insert a 'My dear Kappus' in the text when he resumes.

'The Enlightenment narrowed the world down to industrial production, in order to increase dependence on material things, instead of giving humans the courage to explore the unknowns within themselves. Thus marginalised, the powers of the spirit that could "get to the bottom" of life and death fell into desuetude and atrophied. The inexplicable had been outlawed, the point of our existence lost. What came from within, moved the spirit, was nulled. Fear and confusion entered to fill the void, and *servitude volontaire*. People accepted that outside forces determined what happened to them. Just as for aeons people were deceived by the movements of the sun, so we still are deceived by the movement of what is to come. The future is fixed, dear Mr Kappus, and we revolve around in infinite space. How could things not be Difficult for us?'

Note (to myself): Kappus would have picked up the nod to Schopenhauer in 'the future is fixed'. But being a good student would have known that Schopenhauer applies the 'stand-still' to 'the subjective *present* of our essential being', not the future *per se*, what will happen to us. He is emboldened to ask how could the future, which doesn't yet exist, be fixed except as a fixed idea? He re-reads the paragraph, and decides that essentially, it was a reminder that, though modern man has lost his way, all he has to do is backtrack into himself. What's sitting in his mind has the means through 'solitude' to bring a better future into existence. This makes Kappus feel better about his own insignificance. 'Somewhere in my innermost being lurks the key to my future. All I need to do is find the lock.' Nevertheless, Rilke's happy thought comes with a breath-taking warning:

'Solitude is not something you can take or leave. We are solitary beings. It's what we are. You can fool yourself into thinking otherwise. Accept it as a beginning. But beware of the vertigo* that comes when our eyes lose the accustomed fixed points on the horizon, and the world's inner-space (*Weltinnenraum*) enters us rather than the other way around. The near becomes far and the distant infinite. It's like someone would feel if magic-carpeted from his room to a mountain peak and exposed to the unknown, the nameless. The disorientation almost destroys him, uncertain whether he is about to fall or be hurtled into space or be pulverised into nothingness. He has to lie to himself that all is as it should be to keep his balance, and recover his senses in order to dispense with all proscribed weights and measures known to him. The man of the mountain then can stand alone in rarefied air, taking in the cosmos, and without visible means of support.

'Solitude obliges us to brave a parallel experience. We must accept that anything can happen, our existence is unpredictable. And that takes courage. Human beings nowadays have settled for the received knowns, and shy away from the inexplicable. Apparitions, the 'world of the spirit', death, not to mention God; all those things that belong to us have been banished from our daily lives, so the senses that could seize their significance have atrophied. This not only impoverishes our existence, but restricts the relation between one another. We have removed ourselves from the riverbed of endless possibilities to squat down on the sandbanks where nothing happens. And so, the boring, self-limiting status quo continues, frightened of the new we don't feel equal to. But someone who is ready for anything, that excludes nothing, even the most inexplicable, will enjoy a rapport with another that's life-enhancing and can be lived to the full...'

Note (to myself): Heidegger picked up the last two paragraphs in his lecture on poets as philosophers (published 1982): 'There are truths in poetry that philosophers do not know', citing Gotthold Ephraim Lessing's, "Uncertain certification... You believe you know, and then you remember it's more complicated". An idea that made Kierkegaard want to be a poet.

Rilke addresses the young man's recurrent plaint about distractions, and reiterates his usual response to it, citing this time Edgar Allen Poe's prisoners in the dungeon and the need to escape into solitude. 'In order to survive on this mountain range and experience the angel or devil thoughts that come to you out of nowhere, you must be properly prepared. So, before tackling the summit, find a corner in your room to pace up and down, breathing evenly, living on less air, to build up reserves that will stand you in good stead on the summits. Even if nothing extraordinary happens to you on solitude's Olympus, you can profit from the exercise when you descend to face the smog of life.'

Note (to myself): *regarding vertigo (three paras above): I fancy, Rilke interrupted himself to look up Montaigne on intellectual giddiness. 'The thinking man is suspended in a cage above the Notre Dame in Paris. He has every reason to believe that the wire is secure and he can't fall, but that cannot prevent him fearing that he will be catapulted into space, exploding into a thousand pieces. What contortions the brain undergoes to support the irrational in order to explain our state of mind!' Rilke excluded the last sentence and, instead, has the man on the mountain peak lying to himself to control the jitters, before elevating himself above all he has been taught to believe.

•

Your Mountain

'My dear Kappus, your mountain is at present the parade ground. And holding your breath there is as much an ordeal and a bounty as on a mountaintop. On concrete, down at sea-level, as much as above the clouds, the world of the spirit is to be found. Fear is the devil you know. Be it for the wars you're being prepared to face, or going beyond the explicable. Courage is the angel you don't know, but will get to. In your solitude, exult in the devil and angel or they will crush you and it's back to the dutiful dead-end life.'

Note (to myself): the young poet would not have known that Rilke was probably thinking of his father, who failed as a soldier due to the infamous chronic cough on parade, a come-down for the family tradition which, nevertheless, released him to concentrate on becoming a poet.

What follows would come as a relief:

'Dear Mr Kappus, spiritual development fortifies us to make the decisive leap into the world outside. Its guardian angel narrows the gulf between one human being and another. Fear of others makes so many hide out in the safe haven of convention, but the spiritual is a way in, not out, and sooner or later the ground will open under you and you can dig deep. Alternatively, if you go the way of 'free spirits' like Verlaine, and throw away your thinking cap, and float in the river letting dredgers flow past, soon enough the floods will come, and you'll be swept away into the ocean.

'I know scratching where it itches with a return to your primal nature has its attractions for a young poet [*pace* Richard Delmel]. But it would be removing yourself from the main stream of endless possibilities to let life pass you by on the sandbank. I once fancied being a vagabond. A night sleeping in the open air cured that. Neither did I find being "drunk with wine and poetry" and "doing what you liked", as Baudelaire decreed (*Les paradis artificiels*), freed the spirits. Not knowing where you are becomes monotonous and that breeds tedium, and you find yourself not lolling beside a scenic river, but stuck in a cramped basement with bars on the window and scarcely any light. You pound the walls of this hell-hole. 'Any Where Out of This World'* You are like Poe's prisoner. In the dark he gropes for the shapes in his dungeon so as not to be a stranger to the horrors that he must live with, down to the last rat.'

Note (to myself): *from Baudelaire's 'Voyage', *Petits Poèmes en prose*. It is a quote in English from Edgar Allan Poe's story *The Pit and the Pendulum*. Introducing Poe was pertinent. Not being able to support himself with his writing, Edgar joined the army (claiming to be twenty-two, although only eighteen). After two years in the ammunition workshop, his attempt to be discharged was only made possible by making peace with his hated family.

'But of course, we are not prisoners. The lock on the door is in our head. There is only ourselves to fear. We can pace up and down in our room, or bestride the wind-blasted heath, in the sure knowledge that thousands of years of evolution have fine-tuned our innermost being to reflect the world around us. It's "the power and beauty of the well-kept secret of oneself" that nobody else is able to conspire against. It can be trusted as long as you trust yourself. You are the vessel that contains, not only life's joys and hopes, but its hazards and abysses. We must learn to love them, so they can be faced and embraced to fulfil us.

'It's the dragons and princesses all over again. We grow up with them on realising that the monsters that frightened us are really humans. Beauty and the beast coexist within us. You live with that reality and can't live with it! So be it.

'My dear Mr Kappus, don't torture yourself because roses have thorns. Such is life and the dark grave. Why distrust the world you were born into? It is on your side. The terrors it holds are your terrors, the abysses are yours too. Try to love them and if you succeed, they will be appeased. Stand firmly in the light and shade that is yourself, without fear of your shadow, and who knows, one day you may find yourself at the centre? of earthly existence, the fulcrum of time, or the centre? of the perfect golden globe of space where the eternal *will* exists, and you won't have anything to fear.

Note (to myself): the string of this mystic kite is grounded by Schopenhauer's 'On the Indestructibility of Our Essential Being'. And augers the symbiosis between life and death that was to become a major motif in the *Duino Elegies*. Life carries its death within from birth, and death is a continuation of life by other means.

'Don't be dismayed by the sadness that looms up before you and overshadows all your doings like a cloud, making your hands tremble. It's all for the better. Know that something new is happening to you. Life has not forgotten you. It holds you in its hands and won't let you fall. You don't need to convince yourself that your feet are on the ground, or up in the air, like Melchior Lorck's *Tortoise above the Venetian Lagoon*, a painting that once troubled me' (and Montaigne?). 'But life's suspension, with its fears and exhilarations, is working to hold you up. Don't ask where it comes from and where will it all end. Just accept what you're going through, and you'll come out of it all the stronger. You want to become something and the joys and woes of solitude are your womb, your incubator. Live with them, give them birth.
'Some people would say that passive acceptance is an unhealthy attitude. Sickness is the means by which an organism frees itself from an alien invasion. You don't give yourself up to it. If you do, it will devour you whole. They are wrong. You must help your body to be sick, so it can deal with it itself. Patience and suffering go together, and recovery comes with trust. Sometimes in the heat of battle against a rampant enemy, to fight the good fight you must sweat it out in the trenches. In

this case you're your own sand-baggers and ambulance team. Keep vigil over yourself. As you know, in any illness there are days when the physician can do nothing except wait. That's what you must do now, more than anything else, and you're in no better place, an army camp in peace time. Your time to go out into the world and achieve something will come.

'But don't watch yourself too closely, dear Mr Kappus, and start jumping to conclusions about what's happening to you. Simply let it happen. Otherwise you'll brood and blame your parents, and all that foolishness. The past made you what you are, for better or worse. It's your backbone. Don't make a hump of it. That one grows up at all is a wonder. What went wrong in a solitary and helpless childhood is balanced by what went right. Count your blessings [*Gerundheitl* – blessing - is the most frequently used mana noun in Rilke's correspondence.] The errors made by parents and the dreams of the child are two sides of the same coin. *Sehnsucht*, our longings/yearnings, are theirs too, born of childhood's griefs and grames. You carry them on and that's all to the good. A happy childhood would have its drawbacks. It is more likely to lead you to a conventional life with all its eventual woes. Your sorrows, and resistance to them, is the past that goes with you into the future. Don't remember your upbringing to condemn it. Resentment only serves to repeat the bad things backwards. Once you turn against what formed you, you become deformed and are in danger of losing everything. You disappear outside yourself, and the codes imposed by dogma will step in to trample you.

'The 'spiritual presences', the strangers that enter your life and become part of you, are the life and soul of what's to come. Let them work on you in solitude. It won't be easy. They break, make, break to make, make to break. That's the circle of renewal by catabolism. You replace what you are by what you become, and back again, in cycles. It's like the seasons. In the dead of winter, you are lifted by the thought that the good days will return. You begin to appreciate winter's privations as a hibernation that makes spring possible. So, the highs and lows are equally desirable.

'When you achieve this state of equilibrium, don't regard it as a victory. Victory is an empty phrase, garnished with bunting and public parades. And it can be ignominious, as defeat can be glorious. But neither extremes are of any consequence in the larger scheme of things. Nature is based on cycles, and humans must go with them. Take the externals for granted and just to let things happen, registering them within yourself. It's more becoming (in both senses of the word).

'In childhood your *Sehnsucht* was for the great-good-thing. Forget it. Someone else put that in your mind. Go for the greater-good-thing-beyond. The one that speaks for you and you alone. Even if this leads you into what others would call vice, a term Rodin dismisses as an amateur concept. If vice is necessary to your life, it will be absorbed by it without difficulty, and virtue will prevail. I know that at present reaching that state seems like a tall order. But, if you oppose your lingering sense of impotence with the satisfying thought that it will not always be so, you'll be well on the way to making the grade. Reaching your greater-good-thing-beyond will be Difficult, like all births, and indeed spring itself. Nature knows that, and invariably makes a space for itself so it can expand and avoid stifling in stagnation or bursting its banks. Women know that all too well. Give yourself time and you too will grow out of your feeling of helplessness. Vines can be trained to encircle the garden of our lives.

'I am thinking of your life, Dear Mr Kappus, with its hopes and fears. Recall how as a child you yearned to belong to the world of grown-ups. I see that now you want to go further than that, and are drawn to a larger world (of war and poetry). That's why your life is bound to be Difficult, but you will grow with it, if you trust yourself and your solitude, and the 'spiritual presences' won't let you down. They will prevail.

'You are not alone in your solitude. Don't think for a moment that he who is trying to console you has it easy. His growing pains were no easier than yours. If he hadn't suffered difficulties in his childhood and the sadness of their subsequence in adult life in which he found himself wanting, he couldn't have shared with you the calm and simple words that sometimes make one feel better, for better or worse.
Yours,
Rainer Maria Rilke'

We are Alone:

The long goodbye

Kappus would have been touched by this final confidence. The seven-year age gap between them seems less. The famous poet was more an older brother getting carried away and excusing himself in the third person. It was funny and sad, but normal. Indeed, this letter must have engaged the young man more than any other as it addresses his immediate concerns. Almost certainly (because of its length and breath) written in increments, the jerkiness gave him a rougher ride than usual. Sometimes the writing is more excited than exciting. This could be taken as a compliment. His master's prose isn't standing on ceremony. This moved him to think that maybe they were getting closer. He would be wrong.

For instance, the writings sent in the wandering packet were not mentioned, and they included some prose appreciations of favourite books. And Rilke wouldn't be best pleased as he had made himself clear on the value of literary criticism. And clearly, he didn't 'love' the poems. Kappus wasn't to know it was more or less the end of their intense correspondence. The next two letters were perfunctory.

Rereading the letter, he would once again have marvelled at the bullet-point handwriting. Despite Rilke's impatience to get his freewheeling thoughts down on paper, his tiny tight-knit script was almost pointillistic, as though he held his pen like a gun. But he must have wondered about Rodin and the Mephisto suggestion that vice, if it exists, is no bad thing. Rilke had not made it clear that the Auguste had the capacity to see the good in anything (or maybe he wasn't clear himself and had mistaken his maître's joke for a principle). As Paul Gsell, Rodin's belated Boswell, wrote in the preface to *L'art*, 'If wronged by someone close, Rodin takes it badly, but soon recovered his beautiful temperament to contemplate with equanimity this choice example of gross baseness.'

Rilke, as an occasional guest of the Rodins, observed the domestic bedlam in 'Les Brilliants', Meudon*: 'I pity long-suffering Rose. Her life is like holding a cup under a waterfall' (letter to Lou). She wasn't the only one to suffer. Rilke was painfully aware how one-sided his relationship with the maître was. Rodin could not read German and so his work remained a mystery to him. He found Rilke quaint enough to develop affection for the timid little hand-kissing young German. But it was a master-and-dog relationship at best, and his carping about the monograph was undoubtably a factor in Rilke's flight to Sweden. Rodin's entourage was another: some saw him as a lacky and others a comic turn. Stefan Zweig, in his lecture commemorating Rilke, said that 'when the younger Rilke was talking, he tended to monologues as his French was not quite up to exchanges with the Parisians, who are language snobs. *Politesse* is a French word but fitfully practised with foreigners. Often they walked out on him mid-paragraph, muttering b*aragouin*.' Rilke confided to Lou that he was sacrificing up such humiliations on the altar of his poetry, repeating what he said to Clara about Rodin and Tolstoy. 'One or the other: happiness or art. A serious artist has no choice but to make his way through an undergrowth of brambles, doggedly dedicated to the task at hand. As for his life – it's an atrophied organ of no further use.'

Rilke spared the young poet such dark thoughts. Or what he wrote at the time to Lou: 'I feel like a pothole in which stale water collects and that speeding carriages drive right through.' The third-person self-pity in the final paragraph was no splash on the rickety road.

Note (to myself): *Meudon, on the outskirts of Paris, could be a dark place. J-P Sartre was brought up there (read his *Words*) and Louis-Ferdinand Celine lived out his post-war shaming (read, his deeds). 'Les Brilliants' was not a happy house for Camille Claudel. It now boasts a hauntingly daunting Rodin Museum.

•

My Wren Winged by Rilke's eagle

Sometimes reading *The Letters*, I feel Rilke, having got carried away with a flight, is desperately seeking to land it. As sometimes he changes flights mid-air, moving on to another, in my transcription I'm tempted to become their air-traffic controller before the original idea disappears off into outer space. In the eighth letter I didn't resist the temptation. It was written in tranches (evident from the flight changes) and so when the flow was interrupted, I spelt out the connections and to sustain continuity I even re-jigged the scheduling of themes in the narrative. But after bringing the flight down, I worried that it wasn't the one that Rilke had taken, but my own!

I had been most at home with Claude Porcell's French translation, richly annotated to fill in the unsaid. Comparing it with the German,

I realised Porcell lightened the tone with the odd *mots justes*, particularly when Rilke directly addresses Kappus. It is a linguistic trait. French politesse as opposed to German *hoflichkeit*.

I found myself favouring the French for my transcription. I don't think apologising to Rilke's ghost is called for. He wasn't averse to question his native tongue. In a letter to Lou that coincides with the eighth, he complained about 'the difficulty in searching for the external equivalents in action for the movements of the soul.' Maybe that would account for the guttural *hoflichkeit*, in what was meant to be a soulful touch.

Note (to myself): He was to write over two hundred poems in French. Possibly it wasn't a rejection of his vernacular, but a wish to be read by the French poets he so admired like Paul Valéry who had no German. During his last visit to Paris he confided to Maurice Betz, his friend and French translator, that he felt belittled as his reputation as a poet was merely based on hearsay.

My transcription, I like to think, is a heart-felt homage to the ideas flying around (and sometimes skimming the runaway). I'm grounding them so they land comfortably for passengers like Kappus and myself. But to do so required cutting out some notional aerobatics; repetitions (a hazard of lift and lay letter-writing); and asides I deemed marginal to the narrative. As a result, my transcription is shorter than the original by more than a half. Textual scholars need not despair. *Briefe en einen jungen Dichter* is in print (and in multiple languages). What I have left out can be checked out.

I have been faithful to Rilke in my fashion, and his fashion too. I read the letter, feeling my way, sometimes with 'tacit knowledge'. That is understanding an idea without knowing why. Michael Polanyi, the Anglo-Hungarian philosopher, developed the concept (1943). He argues that 'tacit knowledge' is facilitated 'by believing before you know' and 'its pursuit demands a passionate outpouring of oneself into untried forms of existence'. Polanyi applied the concept to counter the logical positivists. Rilke would have been more positive without the logic, being amongst the leading poets of mystical ideas. And so, when puzzled by a meaning, I tacitly went beyond his words. It was a literary transmigration of sorts. Possessed by what I believed he was desperate to make known to Kappus, and indeed himself, I dared to become on occasions his master's proxy voice, to round off what he hadn't the time or patience to complete. Forgive me my 'trespass', dear reader. I was only trying to help.

Chapter Eleven

The New Love

•

Mother envy

The young poet returns to the seventh letter. His studied response to 'the sealed package' of love was answered by faery tales in the eighth. 'Perhaps all your dragons are really princesses, and so love them despite appearances.' He was in a Military Academy, not a nursery. Rilke had prophesised a future when women, empowered by recovering their primacy, would take the initiative and readjust the gender balance. A utopian fantasy that he was no doubt wowing the New Women in Sweden now. But on second reading, he wryly recognised his relations with his mother in Rilke's marriage of two minds: 'Two solitudes protecting, *circumscribing* and acknowledging each other.' By setting limits to love, she had sealed the 'package' once shared and left it in a cold place.

Rilke ought to have been sensitive to the boy's feelings. He has 'Oedipal problems' himself (Lou told him so). By all accounts, Sophia ('Phia') Entz-Kinzelbergers-Rilke was a spoilt, frivolous schemer, who liked to play the diva with people, not least with her 'useless' husband and eager-to-please son. Her literary transmogrification into Malte's bed-bound, ethereal mother who dies while he's a boy, is not so strange if you allow for wistful thinking, a trait he hazarded in the Xmas letter to Kappus cultivates unconditional beliefs in childhood, sadly regretted once innocence is lost…

The reinvention owes something to Stendhal's mother, who died when Henri was seven (the same age as Malte's). Little Henri loved her so passionately that he was prone to crawl on top of her in bed and 'kiss her all over'. She couldn't bring herself to discourage him, but when spied on by his enemy, Aunt Sèraphie, their profane pietàs became a family scandal.

Stendhal claimed his mother spoiled him for other women. 'I was not loved by those I loved. Seemingly, I loved them in my fashion and not theirs' (*Diary of an Egotist*). And his *De l'Amour* is about being always in the wrong with women. Love of his mother was the only

The New Love

lasting one in his life.* Whenever he heard the bell of the church in Grenoble, where as a boy he saw her dead body, he clenched himself in the grip of 'a dull, dry, emotionless sorrow that is neighbour to anger'. Rilke would have wanted a mother who made him feel like that.

Note (to myself): *while Stendhal was writing the painfully romantic *De L'Amour* (after Princess Matilde hadn't taken his passionate advances seriously), he found time to enjoy the mature charms of the opera singer Madame Pasta. When she sang Vivaldi's '*Il Cimento*' to a full house at La Scala, he thought she was publicly celebrating the 'cementation' of their love, confusing the French word with the Italian for 'ordeal'.

So many writers have delicate mothers with artistic inclinations, and inadequate fathers, that it almost seems like a necessary prerequisite. D. H. Laurence and Frank O'Connor are only the tip of the iceberg. Scratch a literary youth and you'll find him in father-freeze or/and mother-meltdown. Poets as different as Rilke and Brecht had the same (dis)advantage. Real enough for Brecht with her tuberculosis, but for Rilke it was aspirational, channelled through Malte. Phia was robustly healthy and outlived her husband by a quarter of a century and her only son by two years. Missing out on the early loss of a mother meant his poetry suffered, but wishful thinking helped with prose and with a rare poem, 'Mourning' (1907) in which after Phia's imagined death he recalls the infant games he played to please her (it didn't in life):

> Out of our play can sometimes come
> real sunshine, flowers, the world's first cause.
> And we can act out life, in sum,
> carried away, not thinking of applause.

Rilke's letter to Lou about the future of love is more restrained. 'Sealed packages' are not mentioned, and he underplays the fertility dimension. Lou would not have tolerated talk of 'the fruity weight of women's *Geschlecht*', not having ever considered herself child-bearing material. She saw it as a peril to be avoided. And so, his vision of the future is more clinical and men and women will reach out towards the same objective like brothers and sisters, in order to carry together the burden of their sexuality.'

The New Love

Sharing 'the burden' with Lou within those limits should have been possible. As two free spirits who are married, but don't want a divorce, they have an object in common. Marriage gives them both an alibi to do what they liked within bohemian reason, and serves as a ballast to keep their relationship afloat without, so to speak, muddying the waters. It is a working arrangement, even for their respective spouses, Carl Andreas and Clara. The dramatics between Carl and Lou are long behind them (her condition for marriage was 'no sex' leading him to stab himself in the region of the groin. But he recovered to make-do with an affair with the maid which produced a child).

Note (to myself): echoes of Kierkegaard's father, who after the death of his wife, begot Søren by the housekeeper. Although in Carl and Lou's case it had a happier outcome. They remained together unto death, despite her late-onset promiscuousness.

Clara's complaisance is more cold-blooded. Not having a choice, she puts up with it. Even when he married her, Clara knew she was second-best (Paula Becker wouldn't have him). Also, as a student, Rodin preferred Camille Claudel's sculptures, and Rilke treated her work with the silence that Rodin did Rilke's poetry. On the other hand, Clara feels free to hate Lou. Intellectually, she comes a poor second to her in Rilke's eyes. Though he condescends to communicate in letters his discoveries in the visual arts in Paris, and the sordid conditions of life there, that is about it. Lou gets the full Monty of art as ideas and ideas as art, plus the romping jollies of friends. Conversely, Lou knows that Clara had more of a hold on him than she has. Not merely due to baby Ruth. The bond is forged by a combination of decorum and unconformist Catholic guilt. The latter Lou despises but she cannot compete with social convention. Not least because it's her modus operandi too.

In effect, although Lou and Rilke might 'reach out' to carry together 'the burden', it could never have been 'like brothers and sisters' in the normal sense. In her youth she experimented with sisterly love on the writer Paul Rée and it ended badly. She renewed the idea with Carl Andreas and, after the violent start, it settled down to a white marriage, mutually free to pursue their diverse obsessions. Shortly before her death in 1937, Lou reminisced on her relations with Rilke: 'We were rather like primal siblings, before incest had become a taboo.' Nearly, or erstwhile (who's to know*), lovers, the flame of passion continues to flicker with flirting without flowers, kept alight by a whiff of jealousy. Not, of course, of their sitting spouses, whose response to the liaison couldn't be more different. Carl Andreas is complaisant for the sake of material support for his peripatetic scholarly work as an Orientalist, often unpaid, and Clara, having mixed her labour with Rilke, is damned if she's going to be junked for an older woman.

Note (to myself): *Kassner commented that Lou wanted to make the young Rilke her lover but he 'defended his virtue'.

The jealousy that fans the flicker is two-way. Lou is unfaithful to Rilke in her fashion (the passionate letters, mainly unilateral with famous men), and he is true only to his work. But sex, other than of the subliminal kind, is out of the question not only because Lou and her libido are in thrall to Freud. She wouldn't wish to tempt the gods by congress with a needy poet fourteen years younger than her. And so, 'What began as a Grand Passion ends up as a willingness to oblige', to quote Ezra Pound, no stranger to threesome's himself with Dorothy Shakespear and Olga Rudge.

This suited Rilke in his belief that love should be separated from possessiveness so that the erotic impulse can be saved for creativity. Moreover, Lou did most of the obliging as a confidant and counsellor. But she knew the score and, while finding late-onset consolation with younger men, stood by her friend, now more mother than muse (*pace* Freud's Oedipal simplification).).

After his death she responded to an adverse critic, 'It's all wrong to think of Rilke the man within the narrow confines of lamentations and self-loathing.' The 'lamentations' were reasonable enough, particularly in the aftermath of the Great War, but identifying with the Prodigal Son because the 'man who didn't want to be loved' wasn't 'self-loathing' but self-protection. Lou loved him by remote (letters mostly), intruding only on his work and sometimes his psychic health (he cherished the former).

In sum, she came to be his surrogate sister, easier to achieve by 'his willingness to show his feminine side'. Her posthumous tribute, 'Rilke made me feel like the Blessed Virgin after the Immaculate Conception', is affectionately funny and probably heart-felt. But the descent of the poet as the Holy Ghost has engendered legends. Recently a German film, *The Audacity to be Free* (2016), intimated that when Lou went blind, her housemaid companion, a severe and controlling presence, was her daughter by Rilke.

•

Size Matters

A word with the all-knowing Joab Comfort is called for:

'The sex-life of Rainer Maria? A very short book,' he says. 'I don't think Rilke thought the act dignified love's mystique.'
'Yet, Joab, he gave sex many incarnations in his poetry. Even in his 'Thing-poems' when trying to get under the skin of lower animals "The Panther", for instance.'
'He had no problem was with the idea. His climacteric moment comes in his "Leda" sonnet. Rilke out-swans Yeats's "Leda" by concentrating on the job in hand rather than bringing Helen of Troy and "Agamemnon dead" into it. The last sextet is hot stuff, the act of possession makes a god mortal:

'Zeus flew down from the skies, gliding, white, and all around her disguising wings stirred.
His neck slid through her weakening fingers,
And he loses his godhead. Now at one,
he feels in every feather the delight
at having in her lap become all swan.'

'On the other hand, Joab, Yeats asks if it was Leda's divine moment, putting on "his knowledge with his power". It is the deification of a woman. W. B. makes her a momentary goddess, while Rilke makes a man of a god through the agency of a generous woman.'
'There is an overlap between the two poems. Yeats's "Leda" was written the year after Rilke's death, 1927. He could have been reading the recently translated 'Thing-poems' and the line "A shudder in the loin engenders there / the broken wall ..." comes from cross-fertilisation between 'The Panther' and "*Du Berg, der blieb da die gebirge*".'
'Which means the silent rising of the ...'
'*Der orgel Mannliche*. Let's change the subject ...'

The New Love

'No. It's important. The last line of the *Duino Elegies* is 'the joy of being astonished at the rise and fall of a happy thing'.'
'See-saw Margorie Daw. Rilke was a pure poet.'
'But what about the sequence of poems he wrote during the Great War celebrating the phallus? What was the "happy thing"?'
'Don't ask, Augustus! Rainer Maria was a little and delicately formed man, and all the women in his life, except Lou, were much bigger and stronger than him. Clara was a veritable Brunhilda. Size matters ...'
'Ah! Maybe that's where the dignity comes in.'
'Yes, he died of shame.'

Note (to myself): Yeats, after reading a book about Rilke's ideas, was so 'annoyed' with his Hindu notions on death (that 'you are born with one's death ...') that he wrote in the margin:

Draw Rein, draw breath.
Cast a cold eye
On life, on death.
Horseman pass by.

(subsequently the refrain in the poem "Under Ben Bulben").

•

Gender Bender

Rilke's impatience with couples married to the conventions takes an abrupt turn in writing to Lou. 'Not having not taken the 'divine risk', 'they don't have a second chance to achieve love, even when the children leave ...' But he offers an optimistic solution: 'If things are to change for the good, lovers' hearts must break, or tear themselves apart in such a fashion as to close the way to all deceptions. And once set adrift from the traditional moorings, the currents are in their favour. What's conceived in the high seas of solitude will give birth to a race who learn to do freely what they felt compelled to do before.' Maybe Lou would have remembered her Kierkegaard. Rilke appears to have substituted 'lovers' for 'poets', and 'the conventions' for 'Christianity'. But she would have found his closure less Kierkegaard than Nietzsche.

'Doing freely what you felt compelled to do before' might suggest a *repetition forwards*, but is most likely to be a boring 'the more things change, the more things remain the same'. Compulsion is stronger than freedom when it comes to love.

In the 'sealed package' letter, Rilke is certain that the gender transformation is only a matter of time. He relays this to Clara, Kassner and, of course, Lou: 'We at the hour before this dawn can see the light of day. As sure as dreams precede an awakening, such ideas are preparing us to achieve the inevitable.' He also mentions to Lou the enlightened groups of people in Northern Europe 'who are now coming to grips with our entwined nature' (through experimental psychology and innovative education). 'This should quicken a collective movement towards universal love.' He tells Clara about the neuroscientist in Sweden who 'talks about an inevitable mutation in the evolution of human relations.' And adds to Kassner, 'However, I don't think a change in our nature will be necessary. The nurturing will be a renewal of what already exists in us all, the primal.'

Rilke privileges women as the source of this nurture. But he is willing to contribute practically by writing a monograph on Ellen Key and her experiments with women's education. He had sent her a letter from Rome (complaining of spring fever) and giving her a moderated version of the gender transformation. Her reply was prompt and friendly. But her inclusion of a detailed questionnaire did not please him ('Who are you, young man'). Still, her open invitation to visit Sweden made him decide to abandon his solitude to accept her hospitality and sit at her feet.

If Clara is jealous of her, and Lou a mite suspicious, there was no reason to be. Ellen Key is almost twice Rilke's age, single in both mind and body and with an impeccable reputation as a serving sister. She was certainly no Joanna the Baptist of 'neo-primal motherhood' and, had she known about his domestic (dis)arrangements, would have been shocked at poor Ruth's father. Ellen Key's most popular book, *The Century of the Child* (1900), anticipates Dr Spock with its bias towards hands-on parenting. Rilke is a sitter at feet by nature and physique. And since Ellen Key is built like Margaret Dupont, the grande dame of the Marx Brothers, he must have looked like Harpo, plucking the strings, her little poet. She would be amused, and touched.

•

THE NEW LOVE

Writerly Retreats

The sojourn chez Ellen Key marks the fourth country that Kappus has received letters from in eighteen months. Rilke makes light of his wanderlust, justifying it to Lou as a rite of passage: 'Growing up is learning to leave your family and *patrie*' (using the French word to avoid *Vaterland*. He's a citizen of the world, and Paris is its capital). But Rilke is being economical with the object of the Key trip. Having successfully dispatched the Rodin monograph, he was offering to write one on her educational philosophy for German readers.

The Ellen Key odyssey is to be a political variation of a pattern designed to avoid having the 'proper job' his father (and Clara no doubt) pressed on him. Strong, well-off women, in effect, adopted him as their poet and, once in residence, he made them complicit in his poetic struggle. All he asked for was to be left to write and think in the hunting lodge (fair game off season), or some eyrie, if it was a castle. But he made himself accessible for dinner, and 'knew how to behave' in polite society. His mother's family, the Entz-Kinzelbergers, considered themselves gentry, and he was brought up accordingly. Needless to say, any gallantry was kept within the bounds of the courtly (flowers for the lady). Husbands didn't need to be complaisant.

Rilke's most favoured patron is to be Princess Marie von Thurn und Taxis. Thanks to pioneering commercial postal services in the early nineteenth century, her family had estates all over Europe. Twenty years older than him and a match for him intellectually, like Lou, though more relaxed. There was no history to live down. In effect, such *deluxe* retreats were to prove a nifty, thrifty way of sustaining himself in the best watering places and cities in Europe. Rilke couldn't live on poetry alone. Not that he would have ever seen this as a way of saving on bills. Samuel Johnson's 'A man unconnected is at home everywhere, unless he may be said to be at home nowhere', would have appealed to him (as it did to Beckett whose bedside reading was his *Prayers and Meditations*). But not the good doctor's rider, 'Solitude is dangerous to reason without being favourable to virtue.'

•

Meanwhile, Rodin...

In the eighteen-nineties, through travels with Lou Rilke had broken with the art nouveau style of his juvenilia, and he dedicated *To Celebrate Myself* (or *The Self*). His neo-romantic symbolist had found a muse ('You alone are real to me'). It was to be short-lived. Marriage to Clara briefly offered him an alternative. But the fruits thereof withered on the vine. Now four years later in Paris, writing his 'Thing-poems' in his new-found modernist mode is a release, but his muse being beasts, objects and blind men is something of a comedown from what he had hoped for ('The nameless storm and hurricane of the spirit' in Duino Castle was yet to come). Still, he grounded his *Sehnsucht* (yearning/longing) to please Rodin, and settled down to cultivate 'deep patience' and 'earthy industry' in order to write the poems which Gretchen Malherbe says every German schoolboy knows by heart.

It wasn't the maître's workhorse shoulders and Moses beard, or even the surprisingly gentle azure in his eyes, often half-closed, that impressed themselves on Rilke. It was the hands, enormous with stubby fingers of astonishing suppleness, as he moulded the wet clay 'like God creating Adam and Eve'. Hands, indeed, are a sub-plot that haunts *The Notebooks*. Even when symbolic or frightening, Rilke grasps their physicality as though sculpturing them. Kassner's remark, 'Rilke was a pure poet even when washing his hands', goes deeper than affectionate mockery. Disquiet goes with the manual. Disembodied hands that torment the boy Malte and Charles the Bold. They surely inspired the German horror film *The Hands of Orlac* (1924).

Rodin told Paul Gsell in his only interview, 'Artists and thinkers are like Aeolian harps played by the wind: delicately sonorous vibrations, prolonged for other mortals and sometimes future ages. But you must not be impatient before the mystery of things. You are chasing a chimera that will only come to you if you approach it with love and respect. As far as the truth of things is concerned, we must know our limits. The great mysteries are beyond us. We can touch but never to grasp them. Art is only scratching the surface to get an idea of what's under it. It's a religion that to practice, the first commandment is know how to incarnate the externals – a hand, an arm, a thigh, a leg, shoulders, a torso. And the last commandment is to respect your materials. You're modelling a world with the clay from which we were formed …'

It was Rodin's mutinous pupil Emile Bourdelle who sculptured him as the Great God Pan, horns and all. The old man laughed, 'Michelangelo gave Moses horns too as a symbol power and wisdom. I'm flattered and gratified.' Lou's husband, Carl Andreas, would have pointed out to Rilke (but they rarely met up now) that Michelangelo had been misled by St Jerome's translation of the dual-meaning Hebrew word *keren*. He chose the literal 'ram's horn' for what rises from Moses's forehead, where the spiritual 'radiating light' would be more apt.

Rodin didn't mind being represented as a horned demi-god, tooting an imaginary flute to startle fauns. It was said to be his dance of seduction, and what happened next was unpredictable. It could be a pas de deux with the available nymph, or an undercover investigation of her surfaces for his next art work, with Narcissus looking on while Echo panics in the kitchen. Mixing myths and metaphors in 'Les Brilliants' contributed chaos to the Dionysian romps. Rodin told Gsell that he forced himself to 'contemplate the perfidiousness his capriciousness could create in order to squeeze some beauty from it, for the only lasting joy in life is in the redemption of what is true.'

He took Bourdelle to see Giorgione's *Concert in the Country* at the Louvre. 'You'd benefit from the studying a Master. There's two naked women entertaining their swains with wine and a little light music. However, the *joli joie de vivre* has its dark side. Nobody is quite in the limelight. The women have their backs turned, and the heavily dressed men's faces are in shadow. A sort of inebriated melancholy pervades the scene. It is the qualified pleasure of the *joie humaine*.'

'So what!' said Bourdelle.

'My friend, one is looking at Giorgione like someone listening to poetry in a language you don't know. The joys of life always have their shady side. Coitus in excelsis is a dirty deed and short, so says the poet's philosopher' (Thomas Hobbes?). 'What is the point of it all, he is saying? After life, there's death and so on, or not, as it may be. There is no straight answer, except in art like Giorgione's. The great unknowns are songbirds secreted in the tree that throws its shadow on the men, representing mankind. Sight unseen, but you hear them.'

'Anyway,' said Bourdelle, 'the painting is nowadays attributed to Titian.'

'If so,' smiled Rodin, 'It's good to know he learned something from Giorgione.'

But Bourdelle wasn't listening. He found the maître's work slapdash, and given to emotional outbursts. His heart was with classical perfectionism, and his mind was with the Gnostics (see Guiding Note 7), who put their faith in learning and speculation as practised by the Greeks. For the Gnostics the concept of personalised revelation was sacred. Each individual has within him a mystery to explore – the God in them – and finding it means salvation. Bourdelle's *Virgin of Alsace*, a monumental sculpture in the Vosges Mountains, completed the same year the *Duino Elegies* was published (1923), has weathered badly. You'd hardly notice it.

Rodin was given to saying, 'Actions speak, words don't act.' As a man of action, the one thing that's sure about him, apart from his genius, is that he never had a need to tell a lie, being shamelessly blunt.

•

Reasons for Escape

Rilke, like Bourdelle, is restless for higher things, and Rodin's 'steadying influence' was holding him back. In his *Letters* to Kappus, he doesn't vaunt his current works. The 'Thing-poems' and the novel don't get a mention. His semi-nomad life is a bid to escape from 'the room with the locked window' of his marriage, but also from Rodin's studio which isn't only work, work, work. Scratch the surface and what's underneath is Auguste's unpredictable domestic (dis)arrangements, not notably happy, at least for the women. Musical chairs without the music. They all fall down when the maître changes his mind.

Since the two reasons to escape from Rodin's grip are associated, this makes the distancing from him doubly necessary. The second was that Auguste had a soft spot for Clara, the stolid German student with a steady hand, who could surprise one with a technical twist of the wrist, but had disappeared back into a bourgeois commune of landscape painters to get married to the little German poet. The whistling Pan in him could have danced for her. His feelings made it easier for Rilke to make the break, being expressed in angry asides.

The Letters underwrite Rilke's restlessness for higher things. Not that he could ever rival the seismic grounding that is Rodin's. But he would at least be different. What he can't possess from solitude only, he must now go out and get, and to do so, he needs to unsettle himself, and his writing, in a colder clime than Rodin's hotbed. Maybe that was the third reason for his break with the maître. The Swedish trip is a bid for freedom from what was holding back his ambition. And he has a novel to write. But the explicit one – to support to Ellen Key –

The New Love

was not merely a pretext. He was seriously taken by her work. Reasons were often multiple in Rilke's life. Or beyond reason. It was as though he was always ahead of himself.

•

Flash forwards

Seven years later, Rilke was staying with Duino Castle. Princess Marie recounts how, obliged to turn his mind to a boring business letter, Rilke paced up and down his room all morning while a bitter north wind (the *bora scura*) raged outside. As the gong rang for lunch, he rushed out on to the battlements and she thought for a moment that he was going to leap over the parapet and into the sea. Gesturing wildly to the sky, he shouted something… Over lunch, he told her that a voice in the wind had called, 'Who, if I cried out, would hear me amongst the 'Order of the Angels.'. It was of course to be the opening line of the *Duino Elegies*, and that night he started the first of them. There were nine to go. It took more than a decade. However, the voice carried in the howling gale had already been lodged in his inner ear when writing the letters to Kappus. Not yet coherent, but audible enough to vibrate in his mind. In writing to the young poet, he was listening to, or for, what was to be the future of his poetry.

Chapter Twelve

Gender Politics in a Cold Climate

•

Feeling for Thoughts

Chez Ellen Key is different from Rilke's usual retreats. The visit was not in self-interest as a pure poet. He called it an 'intellectual homecoming', and is making himself comfortable in order to contribute his brain to her campaign for women's rights. While writing the seventh letter she was very much on his mind. He sees her work as a refreshing break from outmoded conventions, offering socio-scientific methods to change the basis of human relations, within a non-conformist Christian context, with women leading the way. He hopes to play his part in influencing those aspects which could be related to primal sex and gender transformation. Rilke could well have echoed Kierkegaard's journal entry when he went on his latter-day attack on the Danish Church, 'I am the ultimate phase of the poetic temper on the way to becoming a social reformer', but perhaps without Kierkegaard's rider, 'in a small way'.

Rilke has universalist ambitions. Thanks to Lou, vitalism, via Nietzsche, and gestalt theory, via Rudolf Kassner, had broadened his mind. But his heart is with mysticism: 'God and death are not mere thoughts but inherent features of nature.' When Ellen Key asks him in a letter where he stands with immortality, he replies, 'Nothing that is real can pass away. But many people are not real.' A humanist he is not.

Martin Heidegger during the Second World War tried to resurrect Rilke for European philosophy. His attempt is more a reclamation of poetry for philosophy, inviting a poet back into the Plato's Cave. By association this damaged Rilke's reputation in post-war Germany, although he was essentially apolitical.

Heidegger denominates Rilke's contribution to philosophy as *Weltinnenraum* (world-inner-space), defining it as, 'a realm of poetic figuration, freed from the referentiality of ordinary speech, that goes beyond mere communication'. Never at a loss himself for incomprehensible formulations, he quotes 'Song is pure being. / O ye gods, it's easy for you' (*The Sonnets to Orpheus* 1 and 3), and defines world-inner-space as the where a man discovers for himself the external world and internalises it. It is a heady concept usually associated with parapsychology (Princess Marie was a keen spiritualist and Rilke attended her seances at Duino Castle).

Heidegger, having thrown in his lot with Hitler, is drawn to the idea of a human being so pure that he doesn't need to protect himself from the world as he contains it. This *felt* thought is hardly in the realm of philosophy but of Gnosticism (as Zbigniew Herbert wrote, 'The weeds of gnosis are rampant in the garden of the natural sciences,' and Rilke is cultivating them). Heidegger goes on to cite the eighth *Duino* elegy, which starts: 'All animals see the open (space). The human eye only looks inwards and is fixed there forbidden to exit. The world outside the mind we only know from the beast's primal gaze. Still, we turn even the youngest child around and force it to look inwards, thus avoiding the openness that radiates from the beast's gaze …. The free animal has always its death behind and before it, God, and when it moves, it moves into eternity …' This accords with 'speech' freed from mere 'communication'. Rilke dedicated the elegy to Kassner, and it was to him he wrote his famous dictate: 'Happy are those who know behind all language there stands that which is beyond words.'

In the 1950s John Ashbury observed, 'Abstract expressionism can be accepted on the gallery walls but not on the page.' The same could said for *felt* thoughts. Although the inverse of abstract expressionism – expressed abstractionism – *felt* thoughts share a heart-felt public dimension with graffiti ('Julie is a dog'). But on the privacy of the page they can raise eyebrows. Heidegger did not blink, but he must have wondered what Rilke felt he was thinking, or thought he was feeling. Speaking on behalf of Rilke's ghost I would respond, 'Think nothing of it. *Felt* thoughts are the most natural way of entertaining thoughts. They are how we daydream or think to ourselves. Sometimes they can be the seedbed of poetry, but are by no means the prerogative of poets. Everybody has them and sometimes they can make more immediate sense than a rational analysis. Moreover, *felt* thoughts are not less meaningful for being fleeting.'

•

Woman's summum

Felt thoughts would hardly have cut ice with Ellen Key. Her ideas on specific educational and political issues were founded on sound logic.

The trip was a quixotic mission from the start. Rilke's atavistic sympathy for the binding cycle of nature and motherhood would not have been in harmony with Ellen Key's commitment to direct action. But though hardly a model 'new man' himself, his love of women in general made him a receptive listener, and Ellen Key and her friends didn't doubt his sincerity when he espoused not only a levelling, but a reversal of gender inequality. Evidently, he was well ahead of most of his male contemporaries and, wisely avoiding taking the extreme anthropological positions posited to the young poet, he proved more than willing to fight the good fight: 'Women are women, not just playthings or slaves of men. They are neither each other's equals or opposites.' Ellen Key could live with that.

Even if generalising women might be considered an escape clause for an errant husband, it doesn't diminish Rilke's prescience. Advanced women like Ellen Key and Lou Salomé no doubt gave him an inkling of what was to come. They were the two sides of the same feminist coin, the sacred and profane. Ellen Key came to women's rights through Christianity of the Kierkegaardian kind (the more fervent it became, the more doubts increased). Lou, very much her own woman, was a female aesthete (who became a psychoanalyst) rather than a doctrinaire feminist, but she was happy to spread the news of her relative independence to less fortunate sisters.

In a concurrent letter to Clara, Rilke expresses the wish that she would learn from such women. A forlorn hope with Lou, given that she and Clara are effectively fighting for his soul, and body, respectively, and the older woman is at present winning hands down. As for Ellen Key, Rilke would no doubt prefer to keep his troubled relations with Clara to himself. Although there were plaints in a letter about drying up as a poet due to the exigencies of marriage, he was careful to promise a photograph of the happy family with little Ruth the centrepiece. Even if she found out they had separated, Ellen Key would have been too much of a lady to mention it. But she would be thoughtful.

•

The young poet's felt thoughts?

Rilke could safely put such personal considerations aside with Kappus, and if he was tempted to further clarify his ideas on how women would change the world, and men, he resisted it. In replying to the letter on 'love' as a 'package', Kappus ignored Rilke's big idea, and instead went on again about his loveless state.

Reservations about his own mother apart, the young man must have smiled uneasily at the notion of returning grown men to the breast to reincarnate the human race as a loving species. He had the usual vague hopes and hesitations of callow youth faced by the 'opposite sex'. In Richard Dehmel, whom he rather daringly described as 'in heat', and Rilke corrected it to 'rut', he found Blessed Virgins could change into Jezebels in the course of a kiss. And now, hearing a famous poet, no doubt surrounded by adoring women, enthuse about a future of unbuttoned amazons unleashing their power and with their knowledge on the male of the species was the stuff of bad dreams. The burden of his 'loveless life' would not have been lightened by contemplating Rilke's grotesque *pietas*, more graphic Jacob Epstein than tip-of-the-iceberg Rodin.

Rodin makes him think of Clara, a former pupil of the maître's. What would she make of Rilke's vision of universal womanised love? Of course, Rilke might not want to share the future with her. But the present was more likely to be on her mind being his contribution to the future movement, in a small way, with baby Ruth. Kappus imagines sending her an anonymous copy of the gender-blender passages and, as a literary exercise in telepathy, improvises her reaction to it. He gets to work...

Only Rodin could make a monument of Rilke's tableau in the sky: men and women, each in glorious isolation, reaching out to the nebulae and to grasp the falling stars that will support them as they drop to earth. There they will find (un)common ground to carry on separately together, to create a terrestrial paradise of twin solitudes and twin-toilets, a world where angels pay the bills and cherubs are seen and not heard... Ah, Rilke, nobody can dream the dream like you, *and dreams exclude others*. Rodin knows that and would submerge the unparalleled couple in the mud of the first circle of Dante's Hell, the one for the futile...

But he tore up the Clara, having to admit from his knowledge of men that Rilke's basic idea on gender politics is sound. If the battle of the sexes is to end and love conquer all, the initiative would have to come from women. And as men are fundamentally weak, *Summum femina* would reign supreme. But when he re-reads, 'Women, in whom life abides and dwells more immediately, more yielding and more at home, have been able to ripen more fully than men into human beings,' the four 'mores' are too much for him, and he feels like a tourist looking up into a roofless Sistine Chapel. Sum-mum-mum, where are you!

He wonders why Rilke continues to write to him. 'It's certainly not my poems and definitely not my essays (sending one was a bad mistake).' Perhaps opening himself up to someone that did not know him gave the master poet free rein to try out ideas as a work plan. Exhilarated by the thought at being the sole confidant, he feels a poem coming on, a long one, a canto for each letter received from Rilke.

Twenty years later, when editing the letters, Kappus would have known from memoirs that he was only one of many portals opening the way into the gnostic garden of what was to become the *Duino Elegies*. The 'spiritual presences' anticipated the 'Order of the Angels', and 'solitude' was necessary to hear their 'subjective hosannas', but Lou and latterly Paul Valéry were the spur. Nevertheless, he had been the prime confident of Rilke's evolution towards gender equity, and in the final elegy it was celebrated in the paean to the 'rise and fall' of love and happiness. His preface tells how flattered and happy he was to have scaled the dizzy heights of Rilke's kite-flying, but relieved that once the wind dropped, and the vertigo of the correspondence wobbled to a stop, 'life having forced me into domains Rilke had urgently wanted to protect me from.'

Reading *The Notebooks of Malte Laurids Brigge* and the passages linking Malte's hopeless love for Abelone to the medieval tapestries of *The Lady and the Unicorn* (Musèe Cluny, Paris), as a homage he writes out a paragraph for Rilke's shade to read as though it was by someone else:

'The lady holding court on a floating island, blue set against a red background of birds and beasts, sentinelled by a fawn unicorn and a beige lion. The unicorn is neat and tidy, the lion shaggy and ill at ease. They are the suitors, respectively innocent and worldly. The first five tapestries represent the senses, and the sixth their consummation. The composition is broadly the same for each, except the lady changes her ornate gowns. She moves easily within the sensual world until in the penultimate tapestry a blue canopy, garnished with magical symbols including three silver moons, encloses her. It is the purification of the five senses into a single wish, that is, for love. In the final tapestry the lion has been sent packing, and the unicorn rests his head on the lady's lap. Love is at peace.'

In effect, Kappus is opening the 'packet' to find Rilke that privileged medieval legend – love as a homage to God-given beauty – over a Freudian interpretation. Certainly, the tapestries play with the sentimental life but they are more about yearning than fulfilment, prayer than performance. His poet master knew the troubadours got it wrong by being too literal, praising an arm or a leg or the golden tresses. Kneeling at the feet of any woman is an act of adoration before an eternal mystery. Kappus smiles to himself, remembering that on receiving the letter it wasn't Olympian pageants he was daydreaming of but, ever so shyly, sexual Olympics.

Of course, dear reader, these are my *felt* thoughts on Kappus's, fostered by reading the *Letters* as though they were written to me (once a young poet who circumstances led to 'other domains'). Rilke's 'package' of love came to me slightly damaged from passing through many hands, but that doesn't mean the contents were. I can feel the width, but am not sure of the quality. Therein lies the ineffability of love. Rilke knew this. I dare to guess on Kappus's part. Like him, I'm trying to read the poet master's mind, a man who, if not impenetrable, is as impervious to the obvious as his poetry can often be. However, through a willed empathy with the perplexed young poet, am I'm getting closer to Rilke?

Introducing *The Lady and the Unicorn* is presumptive. The tapestries are not mentioned in the *Letters*. Kappus only knew of them a decade or so later when reading *The Notebooks* where they figure large as a tribute to Malte's first love, Abelone. He was probably impressed enough to seek out prints. But, given the embarrassment of evidential poverty, I excuse myself by invoking Olsen's 'trespass vision', and carry on, but not regardless. As in life, my inscapes into others minds will always remain provisional. Dream on *felt* thoughts.

The lady and the unicorn are comfortable together. But Rilke wished for more. Absolutes were the horizon he was looking to. Maurice Betz, in his memoir, *Rilke a Paris*, wrote, 'The relativity of realities tormented him so much that the tremors that quaked within him erupted in pain and suffering.' Rilke only settled for relative calm after the Great War when writing the *Sonnets to Orpheus*, though rounding off the *Duino Elegies* came in a reprise of 'the hurricane of the spirit' that gave him its opening line (letter to Princess Marie, 1922). In its aftermath, he wrote to Lou that 'everything that was resistant in me, every fibre, every tissue, bent and cracked. Eating wasn't to be thought of.'

The creative storm lasted three days, but afterwards, his Great Work completed, the calm, as death approached, prevailed. He wrote to an admirer that everything, from petals shorn from broken flowers to the rough-hewn walls of his rundown castle, was sensitive to his touch. Hands, so much a part of his writing, were also his grip on life. It helped that he believed in death belonging to the disease and not the person.

•

The Key Question

Rilke settled with accustomed comfort at Castle Borgeby, where Ellen Key was a fellow guest. What they spoke about is anyone's guess. One thing that's certain is he always addressed her as 'Frau'. 'Fraulein being a diminutive is not in keeping with her status' (letter to Clara). Needless to say, the conversation was unlikely to have been anything like that with Lou or what he let fly with Kappus. By all accounts, Ellen Key was a sensible, pragmatic person who realised the liberation of women could only come about when men changed, and that included Rilke (his letters to her often veered from the enlightened to the chauvinistic in the same paragraph).

On noticing that his deckchair reading on the terrace is Thomas à Kempis's *Imitation of Christ*, she is intrigued. He tells her that if you substitute 'Art' for 'God' in the text it takes nothing away from the wisdom of the book. This made her thoughtful. But the young poet is the least of her worries. The established Church continues to patronise her educational experiments with a *faux* complicit smile ('There, there, dear. Don't forget the flowers for Sunday'). Worse, suffrage for women was only raised publicly in the unpopular context of female tax-payers, and controversial family-planning (Malthus be damned!). Reluctant to distance herself from the Christianity of her childhood, after an unrequited romance with a married colleague, she veered towards a Roman compromise, noticing how Catholic feminists gained some sincere support from the Church through the Marian Doctrine (marriage annulments could be arranged). Moreover, the Immaculate Conception may not have been birth control, but it was an assumption in the right direction.

Although, one of her wilder Catholic 'sisters' gave a lecture to Key's followers on how the Holy Ghost put Joseph, Mary's husband, in his place, and for a time the issue of blasphemy replaced women's rights amongst both her cloaked enemies and fellow travellers.

Ellen Key's proto-feminism was ladylike but effective. 'As good works are the traditional role of progressive women, real work is their future. Men must bow to them, and not only on one knee with a bunch of flowers'. Of course, she proved less radically universal than Rilke had hoped. She wasn't ready for 'the purification of women's true nature from the contaminations of the other sex'. But as her house guest he could hardly make a thing of it. And when she moved to a friend's mansion in Denmark to get away from the claustrophobic atmosphere of her 'sisters', Rilke accompanied her.

There he completed his monograph (letters to Lou and Clara), not, as expected, focusing on Ellen Key's practical works, such as educating women into earning their own living. Whether Rilke took the withering remark on cut flowers personally or not, he deviated from an advanced position, opining that women's liberation from male dominance is only a 'stage'. However, their 'masculinisation', through professions, costume and manner, endangers 'a distortion of their unique nature'. Rilke is covertly reining women in to look after baby, sighs Clara. He's putting me in my place...

Needless to say, he didn't include his theory of the future when 'men and women will reach out towards the same objective like brothers and sisters in order to carry together the burden of their sexuality'. As though to balance any perceived backtracking, he dwelt on the metaphysics of human relationships with an emphasis on a reduced role for the family. The latter would not have pleased Ellen Key, whose latest book was *The Century of the Child*. It's doubtful that he showed her the manuscript. But although they would have talked around it, she would have had an inkling of the likely content from his many letters to her. It was never to be published and their friendship did not suffer. When they finally parted company, he had an open invitation to return. Thus, ended Rilke's brief period of political activism.

Rilke moves on to Denmark, lodging with one of Key's well-off friends. He maintains that northern climes are where ghosts only really belong, and they are needed for his novel. He also confides to Lou that he is thinking of writing an essay on J. P. Jacobsen, the Danish novelist closest to Kierkegaard. Nothing came of it, bar the eulogy sent to Kappus. Instead, he returns to what he admired in the Russian peasant poet, Spiridon Drozhzhin, 'his profoundly apolitical focus'. On his first visit to Russia (1899), his praise of Spiridon annoyed the author of *What Then Must We Do?* Tolstoy's tetchy 'Just write, write, write' when young Rilke confided his unconvincing writer's block, probably really meant 'scribble, scribble, scribble'. Tolstoy had no truck with the 'Art Is All' brigade. Starting out on *The Notebooks*, Rilke made a note to himself, 'Malte is to be Leo Nikolayevich's opposite'. But he thought better of making Tolstoy the whipping boy of his book.

Note (to myself): Spiridon Drozhzhin was to prove Rilke wrong. When the Revolution came, he welcomed it and wrote hymns to Lenin.

But the Scandinavian sojourn gave *The Notebooks* renewed life. Ellen Key comes to visit her Danish friend and they enjoy congenial chats on neutral ground. Key shows him a painting on the wall, *At the Vestry Door* by K. E. Jansson (1874. Now in the National Gallery, Helsinki). It depicts a dishevelled parson looking into his church at a rather frivolous chandelier above a plump woman worshiper. He is caught at the moment just before returning to finish his sermon in the dark, dismal vestry. 'The poor man is rejecting the light,' Ellen Key says.

Rilke can't believe his eyes. The parson is the dead spit of Sigbjorn Obstfelder, a Norwegian poet he used to see around Paris. 'What happened to Obstfelder?' he asks.

'Sigbjorn died of tuberculosis in Copenhagen in the millennium year' (1900). 'Collapsed in the street. People thought he was an old tramp. He was only thirty-three.'

'The christic age,' says Rilke, and recalls for Ellen Key the demented soul that haunted the vagabond world under the bridges. 'A transient amongst the transients, passing from alcoholism to madness, and back again. But Sigbjorn Obstfelder was not one of them, or anybody's, sidling around as though he was lost and too timid to ask the way. Only once was I face to face with him. His dead eyes still had some light in them. Dim but not extinguished. All it needed to rekindle them, I thought, was for someone to put a comforting hand on his shoulder. But, when I touched him, he went into a St Vitus dance.'

'Yes, poor man, on top of everything he was epileptic. Yet astonishingly he had written a rather good novel, *The Priest's Diary*,' says Ellen Key. 'It was found in his pocket when he died. It's as sad as Jansson's picture.'

Alter-ego

Rilke decides there and then to make Sigbjorn Obstfelder's story the cover for his alter ego Malte. He would begin with the derelict poet handing the narrator a bundle of papers with the words 'I am going to perish'. How he would die would lend the plot tension. Suicide, or syphilis, or simply starving to death. *The Priest's Diary* tells of a defrocked parson who sustained himself against the chaos of life with the conviction that an ordering principle is just around the corner. Malte, a hopeless holy fool, also vaguely expects that something miraculous will happen.

Although the opening paragraph was transcribed directly from a letter Rilke wrote to Clara, it is pure Obstfelder. 'So, this is where people come to live? I'm more tempted to believe it is to die. I've been out and seen the hospitals. A man collapsed in the street and a crowd gathered around him, sparing me the rest. I saw a pregnant woman ...'

A few years later, Rilke wrote an enthusiastic review of Obstfelder's posthumous fragments, implying he had seen him in Copenhagen rather than Paris. Most likely it was neither, a case of mistaken identity. Obstfelder was already dead when he first came to Paris or Denmark. It could have been his ghost when Clara pointed this out. However, as the novel took shape it was the ghost of another *maudit* poet that haunted his imagination. Baudelaire's manic persistence provided a better ordering principle.

Rilke soon discards the initial framework of the 'found' papers of a fictional character. It was Kierkegaard's stock-in-trade literary trick, designed to give his perspective an editorial dimension. A diary fished out of a lake, for example, in *Stages on Life's Way*. It has been picked up by Knut Hamsun, Andre Gide and Robert Walser, and vulgarised by many other lesser authors. Indeed, it is so much in vogue that another by a first-time novelist would be one too many. And he needs the money.

Even the meagre monthly stipend from his father has now dried up. Josef, in the letter informing him, hectored as usual: 'You were imprudent to throw away a good career in the army. And for what? Poetry.' Whenever Rilke was tempted to daydream of greatness, the word *Unklug* (imprudent), pronounced like a gunshot, stopped him short. In the *Duino Elegies* he was to say that the poet protagonist loved his father when he was an embryo but, on being born, he turned away from him because 'the space that I saw in his face was a blank'.

He is kinder in a letter to Clara, 'My father has become patient with me in a sad way', and expresses guilt at not getting down to real work. 'It's made worse by Ellen Key and others here who have confidence in me. If I cannot be happy in my own eyes, I can never be happy' ('Pleasing yourself is Difficult, Rainer Maria,' she might have smiled).

In fact, Rilke's pilgrimage to Ellen Key had kick-started the novel. Since visiting Tolstoy, discovering Kierkegaard, and Worpswede, his work rate has slowed down. Apart from a failed play, the two books published (*The Book of Images*, *Tales of the Good Lord*) were a backlog warmed up. In differing ways Tolstoy, Kierkegaard and Worpswede were touchstones to his marriage. On his first visit to the Tolstoy's Yasnaya Polyana, it seemed to him a haven of domestic bliss (he was to change his mind after the second); Kierkegaard was a reminder of the pains of self-imposed celibacy; and the girls in Worpswede, Paula Becker and her friend Clara, gave him ideas. However, the slowdown proved more a stand back, a *reculer pour mieux sauter*. The three encounters contributed to putting him back on track: Tolstoy's advice, 'Just write, write, write', was the bottom line; Kierkegaard's 'live the idea' gave meaning to the life of a pure poet; and Clara's role as his Penelope offered him the freedom to absent himself, like Du Bellay's Ulysses 'on a voyage overflowing with thoughts and experience'. And so, a prolific full-time poet free to roam, his future had the makings of Richard Brautigan's 'fine trip with some splendid scenery'. His optimism, alas, was to prove premature.

•

The Key Answer

Six years after the visit, Ellen Key did Rilke the honours by reviewing *The Notebooks* in an educational journal. The review is favourable but sharp ('A spiritual condition, such as Malte's, bears within it suffering so great that it occasions suffering in others'). They kept in touch. A contact that began with confessional letters from a young poet grew over the years into mutual admiration. Of the women in his life she was probably the best for him (Princess Marie comes a close second). She made allowances for his poetical temperament, and he didn't have to flirt with bouquets of flowers. And, as his letters show, he was at his most truthful with her. Although there were omissions, his letters did not play with family pretensions or legends, and he only went back on his word with the ill-judged monograph. True, Lou and Clara tie for third and fourth place, respectively. But they were burdened with baggage. Ellen Key travelled light, and Princess Marie had servants.

She died the same year as Rilke in 1926, and is still venerated in Northern Europe for her championing of women and children's rights and education. Amongst her successes was empowering women in the professions and including them in the suffrage. Through her agency, Denmark was the first country in Europe to extent the vote to women (in 1908, coincidently the year Rilke completed *The Notebooks*).

Scandinavia didn't disappoint Rilke. He exploited the 'spiritual presences' he felt in the air to extraordinary effect in the novel. Ghosts and objects with a life of their own pervade it. According to Lou, Rilke gave Ellen Key a walk-on part in a haunted house episode 'as one of the Schulin sisters'. It seems like a snide remark. Ellen Key's educational ideas were in conflict with Lou's passion for psychoanalysis, but they were not really rivals. Rilke loved Ellen in a different way to Lou, more as a queen of spades than a queen of hearts, but he was happier with Ellen to be the joker. Re-reading the section, Lou's observation is softened. The Schulin sisters were kind to the boy Malte, as Ellen Key was to Rilke. The story, indeed, could be a metaphor for his Swedish adventure:

> The sisters live in the outhouse of an old manor recently burnt down. Yet their hospitality is impossible to refuse. Even Malte's reclusive mother comes on the visit. As the family arrive, she announces, 'Where is the house? It was there a minute ago.' The laughing, warm-hearted sisters let the remark pass, and make a fuss of little Malte, who wishes they'd leave him alone. He wants to see the house his mother glimpsed. Slipping under the table, he crawls amongst all the dresses like a dog, and makes a bolt for the door.
> One of the sisters catches him and, thinking he has 'an urgent need', takes him by the hand to the outside toilet.
> Once back in the makeshift drawing room piled up with surviving objects from the old manor, Malte notices his mother has not joined in the general jollity. Others notice this too and the party falls silent. Someone asks her what's the matter, and she says, ever so quietly, 'I smell something on fire.'

One of the sisters, 'raising her eyebrows until she is all nose', says laughingly, 'It is the ghost of a smell.' Malte clings to his mother, who is sitting very upright and trembling, and together they see the old house burn down again.

Chapter Thirteen

A Cold Reception in a Hot Climate (Rodin and Rilke)

Being a poet diminishes the man (Ibsen)

•

Northern climes gave Rilke ghost stories for *The Notebooks* and when they appear the sagging narrative gets a lift. The instability of Malte's mind is reflected in the uncertainty of people and objects in the world which he is trying to navigate. The spooks put Rilke's 'some people are not real' in a different light.

Rilke's youthful passion for Ibsen's *Peer Gynt* (1867) with its explicit Kierkegaardian influence, left its legacy. Peer is a poet-manque, in love with himself, a seducer and a master of self-deception. But he's a loveable rogue whose reckless charm passes for innocence. He falls amongst a subterranean tribe of trolls (Norse tricksters not unlike Irish leprechauns). The troll king sets Peer on a quest to find the difference between a man and a troll. Eventually the Old Man of the Mountain gives him the answer: 'A man lives in the sun, and says, "To yourself be true." A troll lives below ground and says, "To yourself be true and to hell with the rest of the world."' Peer decides the self-centred troll has the secret of how to become a real poet, and takes to the road to live a feckless, ego-driven life true to himself alone. Leaving behind him a trail of woe, he returns to the trolls to deliver his quest findings and the king troll stops him: 'You've lived the answer, and by choosing for the most part the life of a troll, you have diminished the man in you to almost nothing.'

The original idea was borrowed from Kierkegaard, most particularly his philosophic novel *Repetition* (1843). A young man on the advice of his mentor abandons all, including his fiancée, for poetry and disappears abroad. Kierkegaard treats what happens as a psychological experiment and, in conclusion, aligns the would-be-poet with the fate of Job who loses everything, including poetry, and yet is happy knowing in the end that God will give everything back. Ibsen, taking the humanist dimension, consigns Peer to an unhappy end. Having rejected the woman that loved him, he ends up a voice in the wilderness, crying out to be returned to the womb so he can be still-born. He has become a poet but at a cost. Being neither a troll or a man is a contradiction he can't live with.

The subplot of both *Repetition* and *Peer Gynt* is that 'the habit of withholding love unfits us for poetry' (Brian Coffey, 'Missouri Sequence'). Rilke is in two minds. He does not want to 'withhold love', only to sacrifice 'being loved' in order to keep his 'self' pure for poetry. The great French Romantic poet Lamartine says, 'To love-to-be-loved is only human, but to love-to-love is to be an angel.' Rilke wouldn't have refused unilateral love with wings.

In *The Notebooks*, Malte addresses Ibsen directly in a section entitled 'Headstrong man', and rages against his later plays which forsake poetry for social realism. His rejection is of the middle-to-late Ibsen who inspired his failed play, *The Ordinary Everyday Life*. Nevertheless, Ibsen was the first of his spiritual fathers, and one wonders if Rilke, like the teenage James Joyce, thought of making contact with him.* Norway isn't too far away from Denmark or Sweden for a visit. The old boy is still very much alive, and is known to be returning to his early poetical vein with *When We Dead Awaken* (1900). But Rilke didn't, even though *Peer Gynt* was written in Danish and his was improving. He is striking out as his own mentor, with 'solitude' as his muse.

Note (to myself): *the eighteen-year-old James Joyce, then author of a play *A Brilliant Career* (dedicated 'To My Own Soul'), wrote to Ibsen, exactly four times his age. 'You've opened the way, and the higher and holier enlightenment lies – onwards.' The enlightenment at hand is of course himself. Ibsen is his John the Baptist. Joyce had been reading Ibsen's most recent play, *When We Dead Awaken*. But it's not Joyce's great short story, 'The Dead' (1907) that is to be the apotheosis of his self-administered baptism. His mediocre psychological drama *Exiles* (1919) is modelled on the middle-period Ibsen that Rilke abhorred.

•

Father and figures

Josef
Rilke's weakness for father figures can be attributed to a brief period in his childhood when he looked up to his own. He remembered to Ellen Key the time as an infant when his father was the only one who showed him affection; 'but I grew up.' At military school the boy Rilke

was soon disenchanted on learning about the tickle in the throat that had ended his father's army career. It was why he made an unheroic living as a railway official.

Yet Rilke often expressed a rather helpless sympathy for his father in letters. The memory of the kindness to him as a child lingered. Moreover, they both hated the same woman. He knew it wasn't easy being Josef, marrying a rich merchant's daughter only to discover a prodigal son had squandered the family fortune. Rilke was brought up in genteel poverty, living in cramped accommodation and his father scrimped to pay for his education.

When he married, Josef secured a job in a bank in Prague for him, which was turned down. Rilke wrote to Ellen Key (his openness to Ellen Key was measured, but his account of his father rings true):

I'd dearly like to offer my father a great deal of love. His kindness when I was little cannot be effaced. But he doesn't understand my life except in terms of paying my way. This is because he is now quite poor. When I was growing up and my mother left him to live in Vienna, he hadn't room in his apartment for me, and so I was farmed out to a mean aunt. I was glad to get to boarding school. As a child when I starting writing stories and verses, my mother approved just to annoy him. He thought it was a sissy thing. Now, since I haven't lost the habit, he thinks it's something for evenings while holding down an honest day-job. At least he worries about me, which is a form of love, possibly the lowest, but love nevertheless. And he supports me with a stipend from his modest pension, even though I know it's a strain with his medical expenses. I wish it were otherwise. Although it's a consolation that he has my best interests at heart, it is one I'd prefer to do without. And him too, I'm sure.

In the fourth *Duino* elegy, completed ten years after his father's death, Rilke talks to him (I paraphrase):

> You who found life so bitter for my sake, do not rest in peace. You looked hard into my troubled eyes. 'Give up verse, my boy. There's nothing in it'. Your hopes for me and mine for myself were hopelessly at odds. And when I stood up to you, you retreated and I pursue my destiny for what it's worth. By absenting yourself you lost your peace of mind, and a son. Once upon a time my infant love had made you a proud father, and it must have been painful seeing me growing up and away. I

saw the face I once looked to for affection disappear into a space where you were no longer.

As you lay dying did you not feel that what you accomplished in life was mainly pretexts, and all the things that happened were haphazard. In my childhood you were a nursery game, a puppet with strings pulled by an angel. Yet you were then my world and not a toy, a father preparing his son for what was to come. But I was ahead of you and couldn't wait to grow up and be amongst the adults. I saw the man of straw in your puppet's dance and looked beyond you. It never occurred to you that our puppet stage was other than a game. But I had moved on. And you were left hanging in the air, aware you had failed to amuse.

Note (to myself): I justify a prose transcription as I'd like the shade of Josef to register it. The original verse is elliptical and Rilke's heart-felt feelings would be lost on a man who famously didn't like poetry. Although moved, he might want to defend his life, by applying his son's flights of fancy to his vocation as a railway administrator, pointing out that trains are not a pretext but a public service, and transporting people across the continent has its poetical side, making the unknown known.

Rilke, with his marionette metaphor, is joking with his father's memory. Josef reputably looked like a martinet in the officers' uniform of the Austria-Hungarian army. As for 'pretexts', as a functionary in the timetable planning department, he was better at them than performance. Outward display and signing official letters were the office furniture which permitted him to do as little as possible, and he was never to be promoted beyond middle-management. This meant a rather meagre pension when he took early retirement due to ill-health.

Retiring to Switzerland, the stipend allowed to his son dried up, and contact was lost except for the occasional letter of unwelcome advice. When Josef returned to Prague to live in a bedsit while receiving free medical treatment as an ex-railway official, Rilke informed Lou that he was arranging to chaperone his 'poor, dear father' on a journey to Rome, taking in Venice and Florence to see paintings together. The reunion is to start from Leipzig (where Anton Kippenberg, his publisher, lived). In the next letter, the meeting place changes to Marienbad and they'll stop in Munich to see his father's favourite painting, a bullfight by a Spaniard. But the planned trip isn't mentioned again. Josef was to die three years later.

The death of a father inspired the most unambiguously cruel passages in *The Notebooks*: Malte arriving too late finds his father's body is being laid out so that a surgeon can drive a stake through his heart. He stays to watch and, though the description of the operation is chillingly clinical, Malte senses it is the closest he has got to his father as an adult.

As an autofiction it is too close to the bone not to be true to Josef. The account is written with a dead-pan hand and an attention to detail that makes it even more intimate than an emotional outpouring. It was as though Malte didn't want 'to miss anything'. He was in for the kill.

Note (to myself): the primordial fear of being buried alive, and waking up in what was supposed to be heaven but proves to be a closed coffin, produced a medical procedure that became not uncommon in the late nineteenth century and later. Alfred Noble (1896) and Bertolt Brecht (1956) both put it in their will that at their death their femoral artery should be severed by a lancet. Electrocardiographs existed but were not trusted. Nowadays, monitoring the heartbeat has been superseded by the brain's electric power cut. The last thing you do before dying is to think.

Rilke writes in an early poem, 'To You, I Pray…' (circa 1900):

> Does one love one's father? Does one not?
> Like you who abandoned me, hardness in your face.
> Should I turn my back on your helpless, empty hands,
> and put your withered words in a closed book…
> with your dated manners and passé attire,
> your wrinkled hands and thinning hair?
> You, who once-upon-a-time was a child's hero,
> are merely a dead leaf about to fall…
> Isn't to call you father a cause for regret
> that cuts you off for ever? Let you be my son
> and I would know you like a cherished child,
> even when you grow up and grow old.

The reversal is double-edged. In the same collection Rilke recovers his 'immovable-centre' with 'You Are an Heir':

Sons are the heirs when fathers die.
Sons stand and blossom
and inherit the verdure
of bygone gardens, and the still blue
of fallen skies...

•

Maître

Rilke must have wondered what had he got from his current father figure, Auguste Rodin? In exchange for flattering him almost to the point of sycophancy, and allowing himself to be trodden on from time to time, Rodin gifted him the grounding idea behind his 'Thing-poems', which would establish his modernist credentials. But Rilke's monograph on him proved a turning of the page, rather than a page-turner. Rodin was not displeased with, 'Sheer hard work, allied with a self-effacing creative patience, makes him a force as forbearing and benevolent as Nature herself.' But despite his filial overtures to the maître, nothing paternal had materialised.

Before meeting Auguste for the first time after his flight to Paris, Rilke declared to a college friend that 'Rodin is an ageless synthesis of greatness and power, a man of a future century and so is without contemporaries'. When they met it was love at first sight (at least for him). He remarked to Clara on the 'nose like a ship's prow, the forehead like a stone Sphinx's, the mouth ringing with youthfulness as he spoke, too fast alas for me to understand. Above all the laugh, the laugh of a child, joyful to the point of becoming embarrassing.' But, on closer acquaintance, he realised that Rodin was like that with everybody. And their friendship was not going to advance beyond that of a master and dog.

Indeed, after the monograph came out, Rilke confides to Lou Salomé that they had had a 'silent quarrel'. But the coldness is due to Auguste's outrage at Rainer Maria's refusal to allow Clara to continue her studies in Paris. His compromise is the invitation to Rome during his winter sojourn there. There is even talk that Rodin accused Rilke of being a *domestique voleur*, nicking art objects in lieu of royalty payments for the monograph. Worse, a friend of Richard Dehmel puts it about that

Rilke told Lou he regretted writing the Rodin monograph, and when this got back to the maître, he burnt his signed copy. Rilke - it was said - send him a hurt letter and Rodin threw it in the fire. All this is poets' gossip. Evidently Rilke is endeavouring to distance himself, but Rodin would hardly have noticed Rilke's standoff. His studio was a crowded place, what with unfinished works, models and artist acolytes. What Rilke wanted from Rodin was attention, yes, with due respect and mutual usefulness. But the attention didn't always come with respect, and the usefulness, he felt, was too one-way. Moreover, he complained to Clara, the monograph only earned him 150 marks (about 70 euros).

•

Ancestral voices

Daydreaming father figures in the family's military past, he wrote *The Lay of the Love and Death of Cornet Christophe Rilke*, a fable of men at war. His claim to have finished it in two nights is compromised by the existence of an early draft, dated 1899. Rilke had been thinking of his own father's inglorious military career, and was perhaps fantasising on his behalf.

He had thought of sending *The Lay* to Josef, who read only war books. But worried it could be taken as adding insult to injury. Lou questioned his sensitivity: 'You never mentioned to him the sergeant's coughing story. So, there is no question of an insult. Send it and he'll read it despite being a prose-poem. It's a subject dear to his heart and it might be the basis of a dual reconciliation, with poesy and his son. If not, you have nothing to lose that hasn't been already lost.' But he held back, and didn't publish *The Lay* until after Josef's death. Ironically, it could be said to be his father's inheritance by the back door. When re-issued in Germany at the beginning of the Great War, it became a cult book in the trenches and was Rilke's only bestseller.

Before leaving Denmark, Ellen Key asks to meet Clara, and he invites her to Copenhagen, the city of Kierkegaard, the presiding 'spiritual presence' during their engagement. The reunion isn't a disaster thanks to Ellen. Two strong women recognise each other's worth. But it changes nothing.

Clara returns to Worpswede, and he travels on, eventually to summer holiday with Lou in a castle in Treseburg, a gentrified medieval hill-town overlooking the confluence of two rivers. Reportedly, when visiting friends Rilke brought baskets of fruit from her garden. Possibly smarting from Ellen Key's remark on romantic gests, he was off flowers for the moment.

•

The Call of Rodin

During his lengthy stay chez Lou, his mail catches up with him and it includes a most unexpected letter from Rodin expressing his admiration and affection for 'a worker-writer with a worker's soul'. Short and to the point. But to what point? It is surely a command to return to his court. Rilke replies by return of post with a verbal genuflection: 'Revered maître, my soul opens to your words so that they might germinate in me. Bless you from all to whom you bring joy, but also the strength to live a more intense existence'; signing off with 'I love you with all my heart'.

But he doesn't jump to Rodin's call for two reasons. Dignity demands a decent interval, and Lou reminds him the old workhorse would be impressed if breaking the back of his novel was his excuse. She is keen to see the back of it. But basking by the river in the sunshine is more conducive to composing poems for the appreciative ladies. One called 'The Parting' concludes:

> Someone is calling me, so let me go,
> leaving behind, as it were, all women,
> growing smaller, whiter: a waving
> no longer for me: a languorous waving,
> already almost inexplicable: maybe a plum-tree
> from which a cuckoo rises in sudden flight.

He attends to some business with Clara in Worpswede and two months later, when back in Paris goes straight to 'Les Brilliants', expecting a prodigal's return. But his loving 'father' doesn't receive him with open arms. A servant asks him to come back on Monday week when the maître isn't so busy. Rilke confides to Lou his disappointment, adding, 'Maybe Auguste sees his own unlovability in me.'

Rilke has no idea why he's received the call, unless it is to punish him more as a whipping boy. What he wants most from a father figure is acceptance as a pure poet, and that's unlikely with Auguste. Maybe in the long run a mother figure would be a better bet. Lou and Ellen Key seem to like him, but are nulliparous (childless), and even Sidonie is younger than him.

Although he doesn't keep the Monday appointment, he gravitates back to the studio without one a few days later. He feels lost in a crowd. Rodin has enough would-be sons hanging around, not to mention the sons that models claimed were his. Instead of sketching the maître-at-work like everybody else, he scribbles away in a corner. Rodin becomes curious and Rilke explains, 'I'm describing in words what I see with the intention of making a *catalogue raisonné* of your studio.'

'Ah! the Balzac story. But don't forget to describe the latrine.' Rodin jokes when pleased. He has a soft spot for this frail, gnome-like man who, when he isn't gushing grossly exaggerated compliments, disappears into himself. Prod him and his downcast eyes show themselves to fix you with a strange amber glow, and he takes up a conversation you had with him last time you met, primly enunciating in school French ideas that nobody else would have thought of. Rodin considers that with his hands joined at the knees he would make a perfect troll at the foot of a monument to Ibsen. And then he remembers why he wrote to the poet in the first place. It was to asks him to be his private secretary as he had never seen such copper-plate handwriting.

Rilke accepts without hesitation. His duties are sorting the mail and answering less important letters. He would be able to bed and board in 'Les Brilliants'. Rilke's only condition is he doesn't want to be called a secretary. Rodin assures him that to others he would be a house guest and, between friends, he would be a working disciple. All his other acolytes, he says, are potential Judases, and they do nothing for him except steal his ideas. Payment isn't mentioned – a mistake. Both Rodin and Rilke had money-pinching childhoods.

Rodin's correspondence is a full-time job. Particularly for someone whose French is challenged by artist friends who share a private argot. Rilke finds himself slaving away, meticulously triaging the serious from billet-doux by day and by evening taking thunder-and-lightning dictation from his stormy maître. It reaches crisis point when Rodin and his wife get the flu and he has to read Alexander Dumas *père* to them. Rodin soon enough realises his mistake. Apart from the finicky questions Rilke poses, he tells Camille Claudel, he senses in the heel-clicking precision of the young poet 'a wheedling batman', one more inclined 'to lick his arse than clean his boots'. He is not being fair, Camille thinks, but keeps her council. She finds Rilke the perfect gentleman, if rather on his dignity.

After five months in the role, Rodin effectively fires him with a brusque note. Rilke replies, 'I understand you. I understand in the wise organism [organisation?] of your working life you must promptly dispense with anything which appears detrimental to maintaining its multifarious functions intact. As the eye must blinker itself against objects that blocks its view, you must turn a blind eye to distractions' (such as the feelings of others, implied but not said). 'But remember, please remember, how so often I understood you, in our happy contemplations of your art.'

Rilke's round-about restraint amuses Rodin, and the last sentence gives him another idea. Knowing all too well how clever worms can turn, he decides to make Rilke his representative in Germany where his reputation is less than elsewhere in Europe. A lecture tour is arranged. Prague, Dresden, Elberfeld, Berlin and Hamburg.

Rilke's talk is entitled, '*Dinge-Kunst*', '*Thing-Art*', and he expatiates on Rodin's 'transformation of conflicting inner emotions into a physical form. His sculptures go further than painting and poetry can. He brings the invisible – the source of all the good and evil in the world – to the subsurface, and what we see is the movement created by the effect of light on them.' Not a start the maître would object to. But he hardly mentions Rodin again. At the end he recommends his monograph (copies on the table). He reads his 'Thing-poems', and is such a success that only his father's death in 1906 interrupted a second tour. On Rilke's return to Paris, Rodin chides him as being a wren to his eagle. It was probably a joke, but Rilke takes it to heart and sulks in his tent.

In later years, Rilke made light of his secretarial role. 'I just helped Auguste with his correspondence.' Indeed, many letters in his tight-little handwriting are extant and show that he was an industrious scribe over five months. Unkind people said that with Rodin's power and influence he used the position to court potential patrons. And, indeed, one of the letters is addressed to an aristocratic lady, who Rilke wrote to on his own behalf and a lively correspondence ensued with potential hunting-lodge perks (now I'm being unkind). One wonders if Rodin was aware of that.

A terminal rupture was never on the cards. Rilke's belief that Rodin was 'the greatest artist alive' (letter to Kappus) or 'since Leonardo' (to Clara) intensified with the setbacks: 'He personifies the Paris that is the centre of the world with its swans and statues', and 'like Hokusai with patient mastery came to understand the form and true nature of birds, fish and plants' (to Lou). His veneration wasn't just for the art. He wrote to a fellow Les Brilliants sufferer, 'but remember how Rodin says "*Bon courage*" on parting. Not for any obvious reason. But he knows how a young man always needed it.' Rilke dedicated the second volume of *New Poems* to him two years after what seemed like the final break, and when, on Clara's initiative, he moved into the attic room of the grand Hotel Biron to finish his novel, learning Rodin was looking for a larger studio, he got her to show him around this former residence of Czars and Papal legates. Rodin rented two floors. The hotel was to become Meudon's Rodin Museum (1919). A building reconciled them.

•

Coda

Rodin certainly took Rilke less seriously than he merited. Not being able to read German, he had to take the quality of the poetry for granted, and perversely regarded the monograph as 'dutiful'. He would have preferred an attack. Polemics sell sculptures. His soft spot for his curious little poet-critic hardened as, at heart, he didn't trust the effusive lauds and modesty (Uriah Heep comes to mind). A few years later, in the epic interview he gave Paul Gsell (*L'Art*, 1911), Rilke is not mentioned, except perhaps indirectly: 'You must be a man before being an artist. Live life to the full, loving, hoping, quivering to the fingertips with emotion. As Pascal said, true eloquence mocks eloquence. So, all true art mocks itself.' He was not a purist when it came to art. Perfecting it was the labour of an artisan.

Rodin and Rilke were opposites, physically and intellectually. But they had one thing in common, a relentless seriousness with regard to the work. Worldly ambition, though not lacking, was secondary to it. Their personal lives served this differently. Rilke in his quiet, polite, stubborn way controlled all around him while Rodin let it fly so the Great God Pan could descend and create havoc. Both let egotism reign supreme. In Rodin's case as much exploiting life as art. Moreover, Rilke's 'angelism' didn't seem much fun to Rodin and Rodin's devilry to Rilke was a nightmare he wanted to wake up from. I suppose Rodin blatantly conformed to the male chauvinistic conventions, while Rilke deployed them more subtly. Either/or they were a pair.

Chapter Fourteen

A Pause for Thought on the Transmigration of Words

•

After almost five years on the trail of Rilke's letters and novel, his style has turned upside down my notion of what writing ought to be and, indeed, for. His prose is more than an annex to his poems and, like them, can be 'tantalising as a receding wave' in resisting 'the grasp of clarity' (Will Stone). He gives thoughts to feelings that, though steadfast as a Keats's Bright Star, make sense without logical support. If asked to explain a flight, he might have fallen back on Robert Browning's reply when asked what a poem of his meant: 'When I wrote it God and me knew. Now only God knows.' Faced by the stellar and the gnostic, my transcriptions attempt to triage what can be rationally understood, and when it can't be, I hazard a speculative synthesis between what it means to me (without quite knowing why) and how he might have put it to Molly Bloom ('O Rocks! tell it to me in plain words'). This risky compromise calls for a moratorium on my method. I draw from glosses made during my reading:

•

Intertextual Glossing

'Writing is not about getting the sentences right' (Martin Amis), but about getting ideas to fit them. Rilke knew that. However, when his ideas are *felt* thoughts, they are prone to be poetical figurations. Sometimes I wonder if the 'fit' is translatable, even into German (as Jules Renard says of Mallarmé's French into French).

This not a joker's aside. Nabokov maintained 'intractable monoglotism' is the highest compliment that language can pay a poet. But it didn't deter him 'insulting' Pushkin into English. His rigidly literal version of *Eugene Onegin*, proves Pushkin's greatness by the same method that he used in his novel *Pale Fire*, which presents an epic poem that merely serves as a prompt for voluminous notes to contextualise it.

Pushkin's wit and romanticism barely gets a word in in the massive four volumes. Edmund Wilson wickedly remarked that Nabokov was making the definitive case for free translation. They ceased to be friends.

Jules Renard called translation 'the crime of dishonest men and women who substitute one language for another and sell it to unscrupulous publishers'. This may be true, but the need for translation cannot be denied. Spontaneous ones in the United Nations, for instance; although it no doubt leads to misunderstandings, they are a necessary evil to avoid communication between peoples being left to flag-waving. Translation can also be a necessary good for cultural exchange. Michel Tournier notes in his *Journal Extime* the change of a key word in the Goethe/Mozart song about 'the land where lemon trees grow': in the received French version, 'oranges are substituted for lemons, because in France the fruit has bitter rather than sweet connotations. Thus, the prix Orange rather than prix Citron at Longchamps.'

Transcriptions, aided and abetted by Olsen's 'trespass vision', are my way of clarifying Rilke's meaning for myself. *The Letters* in particular I can find elliptical. Reasonably enough. They were not directly intended for me and, moreover, have arrived a hundred-plus years after being written. The language and culture have moved on. And so, for exogenesis it is necessary to choose a milder form of the Nabokovian method, with occasional notes (to myself) to indicate how things have changed. Indeed, this offers the contemporary German reader the possibility of a 'translation' within the original language. Even then what has changed does not necessarily show how things were. Other tongues can only get stuck in a Nabokovian impasse and so, I think, must depend on the freefall of inspired guessing; rather than drown the meaning in surplusage of notes, I have incorporated some of them into my transcription.

My textual scholar friends usually give a reluctant nod to the free translation of poems, but baulk at what they call 'intertextual glossing' for prose (See Guiding Note 11). They allow that with letters, being hastily written, there is a case, but questions of intellectual property can be raised, not to mention basic accuracy. It all gets too contentious if everything that stains a white page is to be considered sacred. So, I throw caution to the wind and point out to them that prose can be poetical, and poetry prosaic, and so they are something of a 'free for all' for readers. The strange looks I get oblige me to revisit the arguments I used in the Introduction:

•

A Pause for Thought on the Transmigration of Words

Justifications

1. Translating a poem is indeed an 'insult' unless you make poetry of it, and that usually calls for compromises in the cuckoo tongue. Being faithful to the original or 'doing it justice' is easier said than done. Most lyric poets don't nest easily. And a songster like Verlaine is best left to his own words and a crib. Some passages of Rilke's letters to Lou, Clara and Kappus read like poems in draft. Indeed, a number of fragments appear almost word-for-word in the *Duino Elegies* (*i.e.*, lines 67-75 in the fourth elegy on 'grown-upness'). And so, in my transcriptions of Rilke in his more elliptical vein, I feel free to spell out what I understand, while keeping the 'tune' more or less the same, albeit with a different arrangement.

But re-arranging the 'tune', particularly when it's a poem, carries the risk of losing it. Rilke's mounting of metaphor on metaphor has more a musical than rhetorical function. He is striving to soften the strident, almost military, beat lingering from the German tradition, or exploiting it with atonal dissonances. Such linguistic tensions give his mature work its distinctive tone, ricocheting recitatives releases the 'arias'.

When in full flow, Rilke can wax lyrical on pain, happiness, sadness and the sights, sounds and smells of the natural world like no other poet. The ringing or jarring or muffled sounds act as an echo chamber for Rilke's extraordinary visual imagination. Kassner, groping to find a phrase to catch the effect, says that his words create 'visual music'. It doesn't quite make sense except as the aural equivalent of Pascal's definition of eloquence: 'the painting of thought'. But it's true that if you listen to some of his 'thing-poems' without trying to understand them and close your eyes, images emerge and they sing! However, in my reading of the letters I have kept my eyes open. I don't want to be distracted by percussion effects, though the blinding light of 'sound-eye' flashes makes this difficult. My transcriptions focus on feeling my way to elucidate ideas more suggested than fully expressed.

2. Reading other people's letters is not good manners, and Rilke wasn't writing them for publication. Kappus waited until after his death to make them available to posterity. Now, a century later, these personal communications need a go-between to put them in context. Footnotes are a cumbersome answer. So many would be needed (*pace* Nabokov) that the text would be in danger of becoming a footnote to them.

Instead, I've submitted myself to Locke's definition of *negative capability* and submerged myself in Rilke's motifs in order to attune myself to their significance and reason with them. Conscious that there can be more to written texts than their rationality, and literary logic has a life of its own, all I can hope for is to make sense of the letters for a twenty-first-century reader, namely myself. Understanding is knowing where you stand.

That said, Rilke had his own reasons for writing *The Letters*. But as he kept them to himself, Kappus's initial assumption that they were for the education of an apprentice poet is widely assumed. Since they were published, hundreds of thousands of others have read them, and what they learned must remain a *tabula rasa* scripted in invisible ink. *The Letters* are cherished, I think, more for the atmosphere of learning along with a beloved poet than any pedagogic transference. Rilke, approaching the crossroads of thirty, wrote them primarily for himself. Indeed, the book could be more aptly retitled *Letters from a Young Poet*.

Through *The Letters*, Rilke offers himself intimations of his future trajectory. Different ways of thinking opened the road. But what happens is far from a clear run. He loses his bearings after coming out of the torturous trek of *The Notebooks* and enters a 'dark wood' tangled by doubts and false trails, and he didn't come out of the thicket until the Great War ended. By then the enthusiasms of *The Letters* aren't necessarily what he had come to believe. Through pain and suffering Rilke learned what he wanted for his poetry. It wasn't to be some earthly paradise with Adam and Eve without The Fall, but the eerie underworld of *The Duino Elegies* and the purgatorial *The Sonnets to Orpheus*.

Chapter Fifteen

Eleventh Hour Redemptions

•

The 'Great Work' accomplished, Rilke is released to write the exuberant late poems. In his last years he relaxes from the tortured expressionism of the *Elegies* into a *repetition forwards* of the 'Thing-poems', freed from Rodin's objectivist strictures. It is as though, the aspirational behind him, the burden of ambition is lifted.

There is a certain lowering of the sights. The titles of his books become more literal (*From Pocket Notebooks and Memory Pads*). He diversifies again into French, probably not a good idea but it showed that he was once more open to suggestion. Perhaps in his last slim volume he had found an answer to Malte's plea 'for strength to stand by my own unworthiness':

> 'O breath, you, poem unseen!
> Regular go-between
> the cosmos and our being.
> Counterbalancing sense,
> I become your cadence.'

He was not only breathing the air of poetry but embodying it. It is as pure as his poems could get. That he arrived at this state of grace at a time when his health was in terminal decline is miraculous. I can see the *Duino Elegies* emerging from a dialectic between *The Letters* and his experience of the Great War. But not this. Could it be that his insistence on solitude and resisting the invasion of others had been reversed?

By all accounts, in his last years he welcomed interruptions in his castle life and entertained in particular women admirers who hitherto had been only friends by correspondence.

> One dies, to know them. Die
> of the smiles' ineffable blossom. Die
> of their light hands. Die
> of women.

At the same time, his prolix letter-writing expanded to include new friends, not least Boris Pasternak and Marina Tsvetayeva. In their tripartite exchange, Rilke surprisingly questioned the idea of being a pure poet (ironically it was what made Boris and Marina bow to him, envious of what they aspired to themselves). It isn't an existential crisis, but Rilke, conscious of how schematic he has been, is counting the cost, not only to himself. If hitherto he had been asked, 'Who do you think you are?' the answer would be, 'I'm in the process of finding out.' His egotism was unique in that he never really thought about himself, but what he wanted to be. Now he had his doubts.

In short, the future has caught up with him and it isn't quite what he expected. Time to revisit the past. But it is burdened with consequences which are too late to rectify. There are reasons to regret, reasons to reproach himself. Still, living his idea has given him what he wanted – he is king of a castle – and at same time, that has turned out to be less than he had hoped – he is lonely. But what can one do?' Rilke postpones the rendezvous with the past to free himself from it. And not having any more future, he must live the idea in the present. This released him to write his purest poetry.

And so, the devil of self-knowledge was put behind him, and the angels of *felt* thoughts had their day. But this may explain his lack of self-awareness in writing his fictive 'Letter from a young worker' (1922), which mercifully wasn't published until long after his death. It is a clumsy tribute to his lived self, which reverts back to the ideas on primal sex, familiar from his letters to Kappus (and Lou), only heightened by a rather embarrassing religiosity. It is obvious that he didn't know many young workers who admired his poetry. But all alone in his castle, he was probably desperate for company and recreated his lived idea for an imaginary fan with a fire-escape twist.

Note (to myself): Gretchen, Joab's German scholar, corrects me: two years earlier he had received poems from an aspirant who identified himself as a 'young worker'. Rilke's response was measured, advising him that the pen is a tool like any other and mastering it requires an apprenticeship. 'Then it will give you the satisfaction of a good job well done.' But the fictive letter doesn't say anything as sensible.

•

Birds of a Feather

As Joab Comfort doesn't believe people have a 'personal identity' ('How does a cat know it's a cat, or a human know he or her is a human?'), I consulted him on self-knowledge and recorded it on tape. In transcribing it I made some modification in the interest of continuity (which he graciously approved):

'Rilke rightly ignored the Delphic oracle's "know yourself", and embraced Socrates's "know what you don't know". It stretched the imagination.

'He had the mind of Coleridge's chameleon poet, and so self-consistency is not part of his make-up. Apparent contradictions are changes of mind. He is not bound to any fixed view, making himself a sponge to absorb and wring out what life throws at him. In his blocked middle period this mechanism went into abeyance. Fortunately, he hadn't lost sight of this working schema, and when expressionism came to his rescue, he adapted it to the new mode, which allowed him to jettison the expected in order to rise above the ordinary-obvious. And so, he was able to evoke an Underworld fit for an Orpheus, and consummate the *Duino Elegies*. When he emerged from this dark place into the light of day, he used the same method to evoke emotion, but the chameleon poet began to question his contradictions. No other could have composed poems like his late work, except perhaps himself during the 'thing-poem' period, when he negated the identity that goes with being a representative person to replace it with what it's like being an object. The difference between the 'thing-poems' and the late poems was there was nobody breathing down his neck, other than the Grim Reaper.

'His aesthetic as developed under the brute influence of Rodin had matured into his own and his alone. A consensual norm with a low standard deviation could be reached by objectivising his writings through a Barthesian analysis of its underlying structure. That is, 'by reconstructing what might be on the writer's mind to permit him to transmit the message. The mind's state pre-empts what it can express.' Rilke has a magpie brain with the wren's opportunism for riding on the wings of intellectual eagles. He is a veritable kleptomaniac of quotations, more often than not unattributed. For example, in explaining to Kassner how to read the *Duino Elegies*, he says it's a matter of 'heightened consciousness', and lends the advice more authority by 'borrowing' Pascal's attack on Descartes's bad faith: 'Give it a fillip to set the world in motion and then forget all about the creator.' Sometimes he is less respectful of the original quotation, modifying it for his purposes. In doing so, all the literary and philosophic world is a stage for him to perform on as he feels fit.

'In the *Letters*, the eagles, as with most of the writings published in his lifetime, are absorbed into his discourse, and become more or less invisible. A surprise eagle to anglophones would be Byron. Gretchen Malherbe tells me that at the time he was more highly esteemed in Germany than by his compatriots (like Edgar Allan Poe in France). He would have been aware of Byron from his youth onwards as the aristocrat of poets, 'pure' in the sense that poetry was his modus vivendi.

'Like Rilke, Byron was a prolific letter-writer, but the contrast in subject matter couldn't be more extreme. His letters touch on every topic under the sun from tooth powder to squeezing money from Murray, his publisher, and as for higher things, they are more sinned against than sinning: poetry is mainly mentioned in relation to declining reputation and sales and as something that he did which was rather infra dig. Aesthetics certainly was not his thing. Nevertheless, his couplet in *Don Juan* on Pope, 'If a poet should be quite consistent / how could he possibly show things existent', would have sung for Rilke. And, under Rodin's influence, he would have been more than sympathetic with Byron's reason for breaking with the Lake Poets. He was reacting against their top-heavy thought systems, believing that the mind is 'fragmented, and you fritter away good time trying to make it whole for poetry. Too much coherence is being sought in their furious egotism'.

'In practice, Rilke was closer to the Lake Poets than Byron. The *Duino Elegies*, his hymn to the Great Ineffables, is akin to Wordsworth's Prelude, a lifetime's work put in a holistic nutshell. His approach though was different from Wordsworth's, an orthodox thinker. The magpie in Rilke means that there is never a dull moment for the tracker of veiled quotes, nay, borrowings. Wordsworth makes it quite clear that he is his one-and-only influence. Rilke did not. He left it to his readers to take it for granted.'

I stop Joab Comfort. Although his discourse makes good sense to me, I feel he's gone too far, bringing in Byron, and now Wordsworth. 'Wouldn't any similarity have been inadvertent? Rilke's knowledge of English literature was hearsay as he didn't know the language.'

'There were thorough German translations. But it's true, Kassner's efforts to teach Rilke English were resisted ("Anglophone culture had nothing to offer me"). He had noted "the affinity with Keats. They share a marvellous Narcissus-like lyricism." Indeed, Keats had meant something special to the young Rilke, though he read him in German, and his *negative capability* had entered the soul of his poetry. But being by nature a chameleon, he was closer to Coleridge's *negative faith* (Trust me, I'm a poet).'

'And, therefore, closer to the Lake poets.'

'Good, you've been listening to me.'

'Some of your ideas come from me.'

'Huh! to debunk. Gretchen says Keats still lingers on, not merely in the visual voluptuousness of *The Sonnets to Orpheus* and some of the late poems, but the eighth Duino elegy, dedicated to Kassner, ends with a loosely translated quote from Keats's "Ode to Melancholy": "Thus do we live, forever taking leave." The original is "And joy, whose hand is ever at his lips, bidding adieu." Rilke leaves out the "joy".'

Not wishing to be the wren to Joab's eagle, I decide to dismiss the influence of the English poets as a superficial empathy between romantics, and revert to Gretchen's observation (which he had endorsed previously) that the predominant influence on Rilke was Nietzsche's *The Gay Science* and the idea of the 'primordial being', *Urwesen*.

'So that's alright then. Life's good, life's grand. Future all planned,' and he went off in a huff...

Note (to myself): I need to recap on *Urwesen* to see if Gretchen's claim should be mine. Nietzsche's *Urwesen* is a return to our primitive selves: quotidian and cosmic introspection disappear and we regain our primal state as part of a tribe rather than an individual, subsisting to survive, perpetuating the species and rejoicing in a communal life.

Rilke touches on this Dionysian epiphany in *The Letters* (the third, 1903), without using the term *Urwesen*. However, he complicates it with a passage on the Difficult; when the heavy (*Schwer*) balances the light (*Leicht*). And I can't make the connection with Nietzsche. I reread the Porcell translation and notice for the first time the footnote on the heavy-light motif has an addendum. I missed it because it was on the foot of the next page. It refers to a fragment, 'A Morning Thought' (1905). Rilke writes, 'The balance of the Difficult becomes the centre of attraction. But it is the destiny of the human being for the force of this attraction to defy gravity and rise above itself to attain a plenitude for God to enter. All then will be made easy (*Leicht*).' I think there is a Hindu connection. He had been reading Schopenhauer. I won't be floating this with Joab, as yet.

•

The Polite Savage

Claude Levi-Strauss, studying the 'Savage Mind', need not have gone to the Indians of South America. Rilke is a tailor-made exemplar, and left a vast archive of written records to prove it. The letters alone would be enough to keep a generation of structural anthropologists away from field work. Rilke's formal education was so at variance with what he discovered for himself that it failed to tame his mind. Despite being a gentle soul socially, he was an intellectual savage.

Note (to myself): I'd like to think Rodin saw the makings of a kindred savage in this demure, polite young poet who tended to break into extreme statements of devotion and put up with his rages without flinching. Here is someone, he laughed, who is capable of anything. And Rilke was, at least in thought.

According to Levi-Strauss, the 'savage mind', untrammelled by intellectual conventions, makes up its own as it goes along. Montaigne's 'terrible bite of necessity' dictates, and 'making do' (foraging) is necessary. Suiting yourself is its salient characteristic, and Rilke is a ruthless pursuer of what others would consider impossible. For example, what Joab called his 'bêtaphorical' ideas (experiencing what it's like to be another species or object). As opposed, say, to the physicist who imposes a conceptual framework to work out a plausible answer to a set question, his do-it-yourself approach draws from what material is at hand and makes the best of it. He's a Barthian *bricoleur*, a tinkerer. If the result turns out hopelessly impractical, put together without common sense, at least the makeshift job can be used to construct a habitation for his poetry and its supporting figurations. If the house falls down, it does so beautifully. For he is an artist of pre-fabs, not an artisan of brick and mortar. And it will rise again, as the components are not readymade. He can reassemble them in untried forms which hold up for the moment. While the walls are a house of cards, the glass ceiling has sky-lights and can open up to project him into the dizzy heights:

> Exposed on the mountain of the heart,
> beyond right reason, knowledge and language,
> I see below the last locality of words,
> and above the final farmyard of feeling
> in unprotected realms of the unsayable.'

Note (to myself): a bonus is that Rilke also makes *bricoleurs* of his readers. For instance, in trying to sort out his advice to the young poet, I have become a tinkerer of sorts.

At the time Rilke was writing *The Letters* and *The Notebooks*, Rodin's influence was bringing his poetry down to earth with the 'Thing-poems'. Rodin wanted his airy-fairy disciple to put more body into his work. Body over mind would give his symbolistic perceptions a more visceral feel, saving him from disappearing up his own air. Eighty years later, Roland Barthes, under the wing of Merleau-Ponty ('*The flesh of the world*'), made the word 'mind' and 'body' interchangeable (*Le plaisir du texte*, 1973). 'My body can't answer that' was his reply when not minded to respond to a silly question. He also made 'nature' and 'desire' one and the same: 'The body, as the instrument of nature/desire, in which the brain is merely a part, is capable of becoming the vessel that unifies everything.' Rodin would have approved, but that's not what Rilke had in mind, or body. He was doing his bêtaphysical best to get under the skin of lower animals to experience by secondary intention what it's like to be a common earthworm. The wretched unloved existence living on the dead led him back to Baudelaire's,

> I am a graveyard, abhorred by the moon,

crawling with worms, which like Remorse,
batten on the dead that I hold dearest...

While Baudelaire's '*Les Aveugles*', 'The Blindmen', may have disappointed Rilke into re-writing it as 'Blind Man. Paris', still he made the necrophiliac '*Une Charogne*', 'A Carcass', Malte's pivotal poem. Baudelaire saw the putrefying corpse as a 'fallen woman' and is redeem- ing through poetry – 'the keeper who preserves the divine essence of decomposing love'. Malte, as Rilke's younger self, comments on the poem:
'I'm beginning to understand it. What are you to do if you come across a rotting corpse? What's terrible is merely repellent unless you brace yourself and force yourself to envisage the immortal soul that inhabits it. It isn't a choice. There is beauty in death as well as life. Take Flaubert's story '*Saint Julien L'Hospitalier*'. The question posed is could a man rise above his fears and disgust, and lie down beside a leper to give him some human warmth? Flaubert's answer is yes, only good can come of this beautiful and true act of compassion. Believe me, I'm not wallowing in the decay and disease of poor Paris to abase myself. I'm surprising myself at how readily I overcome revulsion and love the reality as it is, worms and all.'

Note (to myself): perhaps by dissociating death from the person to the disease, Rilke was predisposed to regard it more objectively. It's not personal.

As we know from a letter to Lou, Rilke had turned his back on the mere pleasing ('Beauty is everywhere to be discovered, even in what some people find repulsive'). But for Malte, Baudelaire either went too far, or not far enough. The 'fallen woman' is left rising above her decomposition like a dangling participle. He sees two death-masks in a shop window and one is of a beautiful young woman drowned in the Seine. Nobody knew who she was. *L'Inconnue de la Seine* had been dragged from the river in the late 1880s. In the morgue a plaster-cast was made of her face because it was slightly smiling like the Mona Lisa. The other death-mask Malte saw was of a knotted-faced composer, who was deaf to the world so that he could only hear his own music. Rilke meant Beethoven, an artist like himself who suffered for his art in solitude.

Note (to myself): when Bettina von Arnim, who famously loved all Great Men, offered Ludwig van herself in marriage, he wrote, 'No, my friend, I must live with myself alone. I'm blessed in the knowledge that God is closer to me than others. The fullness of the sensual pleasures has been refined into the spiritual plenitude where I can only be together with Him. Alas, you women are a snare, a trap, to divert me from this lonely but blessed path, and won't stop until you get what you desire. Please rest satisfied in being my eternal beloved. I'll make you into music ...' Rilke in *The Notebooks* had his doubts that this unsent letter (ten pages) was written to Bettina von Arnim. She is only one of the seven muses that scholars have identified as the possible 'eternal beloved'. Rilke thought that Bettina was her own muse. For instance, embellishing the poet's side of her Goethe's *Correspondence with a Young Girl*.

•

Duality

In '*Le confiteor de l'artiste*', 'The Confectioner of the Artist', from his *petit poémes en prose*, Baudelaire wrote, 'The study of the beautiful is a duel in which the poet cries out in terror before being vanquished.' Rilke accepts the challenge. But his rival isn't to be the soul rising from morgue fodder, or rather their vermin. If he was going to worm his way into Rodin's good books, he would have to move up the evolutionary tree. He chose an animal which inspires fear and is captivating even in captivity. And so, he composed a 'Thing-poem' getting under the coat of a caged panther:

> His eyes, smarting from the blur of bars,
> barred in, fixed, vacant, no longer see
> beyond the cage to the world of stars.
> Bars, bars, bars are his infinity.
>
> Pacing round in narrowing circles,
> his ponderous strides, though powerful still,
> slow down his animus, and his will
> petrifies into paralysis.
>
> Yet, now and then, the drooped eyelashes
> raise a lid, seemingly to reclaim,
> with an impulse of muscle from brain
> to heart, a thought. The moment passes.

It defies a single interpretation. Welsh, my artist friend, says the protagonist is 'a large cat trapped in the body of a failed intellectual. Or the other way around if you like.' According to Joab Comfort, it's 'the finest poem ever written on *coitus interruptus* with oneself.' Either/or, for Rilke it's a change from what came before in that he didn't know what to think of it, a rather thrilling modernist advance.

'The Panther' appeared in the *New Poems* (1907), which Herbert Gunther said 'dragged German poetry into the twentieth century.' Not screaming and kicking. Friedrich Hölderlin in the early nineteenth century had already anticipated modernism in his fragments and between the lines in 'Bread and Wine':

Night, the epic improviser, is coming
and doesn't give a damn about us.

But as Hölderlin didn't come into his own until his rediscovery circa 1912, Rilke's 'Thing-poems' set the pace for German modernism and beyond. The concept of poems as things rather than vehicles for ideas spawned, knowingly or not, objectivist schools of poetry such as Imagism in the anglophone world and Acmeism in Russia.

However, Rilke is still enough of a neo-romantic symbolist to endow a dumb animal with human potential. The central motif is a thought. One feels it coming on, but it's not explicated. Indeed, 'What the panther thinks could I reckon make a neat subject for a post-modern analysis of animal cognition by one of Joab Comfort's postgrad students. Joab's claim that 'the panther's muscular spasm produced a dirty thought which he represses' is unworthy of him. But Joab may have been joking. And so, I keep the reproof to myself. Instead, I send him my translation and, he who knows everything, remarks, 'Rilke is countering the deadly coherence Byron objected to in the Lake Poets, and which also dominated late nineteenth-century German poetry, by getting into the persona of a rather prudish animal in order to "be somehow other, or more, than oneself", to quote Byron.' I'm not displeased as it shows Joab's still sore at my Nietzschean reversal of his English argument.

•

Is Rilke a Girl?

Still annoyed that he has said nothing about my translation, I take a chameleon stance: 'The poem is perfectly clear to me. The noble beast's unrequited plod around the cage represents the burden of sexuality that weighed heavily on Rilke.' Joab reversed his strange look, realising, somehow, we are in closet agreement, and with 'Yes, everybody has something to hide', shoots off. But he returns next day. 'Gretchen Malherbe says you could be right. Rilke was apparently a closet girl. As a child he dressed himself in a frock for his mother and claimed to be Sophia, speaking with a lisp. It must have sounded like Toffee.'

'No, Joab, Rilke told that story to annoy Lou, a failed tomboy. True, his mother always wanted a girl, and when she saw him in a nightdress, he called himself 'Toffee' to please her. Nightdresses were quite normal in those days for boys. Not to spill the deeper secret, Rilke turns it into a pathetic little story about a good little son playing up to his mother, who probably didn't realise that 'Toffee' was meant to be a girl's name, and thought he was asking for a sweet. But the deeper secret is obvious. Shame at not being loved by his mother makes him shameless, and it doesn't work, partly because of his incompetent lips (due to a prominent jaw). Lou, like Gretchen, would have taken it straight and talked to Freud: "Rainer Maria has just let slip his 'secret shame', and it's what I love in him, his feminine side."'

'What Rilke had to hide was nothing to hide,' jousts Joab, bouncing back from our near agreement. 'That was his real "secret shame". After Byron, a "secret shame" was *de rigueur*. No self-respecting romantic was without one. Although Byron was devilishly costive, and was more interested in the hiding than what's hidden. He was a true romantic hero in that. Keeping his "secret shame", even from his closest friends, and so they thought it was something unspeakable. All the better to amplify his reputation as the son of Satan. Even his so-called incest was mitigated. Augusta Leigh was only his half-sister. She was unhappy, and he was kind to her, that's all.

'Since big ideas seemed faintly ridiculous to Byron, hiding his feelings was a little one that amused him. After his first fine, careless rapture with the sincerities of "Child Harold", satire and irony took over, concealing more than he revealed about himself. Hiding added spice to misunderstanding him (his mistresses never knew quite where they stood). Also, it gave life a mystery unto death. He would be taking his "secret shame" to the grave. I can imagine him thinking, my "secret" is safe. Nobody will find amongst my papers a single clue as to what I am ashamed of. I can trust Tom Moore to burn the journals, though he'll read them first. But the spoiled priest in him won't break the seal of my confession. He will be shocked to learn that all my life I've been conventionally weak at the knees when faced by wounded birds and women. I can see him stoking the ashes and thinking, the awful truth about Lord Byron is that, despite his despicable character, he was really quite a nice man.

'The "shameful secret" in "The Panther", is that it loses its nerve and regresses into Rilke's pre-modernist vein. The neo-romantic symbolist has the last word. As the "object" is sexual it leaves a lot to desire. It's the story of a caged beast that lacks a mate, and wonders what to do. The body prompts him. But Rilke couldn't keep the subjective out of it. He vibrates with the spasm that convulses through the panther's body, but has second thoughts at the last minute. And so, he holds back, and accepts the frustration, thus keeping himself pure for something more dignified. In short, the poem could be said to be a salute to primal sex cut short by a homage to self-control.'

Joab parted with a flourish. Agreement reached.

•

Topping the Tail

Rilke's subsequent 'Thing-poems' are truer to his new-found modernist credentials, objects in their own right (slightly shop-soiled by human fingerprints). They have stood the test of time, and are the Rilke poems that every German schoolboy knows. However, 'The Panther' is the one that means something special to them. As it did for Rilke as Rodin's German-speaking followers praised it to the maître. But ready acceptability warned him that to measure up to Hölderlin and Heine (and even Trakl, and Stramm, not to mention Dehmel) he needed amplify his ambitions and write poetry with what Byron had rejected, a thought-system to make the whole greater than the parts. But not yet; as the 'thing-poem' experiment was being talked about in Paris, it would have to do until the real thing came along. Meanwhile, writing *The Letters* and *The Notebooks* is a release. Big ideas can be given a free hand.

Chapter Sixteen

The Short Goodbye:

Ninth letter (4 November 1904, Sweden)

The ninth and shortest letter (barely three pages) was written nine weeks after his last. Rilke is staying in Furuborg, Sweden with another of Ellen Key's well-heeled followers and doesn't lack for home comforts. Just as well, as the Nordic winter is setting in. He claims to Clara that he is getting down in earnest to the novel, and to Ellen Key that Sigbjorn Obstfelder is proving too mature as a working model for Malte. Concurrently, in a letter to 'a young girl' (unidentified, but no doubt Swedish), he wrote, 'Obstfelder once described a stranger's face 'as though there was a woman in it', adding, 'It seems to me that that would fit any poet who begins to speak.'

The letter to Kappus is curt, and rather take-it-or-leave-it (the italics are mine):

> 'I've written so many today that my hand is about to fall off. If I had someone to dictate to, I'd have plenty more to say in response to your *long* letter… I'm thinking about you, willing you on with such an abundance of good wishes that that in some way that should help. But I have my doubts that my letters themselves make any difference. Don't contradict me! I am not looking for gratitude.
>
> 'There is no point in my dealing *again* with the problems you raised: your propensity for self-doubt, or inability to bring *your inner and outer lives into harmony*, or other matters that oppress you. Maybe you need to read my letters again and, without trying too hard, let them sink in and wait for what happens.
>
> 'It all comes down to finding the patience to simply put up with life, believing in yourself when the going gets rough or when you feel lonely in a crowd. Take things as they come, and believe me life is always right, no matter what.'

The young poet must have been taken aback by Rilke's directness.

Hitherto, the letters had been expansive, energetic and upwardly inclined. He must have wondered what he'd said to deserve the hand-off. Evidently it hadn't gone down well that he had persisted in reiterating his doubts and fears, and at length, and pressed for answers to questions that Rilke thought he has answered already. But 'an inability to bring your inner and outer lives into harmony' hurt because it was true!

In fact, Rilke has no further need for the young poet. He had said all he wanted about positioning himself as a poet for future work. Moreover, his novel no longer needs a prototype. Even Sigbjorn Obstfelder is becoming surplus to requirements. As Flaubert was Madame Bovary, Rilke is Malte. Ten years later he told Maurice Betz, 'At times I merged into Malte, and at others lost sight of him. If I went on a journey, he was out of range. But once I returned to Paris, I found him again, more present than ever… We were reunited, sharing the same childhood, doing everything together… and gradually he became myself, myself *and* someone else. 'In short, Rilke and Malte may be one and the same, but more than their sum.

Rilke might have been tempted not to reply ('The boy has not been paying due attention'). But, having mixed his labour with Kappus, finding him a useful wall to bounce his ideas against, he owes the young poet the courtesy of a wave, and himself the last word. However, the 'wave', far from being dismissive of his advice, despite his reservations on its usefulness, puts together a summation of the salient conclusions. One wonders if he kept copies as it's a fair round-up. And, indeed, brevity clarifies the complexities. He bumps along the ground rather than soars. Perhaps Rilke is imitating Rodin's bluntness with young artists when they came to his studio for counsel. In effect, he puts together a wish-list of what is necessary to become a poet like himself.

•

Resume of advice

'I wish you enough patience to endure what oppresses you.

'Enough simplicity to have faith in yourself so you can gain confidence in dealing with the Difficult and your alienation amongst other people.'

'Go with the feelings that brace you and lift you up. They are pure. Unlike the feelings that grab one side of your being and twist it out of shape. They are corrupt, and will pull you down and tear you apart.

'Everything that brings you back to your childhood in order to face it is to the good.

'Everything that makes more of you than you have ever been before, even in your happiest moments, is to the good.

'Every concentration of your being which is joyous and full-blooded, and not artificially stimulated, or muddied by sluggishness, is a blessing. It clears the waters for the joy of seeing to the bottom of yourself. Do you get my drift?'

Note (to myself): Gretchen Malherbe points out that, curiously, Rilke uses the word *Einfalt* for 'simplicity'. It suggests 'simple-mindedness'. This is not, she says, unkind. More like what Dostoyevsky applied to the Holy Fool in *The Idiot*. Also, she affirms, the word for 'faith' (*Glaube*) is religious rather than existential, and chimes with the *pur Glaube* that Goethe gives Odile in *Elective Affinities*, in which scholastic babble is an overture to speaking 'divine sense'.

•

Doubting Yourself

His penultimate paragraph, a homily on self-doubt, makes good sense to Kappus. 'As soon as self-doubt begins to spoil your peace of mind, get to know your enemy and then take it on with a strategy of attrition, attending to every detail with a constructive and disciplined critique, until the tables are turned and it becomes an ally in moving on...'

Nevertheless, the young man, given his master's evident lack of self-doubt, finds this advice difficult to take wholly seriously. His own experience of self-doubt is not as an ally but as an agent to a stasis of spirit. He doubts himself rather than doubt as a dubious factor in itself. Still, military school tells him that the only losing battle is with one's ego. And remembering his improvisation of Clara's imagined response to Rilke's passage in the 'sealed package' letter, he thinks of making a transcription in kind ...

Rilke signs off the valedictory letter, 'That's all, dear Herr Kappus, for today. But I enclose a little poem I have just published in *The*

The Short Goodbye:

Prague German Worker. Through it I continue to speak to you of life and of death, and of how both are great and glorious.' The all-purpose poem is perhaps meant to discourage further intimacies and questions. If the young poet misses the point, Rilke could feel justified in ignoring his reply. However, it's a pity Kappus did not specify the poem when he published *The Letters.* Needless to say, the Prague newspaper has long closed and if an archive exists it is buried in a bureaucratic massgrave. Nothing as grandiose has survived into Rilke's *Collected Poems.* Possibly it didn't live up to Rilke's heralding? But it sounds like a premonition of what was to become the *Duino Elegies.*

Kappus' transcription, if it ever existed, hasn't survived. And so, I've decided to imagine it:

> *As for doubt? Doubt dogs us all, but it is useful if you keep it on a lead and train it. You must play with it, to let it get to know you. When the dog of doubt barks, you must observe it closely. At first it seems gratuitous, stupid, an ugly performance, and you want to kick it, or lock it up. But that would be foolish. Something is spoiling your peace and quiet, and you ought to know what, and why. Your hard, questioning stare will make it whine and pull on the lead. But don't relent. It has something to say that needs to be heard. Anyway, turning your back on doubt, ignoring it, won't shut it up for long. Renewed barking will wake you up during the night.*
>
> *It's necessary to make the dog of doubt work on your behalf. Reward it with a pat and a bone now and then, and it will cease to work your annoyance, and even become the guard-dog of your inner life, and in time, a good friend, an intelligent one, your sharpest critic, certainly the most honest. Eventually, if you treat it right, the dog of doubt will be your faithful retriever in hunting out what you want from life.*

In order to make it more heart-felt, my transcription draws from an episode in *The Notebooks* (which Kappus wouldn't have seen yet). It is Malte/Rilke at his most vulnerable. Malte's only childhood friend was his dog, and its death moved him more than his mother's:

In the dog's last agony, the plea in his eyes, 'Do something, young master,' gave way to fear that nothing is going to be done. If only he would whine inconsolably, I thought, my father's hunting gun would put him out his misery. As it is, the dog distanced himself with an aggrieved look that becomes a look of 'infinite solitude'. I still live with his loss of faith in me. I let him down.'

It is not known if Rilke had a dog as a boy. But I can't believe he hadn't. His sentiments on man's best friend as transferred to Malte boomerang back to me not merely as a punning game. Dog lovers will understand.

I confess the analogy is also a nod to the tramp's dog at the theatrical performance of *The Letters of the Young Poet* which got me started on the Rilke trail. The bark then was to break the silence before the applause. This time it is the other way around. It applauds the silence to come, a four-year break in the correspondence.

Note (to myself): dog psychologists use animal magnetism and the language of love and affection to understand how owner and pet are relating to one another. A pity Malte did not go beyond words with his only friend. He could have come to realise that the dog was responding to *his* distress, and not his own. Yes, he was feeling pain, but animals by and large have no fear of a natural death. It is the owner's fear that make it seem so.

•

Living Malte

Meanwhile, Rilke progresses with the novel, and Malte's diary begins to vacillate between things happening to him and childhood memories. Other than that, Rilke hasn't worked out where the narrative is going. He is conforming to Michael Polanyi's 'tacit knowledge' with its rider, 'a passionate outpouring of oneself into untried forms'. Although the 'outpourings' aren't taking him into 'untried forms', as of yet.

Lou asks him about the structure, but he is cagey and quotes Manet: 'The creation of every work of art should have about it something of the secrecy of a crime or vice.' He sends her some samples nevertheless. Her response is cautious: 'I'm glad you've taken Tolstoy's advice' ('just write, write, write'). Still, he had every reason to be pleased with himself. The early diary part of *The Notebooks* came like a letter through the post (Literally, thanks to Clara). The inchoate delirium of Malte's entries, with their manic detail, close to the cobblestones, would please Rodin. His submerged version of *negative capability* is the order of the day. Malte is a sponge in the gutters.

THE SHORT GOODBYE:

A lost soul, he lives in a state of uncertainty, but grasps at the rails of the notion that the only future he has is in the present. Rilke has taken to heart Kierkegaard's tenet that ideas must come from immediate experience. By living an idea, Kierkegaard was a practising existentialist before it became a theory in the first decade of the twentieth century (See Guiding Note 8).

Malte is living the idea that he is a poet, and so literary references, mostly veiled or blind, keep leaping off the page. An unfair critic might say it is less about the existential life than literature. But books are a real enough part of experience, and for a writer they're his life's blood. Rilke was never more alive than when alone with books ('They harmonise my inner and outer self'*). After reading a good book, he itched to tell someone about it and would write a letter or a poem. Now he has his novel to confide to as well, and it's more satisfactory. Not only does it not answer back, but it could surprise him; like with words appearing on the page whose origin is unknown.

Note (to myself): * the poem 'A Man Reading' (*The Book of Images*, 1902) treats with reading as seeing. He sees into books in the same way as looking at a mirror, or out the window. This idea reoccurs in another poem in the same volume, 'The Man Looking'. Both poems start with the sort of bad weather it is best to stay in from and read a book. The landscape outside is stilled as though transformed into papyrus, 'like 'a verse of the Psalter'. The words on the page offer the final visual image. In a later poem, 'The Reader' (*New Poems*, 1908), the poet is so absorbed by a book that he becomes invisible.

But the narrative loses its grip on the rails, much like that of the titular servant in Diderot's *Jacques the Fatalist* whose story is constantly interrupted by his master and ultimately never told. Except Malte is interrupting himself with extended flashbacks to childhood. The infant Malte is described by Rilke with loving pathos. Servants occupy themselves with keeping the boy clean and fed. Grandparents teach him the social graces. However, his governess, Abelone, a poor relation, amuses herself with him but leaves his education to himself. In his grandfather's library he flits like a hummingbird from shelf to shelf. What wasn't quite understood didn't deter him, confident that, if he stuck to his books, one day it would all be clear.

The boy, Malte, is a romanced paradigm of the boy, Rilke. But

Rainer Maria didn't have his freedom in isolation. Solitude was not encouraged by his mother. His early years were banally normal for a child only half-loved. Passing his formative years in a Military Academy taught him discipline, and how to discipline others, if necessary. But, also, its hierarchical emphasis left an indelible mark. He was always looking for a higher authority in closet quotes to stamp his performance as a reader/writer. Now the exigencies of the novel put him on his mettle. On the parade ground where his writing is drilled, he's saluting the superior officers of his reading, and submitting his claims to his own personal quartermaster, *The Notebooks*. His literary superiors function as invisible powers, loud-speaking orders that are often misunderstood, but contribute to the forward march of his novel. If the parade display passes muster, Rilke, the cadet author, can pass out with honours. Vice or crime are irrelevant (*pace* Manet). It's all about discipline, and 'grace under pressure. A work of art, like love and war, is a battle with yourself.

Obstfelder's *The Priest's Diary* served as initial scaffolding that was taken down when the edifice began to stand on its own. But the priest's idea of 'an ordering principle just around the corner to give meaning to the chaos' surfaces towards the end. Other influences are saluted, if not stamped. For instance, there is a striking resemblance between Malte and the anti-hero of Knut Hamsun's *Hunger* (first serialised in Denmark in the years Rilke began reading seriously as a boy). Both are in their mid-twenties, benignly inclined to a world that's malign and blind to them. The reader worries what's going to happen to these holy fools.

But Rilke doesn't know quite yet what to do with Malte, and it's holding him up. He could send him off to sea as Hamsun did his nameless anti-hero, 'Always to be a stranger in life, haunted by vague fears, and the meaningless details of reality.' He isn't ready to condemn him to the limp-wristed nihilism of the Scandinavian set in Paris (Rodin's student Edvard Munch hadn't the hands to mould clay and returned to the brush. Strindberg put off committing suicide because he wanted to know the results of a French Assembly Election. And they were the tip of the iceberg). Unlike Hamsun, who knew his limits, if Rilke had Malte signing up on a ship in Le Havre, it would have to be a whaler so that he could *fail* to write *Moby Dick*. Besides, a graphic storyline would be burning his boats with Rodin and his modernist friends. A Balzacian plot laid out like an artist's studio would be more their style.

THE SHORT GOODBYE:

Rilke recycled morsels from reviews of Scandinavian novels that he had written at the turn of the century into poems and *The Notebooks*. Particularly those related to death and/or marriage, which he considered a Nordic seed-bed for malicious spooks (*Peer Gynt*), incendiary climaxes (Jacobsen's *Mogens*) and existential dread (Kierkegaard). That is, folktales dying into a *recollection backwards*. Malte, despairing of his poetry, blames 'remembering: that is, failure to forget the past by internalising it'. It's an idea lifted straight from Hermann Bang, one of the Danish writers reviewed, and some might say as convenient a one as Saint-Simon's forgetting being 'the lynchpin of diplomacy'. I prefer Mathew Arnold's 'we forget because we must'.

Kassler, as a good friend, counselled Rilke that if he was serious about a bestseller, he ought to take a leaf from his august contemporary, Thomas Mann, and make *The Notebooks* a family saga realistic enough for popular consumption, like *Buddenbrooks* (1901). He could do this while slipping in the odd Rodin-like iconoclastic aside as a nod and a wink to the knowing, weary of Mann's moral pomposity. It would be the best of both possible worlds, and round itself off by Malte and the main characters all meeting up in Venice. This would have the added value of a mock-Gothic novel, with the reunited cast either ghosts from the past, like Malte's mother, or surreally remembered archetypes from his childhood reading of potted history and the bible: ill-fated Anti-Popes, False Tsars, parable fodder such as Job, Onan and the Prodigal Son. All dead to Malte's world, except Abelone, who is very much alive. She could be a younger Lou Salomé or a resurrected Bettina von Arnim, a multi-talented minx. The Lou/Bettina would whip up the wobbly spinning-top that is Malte. But Rilke hadn't yet a love story in mind. He was torn between Archimedes's 'Give me a spot on which to stand and I'll move the earth' and St Augustine's 'Hear the other side'. Where would it all end? The draft sent to Lou (with Malte fearing his rudimentary soul would languish for all eternity like a 'premature baby') had proved a dead end. He was in time to relent and give Malte a surprise reunion with Abelone in Venice*.

Note (to myself): *where Rilke himself sat at the feet of the aging diva Eleanora Duse two years after finishing the novel, in which he had given her a walk-on part as a timid child actress wearing a mask. As the child grew older, her parents persuaded her to take it off. Now face to face with the audience, she saw the sea of leering eyes lapping her up as though she was a naked mermaid and decided henceforth to hide behind the character she was playing. He didn't tell Eleanora.

Meanwhile, Rilke, like Malte, is living the idea of being a pure poet, and Jean Cocteau could have him in mind in the film *Orphée* (1960): 'The poet is someone who uses language neither dead nor alive, a language few speak and understand, in order to face and unravel a world where only the blind previously exhibit their soul.' In short, when the medium of the subconscious is the message, the poets are 'the unacknowledged legislators of the world' (Shelley). He is working, if not blindly then partially sighted, towards a schema driven by a stream of subconsciousness. But he knows that pure prose writers do not exist for plot imperatives and, indeed, sales pitches play havoc with the soul. A stream of self-consciousness tends to take over.

Chapter Seventeen

Rilke on a High

•

Rilke's 'short goodbye' to Kappus is followed by two years of consolidation. He is publishing his backlog: the second part of *Tales of the Good Lord* (1902-4), holy fairy-stories composed some years before (and dedicated to Ellen Key); the slow-boil *Book of Hours* (1899-1905), a verse cycle on St Francis's search for God; and a reissue of *The Book of Images* (1902-06) with some additional poems in the tried and tested early vein. Kappus and the German public must have been overwhelmed. Then he has *The Lay of the Love and Death of Cornet Christophe Rilke* incubating. It is finally finished and published in 1906 after his father's death and marks Rilke's goodbye to his neo-romantic youth and hello to the first volume of 'Thing-poems', due out the following year. The contrast between them would serve to highlight that the 'immovably-centred poet hero' was now a cutting-edge modernist. The gestation of the novel stalls as it must not be a backtrack into a conventional mode.

When Kappus read *The Lay of the Love and Death of Cornet Christophe Rilke*, did this dreamatic (sic) fable bring back the romance in soldiery for him? It tells the reverie of a young warrior on the eve of battle, bivouacked in a castle, who encounters the resident Countess in a dark corridor. 'They feel their way blindly towards each other as one would a door. He doesn't ask, "Your husband?" She doesn't ask, "Your name?" For they had found one another, to be unto themselves a *virgin* consummation' (for him?). Afterwards 'they try on names like earrings to amuse themselves ...' The young soldier wakes to find the castle on fire. The Turks have attacked. He runs at them with a burning flag and perishes. Once-upon-a-time, sighs Kappus, going to war was a noble calling.

In 1905 Rilke travels mostly in Germany, visiting Anton Kippenberg to make sure he is prepared for the new Rilke. It doesn't go well as *The Lay of the Love* and *The Book of Hours* had come out from a rival publishing house. However, Anton's wife, Katharina, is charmed and becomes one of his regular correspondents. In a memoir after his death, she quoted him: 'We are all hunters. It is our destiny, forever on the march, step by step with Narcissian purity.' His long-suffering editor Kippenberg must have sighed; loving your reflection in a pool is not necessarily pure.

The previous year Anton had wanted Rilke to write a short piece on Goethe for a popular series, and was to be disappointed. The reason is clear enough from a letter Rilke sent to a lady admirer (1904) apologising for his deprecation of Goethe in a conversation: *'Je n'ai pas d'organe pour Goethe'* ('I haven't the organ for Goethe' anticipates Barthes body/mind reversal!). In fact, the only direct mention of Goethe I could find in Rilke's work is in *The Notebooks*. Abelone is reading Bettina von Arnim's Goethe's *Correspondence with a Young Girl*, an exchange in which the poet, now turning sixty and already being commemorated all over Germany with statues, doesn't show to advantage ('Don't read his replies,' says Abelone.)

The 'call' from Rodin had interrupted his strawberry summer chez Lou. He makes a brief trip to Worpswede to talk to Clara about money, and to meet up with Karl von Heydt, a wealthy writer acquaintance. He is duly bankrolled, and it covers his first-class train fare and stays at fancy hotels en route to Paris. Though frugal with his own money, Rilke didn't spare himself with others'. Heydt's patronage dries up shortly after when he asks for more.

The less-than-glorious return to 'Les Brilliants' ends happily enough with the lecture tours, and he still hopes to make it up with Rodin, whose work ethic, he felt, would incite him to finish the novel. His love and esteem for the maître knew no bounds or rebuffs, and indeed the portrait of him in a letter to Lou achieves Jules Renard's aspiration 'to write like Rodin sculpted': 'Short and strongly built, forehead like a memorial slab, nose like the prow of a ship leaving port.'

Rilke manages to meet him accidentally-by-mistake and says, 'Maître, you will always be an inspiration to me.' The response isn't friendly: *'Inspiration? Elle n'existe pas. On fasse le boulot comme une ouvrier honnête'* ('Inspiration doesn't exist. One does the job like an honest worker'). Rilke licks his wounds and wanders off to stay with one of his lady admirers somewhere nice in Belgium, winters in Capri with Alice Faehndich, Baroness Nordeck zur Rabenau, and then Paris in the spring, Venice in the fall...The complete itinerary of this nomad *deluxe* is too exhausting to detail.

In Capri, fellow-guests include the young Countess Manon zu Solms-Laubach, with whom he climbs a mountain 'to get a better view of the sea and sky' (letter to Lou). He is accorded the exclusive use of the Rose Lodge, and Baroness Alice makes herself more than useful by providing him with a literal translation of Elizabeth Barrett Browning's *Sonnets from the Portuguese*, and so he has another book of poems to pacify Kippenberg who is harassing him for the novel.

His journeyings go with prolix writing. Poems increase and multiply in transit; prose requires interim stops. By the time the second volume of the 'Thing-poems', Der Neuven Gedichte Anderer Teil, More *New Poems* (1908), came out, he had all but finished *The Notebooks*. This was only the half of it, when one considers the prodigious letter-writing. It was as though he must be everywhere and nowhere to locate himself. His baggage tag could have been the English title and final line of Baudelaire's last voyage poem, 'Any where out of this world' (a misquote from Edgar Allan Poe). It would have been a prose poem that meant something special to Rilke as it chimes with his wanderlust:

> Life is a hospital where the sick are possessed by a desire to change beds. One would like to suffer behind the stove. Another thinks he would recover if he were near the window. It seems to me I'd always feel better where I am not. The question of changing where I am is one I discuss incessantly with my soul.
> 'My poor chilly thing', I say. 'What would you think of moving to Lisbon? It's warm there and soon you'd be as frisky as a lizard. It's a city on the water, built of marble and the people hate vegetation so much they uprooted all the trees. There's a place to your taste, pal. A prospect of mineral perfection with water to mirror the light.'
> 'My soul says nothing.
> "Since you're fond of peace and quiet as long as you have something to observe, maybe Amsterdam would make more sense? You've seen all the pictures in the art galleries. Or Rotterdam? You who love forests of masts and ships moored right beside the houses.'
> 'My soul remains silent.
> 'Bavaria? European but wedded to an exotic beauty.'
> 'Not a word.
> 'My soul, are you still there? Or too numb to enjoy even your

misery? If so, we must go somewhere far away from life. Let's pack our bags for Tornio, or the further reaches of the Baltic. Somewhere that is dead. We could set up house at the North Pole. The sun barely touches it. Day and night are the same. And so total monotony dwells there. It's the other side of nothingness. There we can plunge ourselves in darkness while, from time to time, surfacing to note the aurora borealis, a roseate wreath which reflects itself in the fjord like fireworks in hell.'

'At last, my soul explodes, and cries out, 'Any where out of this world.'

Meanwhile, in *The Notebooks*, Baudelaire is deliriously down-at-heart and living in Malte. Or rather in the other self that Rilke is merging with. While everyone around him is advancing into a new century, he is in a bubble, going backwards in time. This retreat from a world that he could not face leads to the public library, where the only light on the horizon is a blank page. When it closes, Malte ventures out reluctantly. The faces in the crowd have fixed expressions as though there is only one look. All the nuances of joy, misery and alienation are frozen into a rictus. He drags his cane along the railings. If he closes his eyes, the ripples of wood on iron penetrate his bones. Instead of the Eiffel Tower, he sees the dead eyes of Baudelaire's 'Blind':

'What are they looking for in the sky? These matchstick-men, vaguely ridiculous, frightening children with the whites of their sockets. The divine spark has been extinguished. Always staring upwards, and not knowing where they're going, plunging further into the infinite silence of their boundless dark. They never stop to take in their surroundings, and nod their heads wearily, thinking the worst. All around them the city laughs, sings, cries out, bent on pleasure. I too drag myself along, numbed by the blind men, asking the same question, what do they see?'

Baudelaire's poem leaves Malte looking up into a fog, but Rilke diverts his glance to concentrate on the hands of by-passers. How expressive they are, even when the arms are dangling. And the feet, no two are the same. The vitality of Paris expresses itself in legs. He takes issue with Baudelaire and gets down to rejigging 'The Blind' as a 'Thing-poem', 'Blind Man. Paris', redeeming these godforsaken souls from interior darkness and restoring them to the limelight. The whites of their dead-eyes regain the 'divine spark', and their look is trained down to the street, and illumines a world within a world, an unseen one which unblinds them. The sight of all-seeing blind men imbues the town with a frisson of feeling that stuns pedestrians into believing they are the chosen ones, honoured if asked to lend an arm to cross the traffic. Thus, he answers Baudelaire's question, 'What are the blind looking for?' A helping hand.

Of course, Rilke was never a lost young poet in Paris. He was as settled there as anywhere in the world, having learned to appreciate its advantages for a working artist. Big enough to disappear into, and when needs be, small enough to be seen. Moreover, Montparnasse was not without its slumming society hostesses. Rainer Maria 'knew how to behave', so invitations to select soirees came his way, doing his reputation no harm and enlarging his circle of readers and patrons…and walking home at evening he could revel in 'the insatiable nights of spices, of life, of music, and dresses' (letter to Clara, 'Morning, 1902').

On the other hand, the political life of Paris passed him by. He might have noticed the growing acceptability on the Left Bank of bearded socialists; Leon Blum and Jean Jaures holding court in the better class of salon. The Dreyfus Affair and the Laicity Law (1905), the secularisation that came in its wake separating the Church and State, ought to have pleased his anti-clerical instincts, but they don't warrant a mention in his correspondence with his intimates. Narcissian purity reigns. Still, nobody can escape politics, and in 1915 when the Great War was raging, and Magda von Hattingberg, the musician to whom he wrote courtly love letters, arranged for a 'sung performance' of *The Lay of the Love and Death of Cornet Christophe Rilke* in order to raise money for soldiers' families, he was furious and wrote to Kappenberg to refuse permission, saying a musical accompaniment belittled his prose poem. His art always came first. But relented ungraciously, advising friends in Vienna not to attend the concert.

Chapter Eighteen

Sympathy by Other Means (1906)

The Lowdown on the Westhoff-Rilke Marriage: a letter...

•

A Stern Letter

Rainer Maria is spending Christmas in Capri. Wife Clara has sent him a stern letter (December, 1906). We only know its contents from his reply. Clearly, absence hasn't made the heart grow fonder, despite weekly letters home generally flushing with beautiful sentiments. She would know that Alice Faehndich, Baroness Nordeck zur Rabenau, has put him up in the Rose Lodge, but not about his early morning climb with the young and beautiful Countess Manon zur Solms-Lauback to the Chapel of Santa Maria where the view 'embraces the welcoming sky and the sparkling twin bays of Naples' (letter to Lou).

Note (to readers): Clara's possible reactions in square brackets.

Rilke prefaces his reply with an unwelcome pack of flattery, commending her hard work in putting the record straight: 'I could read your letter over and over again... It calls to my heart each time afresh... It must have been laborious, finding the words and arranging them, and you're so busy' ['patronising the family drudge']. 'You are clear-headed, standing back and above a situation that seemed hopeless, confronting Lou and, by doing so, defending what has so often attacked you when you yourself were without defence' [It's a losing battle'].

His tone is coldly affectionate, as though quietly reproving her for disturbing his peace of mind at a time when he is preoccupied with more important matters. But he chills to the task: 'If only Lou knew how many letters like that I've written in my head and never sent... The same old difficulties loom up and come so close I might as well be blind. But there is something new and sharply focused this time and it is an eye-opener. For this I thank you' ['Glad you noticed'].

'I've only myself to blame for prompting your objections with my desperate exaggerations that seek to get to the bottom of Sincerity' ['that recurrent phrase of veiled vindication recycled']. 'Thus, causing pain to us both. And so, now I'm putting time by to give the matters you raised all my attention. I had wished to tell you a little about the Cézanne exhibition, but it will have to wait.'

His defences are as uxoriously poised as ever, and Clara, who can read them only too well, might feel piqued ['Why doesn't he respond to my brutal honesty without the frills?']. One sentence stands out for her: 'With me it is like this…' Clara sighs. Tacit knowledge tells her she is in for an outpouring of himself in tried and tested forms ['Reminding him of his responsibilities has rebounded. The only ones that matter to him are to himself as a poet purée'].

> 'I'm eager not to miss what is voiced around me so I can respond with my heart exposing it in all its fullness, not only touched on one side and from a distance. At the same time, I can't abandon my hazardous and sometimes irresponsible position for a more obviously reasonable one. I'll pursue my destiny until the ultimate voice has spoken and then I'll obey it as absolutely as I'm now resisting the bourgeois role. Meanwhile, my real duty is not to render myself useful, but to rise above the expected and go with the overwhelming forces that drive me with a rhythm that promises a new order, for better or worse. Lou thinks one has not the right to choose between age-old social duties and the immediate artistic imperatives.'

If 'ingenuity is the intellectual form of generosity' (Levi-Strauss), what follows is a charitable work. Several pages that appear to ramble but the royal road is clear. Despite admitting more or less that the estrangement is all his fault, he absolves himself of responsibility by reassuming the high artistic ground, while at the same time engaging in some inspirational soft-soaping to take the sting out of her urgency.

An aura of indefiniteness prevails. Instead of coming down to earth, and acknowledging the harm done in breaking up the family, Rilke asks to be pitied as he 'strolls all alone amidst the ruins'. Whether it's the ruins of their marriage, or Villa Jovis, Capri's ruin for tourists, remains uncertain. Rilke's self-pity isn't merely self-serving. He clearly doesn't want a messy break-up, not so much for the marriage itself but for his peace of mind. But even before Rilke goes all pathetic, his deceptively reasonable self-analysis suggests that Lou Salomé was probably right. He needed to talk to her friend Sigmund Freud.

I read the letter with an amalgam of outrage and admiration. Outrage because its raptures are so insensitive to the feelings of the injured party while, at the same time, he glories in a certain self-satisfaction. Admiration for his insouciance – never short of a word in defence of his entitlement as a poet. It comes with a sporting interest in how far he will go.

That I'm less indulgent to Rilke than Clara does not mean I'm unfair to him. True, I sometimes round off thoughts that are covert on the page. Yet nothing said or half-said could be to her advantage. Her exclamations (as imagined) are a throwing up of hands. But in going beyond the letter in order to pick out the spirit, I'm hard-pressed to balance the scales with a *Schwerleicht* (heavylight). I say that lightly with a heavy heart because, like Mathew Arnold's forgetting, 'I must'. Rilke had just published a revised *Book of Images* with an additional poem ('Loneliness is like rain…') in which the line 'people with hatred for one another sleep together' no doubt caused Clara grief.

•

Creative Disasters

Intimate unions between artists are often marriages of heaven and hell. * The further you look into them, intermittences of the heart clip the angel wings and prick the devil tails. It's probably why Rilke did not trust mind doctors with his relation to significant others, and Brecht dismissed the philosophers ('Couples on their way home from the cinema could teach Romeo and Juliet a thing or two', 'Socrates's Clients'). The common run of lovers take the rough with the smooth. And the rough usually is the man, certainly then (it was the other way around with him and Lou. She could be rough). The Westhoff-Rilkes hit the rough once a baby was born and responsibilities loomed. But it would be disingenuous only to see the smooth in Clara. And, for both their sakes, not to acknowledge that even unhappy couples have their moments. Although finding them with the Westhoff-Rilkes is a challenge.

Note (to myself): *a random selection would include Robert and Clara Schumann, Katrine Mansfield and Middleton Murry, Bertolt Brecht and 'Helli' Weigel, and the best documented example is Jane Welsh and Thomas Carlyle, as she wrote it up in marvellous letters.

Despite Rilke's general air of 'I can't help it', he must have felt some self-doubt at absenting himself from a young family. At the same time, though Rilke prides himself in being above the ordinary-everyday, he doesn't lack for common sense when it threatens to interfere with his life and work. He has an angry Clara on his hands and, at the same time, a need to wash his hands of marital responsibilities towards her and Ruth (in the nicest possibly way). Still, his high-minded humouring of Clara makes her seem like the conventional little wife that she evidently is not.

Why she puts up with him is a question her parents might well ask, but not Clara. She married him for love, and stays tied to him out of pity. Pity because she can see through him. That must do wonders for her self-esteem. He is one of the most celebrated poets of his generation in Germany. And dancing a tango with a shadow partner, who intrigues you with his cosmic ways and self-absorption, would have its satisfactions. But the explanation could be more banal. Like in so many broken relationships, the one left behind tries to make the best of the mistake, as to do otherwise would reflect poorly on his or her judgement, and annul the first fine rapture. It's perverted Romanticism. The happier days with the absent one is something to hold on to in the cold, dark evenings, a bitter-sweet consolation that lulls you to sleep. In the morning you wake up to the reality, another day to mourn your fate. You get used to it, and something akin to the indulgent false memory of the dead makes life bearable and the dignity of the grass widow(er) prevails.

But Clara in her staunchness is the opposite to that. Indignation is her dignity. There is nothing pathetic about her. 'An exceptional woman whose idea of Rilke is clearer than his own idea of himself,' says Paula Modersohn-Becker. After their marriage, Paula wrote to Rilke to complain that he was monopolising Clara under 'the false premise that married couples must guard their solitude. A superficial notion, true solitude is open and not guarded.' Clara immediately contacted her and their friendship continued as before.

Rodin evidently liked her, and took Rilke aside after the separation and offered sentimental advice – a second honeymoon in Rome, the pretext being to study the statues of Bernini – that only made things worse. The Rome trip proved a trip up. Even those who didn't particularly like her, acknowledged her 'straight-forwardness' (Lou) and 'level-headedness' (Friedrich Huch). Rilke has reason to be wary of Clara, not for what she would do, but for what she thinks of him. This recognition could be the strongest bond between them.

Whatever Freud might have made of it, Clara proved to be the second most enduring of his women friends. Lou had squatters' rights, having met him several years before he encountered Clara in Rodin's studio. When Rilke became engaged to Clara, Lou broke off relations with him with a cruel riposte ('Your silhouette is lost like a little detail in the landscape'). But as soon as the marriage was evidently on the rocks, it resumed with renewed fervour.

Note (to myself): there is a mathematical symmetry between Lou and Clara. Both outlived Rilke by twenty-eight years (in Lou's case if you add in their age-difference), and died at seventy-six. If I was a numeric spiritualist like Plato (who thought God was a mathematician) or a proofreader of digits for divine purposes like Pascal, or even a *gematria* character interpreter (the Hebrew matching of letters to numbers or vice versa), I might be able to make something significant of this. Suffice to say, they were strong woman who 'endured' the best and the worst, like Faulkner's Dilsy (*The Sound and the Fury*). This did not escape Rilke's pen. *The Notebooks* contains a powerful paean to strong women who do not allow themselves to become the victims of useless men.

•

Loose Bonds

Although geographically Rilke and Clara went their separate ways, she never quite lets him go, and remains in his life at one-remove. Clara is his Penelope, the waiting wife, to whom he only returns to by post, and the odd lightning visit. A divorce is refused. Rilke waves a Catholic flag of convenience (he hasn't practised since childhood). It could never have been a case of 'If you break it, you own it' (General Colin Powell). Clara was formidable, and civility with him was her best defence. But her family must have felt that he was playing her along, holding on to her by remote control, in order to have a fallback should needs be, and they had a point.

He keeps on friendly terms with her brothers Helmuth and Friedrich. The younger Helmuth was training to be a painter, and aesthetic encouragement is generously given. Friedrich appears to have been troubled by problems not unlike the young poet, and the advice he gives is similar (the following letter coincided with the seventh to Kappus): 'We are alone... and must work things out for oneself in solitude.' He also mentions that 'one day when I'm older and wiser I will write a book for young people. Not because I've done better than anyone else. On the contrary, from childhood through my entire youth everything became more difficult than for other young persons.' When he confides to Friedrich that Clara and himself are 'guardians of each other's solitude,' the irony could hardly have escaped him, but he had to concede that Rilke was making the best of the worst of marriages (or the worst of the best, Paula might have told Clara).

Extant clues to being 'guardians of each other's solitude' include a bevy of photographs from the Worpswede commune. Other than arm in arm, only one of them shows them touching. It is shortly after Ruth's birth. His hand is on her shoulder and she's stiffening, as though suppressing a flinch. In most of the others they are hardly together, more like inserts in one another's picture. He appears otherwise engaged, looking ahead or beyond, or head down reading a book. Sometimes she appraises him with a sidelong glance ['What is the old world-turner up to now?']. Her pursed lips could be holding back a stoic sigh. They are never face to face. Awkwardness before a camera may exaggerate the remoteness of the two, but their difference in height and build (Clara is a fine strapping girl, Rainer Marie is small and perfectly formed) makes me wonder how they got around to conceiving Ruth. I perish the thought.

Paula Modersohn-Becker's portraits of Clara reveal far more about her than when Rilke writes to, or about, her. Not surprisingly, they were childhood friends and sketched each other often. The first painting is of a pale wide-eyed girl dressed in a checkered red-and-mauve blouse against a blue and vermilion background. The startling beauty of this colour fest is countered by the unnerving frankness of the child's expression. The culmination of Paula's portraits of her is two paintings dated 1905 when Rilke was distancing himself from them both. The first is an expressionist masterpiece and shows a statuesque young woman in yellow facing the world with mistrust, symbolised by a red rose protecting her modest *décolleté*.

Note (to myself): is the flower a reference to happier times? Rilke's flirting with floral tributes to young women began in Worpswede. 'I invented a new form of caress, planting a rose gently on a closed eye (of Paula and Clara), until the coolness can no longer be felt. Only the petal will continue to rest on the eyelid like sleep before dawn.' (Letter to a female admirer, unidentified.)

Clara's other major portrait is not colour-coded and less formalised. Although the jut of her jaw suggests she had more character than beauty, and knows it, her handsomeness is not in doubt. As in the photographs, she doesn't smile. Like the Mona Lisa it could be a matter of teeth rather than mystery. As a sculptor of talent, she would know that a discrepancy between her Hapsburg jaw and petite incisors would not accord with a serious person. It is also possible that Rilke might have quoted to her something Jules Renard said: 'A woman that shows her teeth, no matter how beautiful they are, makes me see her tête-à-tête with death.' Paula is seeing her as the friend she could rely on and not a cypher for how things have turned out with their poet.

Around this time Paula took the most telling photograph of the Westhoff-Rilkes together. Rainer Maria isn't his usual prickly self when caught off-guard by a camera. The ears of 'the hedgehog with a foxlike cunning at keeping the hounds at bay' (Clara) are pricked up as though the world is on to his scent. Despite the suggestion of a diptych in the composition, a charge runs between them, the tension of two backs turning away from some unfinished business. Young Kappus, had he seen the photo, could have hazarded that 'primal sex' and 'universal love' were not quite meeting. But, in fact, it was taken in Clara's workshop, and she is modelling his head in plaster. Both appear deep in thought, a solitude not shared but contained within the same bubble, or bubbling pit, as though what cements them together is half-buried in molten rock, a volcanic eruption so slow-boiled that their union is made to last the drag of time. It proved prophetic.

There was to be no eleventh-hour boil-over for the Westhoff-Rilkes, unlike the Tolstoys. In 1910, Count Leo's dictum, 'Happy families are all alike. Each unhappy family is unhappy in its own way' came home to roost. Sophie, his wife of almost fifty years, mother of thirteen children and his copyist, sick of the plumage with which he flaunted the simple life as a landowner who didn't believe in property and disinherited the family, started 'plucking the old goose's feathers' until, maddened, he ran naked into the night. His youngest daughter brought him back in a coffin. Sophie knew the great man got it the wrong way around with his dictum. It's unhappy marriages that are all the same, based on evaded confrontations, realities not faced, responsibilities ignored, and the weaker spouse taken for granted. She had made herself indispensable, and now it was his turn to dispense.

Eleven years earlier, Rilke made the pilgrimage with Lou and her husband, Carl Andreas, to Tolstoy in Yasnaya Polyana. It was the year he published *Resurrection*, his last novel, in which he forgives himself for his dissolute youth. Both Lou and Rainer Maria were charmed by the peace and quiet Leo had created for himself. Carl, on the other hand, found the uxorious atmosphere oppressive and didn't return with Lou and Rainer Maria for their second visit the following year. It didn't go well. The redemptive novel hadn't got him the Nobel Prize, as expected, and his attempts at poetry had turned him against poets ('They dig and sow at the same time and force their lines to rhyme'). Rilke's attempt to discuss 'spiritual presences' with the mystic of the soil fell on thorns and, in despair, he rather overdid it in abasing his work ethic. Tolstoy's 'Just write, write, write' was barely polite.

Still, Tolstoy's dictum isn't wrong for the Westhoff-Rilkes's marriage. The photos and portraits show that we are in the presence of the exceptional rather than boring sameness. The pursuit of happiness doesn't come into it. Happiness was the only 'Ineffable' that Rilke embraced half-heartedly, and once Ruth was born, he seems to have given up on it for art (until its surprise comeback almost twenty years later at the end of the *Duino Elegies*, and, also, for his epitaph). They are equal partners in what took over instead. Although Clara hadn't a choice in the matters, she had the character for it. Paula's photograph of them in the garden terrace represents their relation as a wrestling match of wills. They circle one another, round and around, holding their nerve, not pouncing. But the moment is delayed too long, and they are frozen in a frieze of their own making. She is moulding his head with her bare hands for a bust while he is otherwise occupied. Rodin ought to have sculptured them. The depths half-hidden in molten rock would have inspired him to an unfinished anti-pietà. But I doubt if the master could have got Rilke to sit as still as Paula caught him.

If Kierkegaard was being cruel to be kind in discarding his fiancée Regina, Rilke, in his reply to Clara's stern letter, is being kind to be cruel. He goes through the motions of complying with the usual marital sentiments; dutiful but without intimacy or complicity. Clara must have realised that she has been put on the back burner in his larger scheme of things. But she stands her ground four-square and takes it on the chin. ['Better to be an albatross around his neck than an ignominious discard.'] I can only speculate on such dark thoughts from her impassive stare in the solo portraits. I will not be moved, it says. Kierkegaard brought Regina to life in his writings and it's no surprise that this sprightly girl managed to live happily ever after with a diplomat spouse that Søren introduced to her. We don't have that literary luxury with Clara, but the visual arts compensate through her friend Paula's portraits, many photographs and a surviving sculptured head. In the joint ones with Rilke, although three years younger, she looks much more grown up than him, and anything but a victim.

Seeing Clara Plain

Worpswede sculptors liked to model her, and one can see why. Clara is 'older than the rocks among which she sits', rock-solid, as no doubt her work was. Her forte was busts, and she had occasional commissions (Rilke's contacts helped bring in some money). All that survives in public view is a plaster of Paula, which was cast in the 1970s for a Modersohn-Becker retrospective in Bremen. Unless we count the inchoate head of Rilke in the photograph, one of art's inadvertent punning moments. Clara as the biblical Salomé (not Lou). Although schooled by Rodin, I don't think she would have had much time for unfinished work ['other than Rilke']. After his death in 1926, she turned to painting and limited her artistic ambitions to bringing attention to her friend Paula. Clara was a serving sister at heart.

I chose the famous 'rock' line from Walter Pater's 'Mona Lisa' advisedly. Clara would have known the prose poem from Paula who had studied art in London and, I think, be pleased to be described as solid. Pater had a formidable aficionado in Hugo Hofmannsthal, who entered correspondence with Rilke in 1902. So, on Pater's recommendation everybody was reading a German translation of Coventry Patmore's *The Angel in the House*. This hymn to a perfect wife was popular in Europe at the time. *I doubt if she identified with the house angel. But Pater's Mona Lisa would sit in state in her mind, 'Like the vampire, she has been dead many times and learned the secrets of the grave.'

Note (to myself): *Pater's reputation in Germany derives from his own personal and intellectual connections with the country. As an undergraduate, he spent time with his aunt and sisters who lived there and studied German philosophy and architecture, which he subsequently taught and wrote about extensively. Paula Becker first studied drawing in St John's Wood Art School, London, and read him in English (*Journals*).

In an early Paula painting of Clara, her right-hand fingers the exact spot where in the first major portrait the defensive rose is posed, and the faint blush in her cheeks reflects the red flower. After Rilke's flight, there is nothing rosy in her portraits and photos. She is as pale as the child in the early work. And the unnerving frankness remains, asserting itself with a frown rather than a smile. Most 'unlady-like', one might say, but perhaps not so to Rilke. In *The Notebooks*, Malte falls in love with Abelone when he hears her singing, 'Her low-pitched voice was how I imagined angels sang: clear and unwavering... Angels are androgynous, and the voice had a virile strain, strong in its celestial purity.' Clara isn't afraid to show her masculine side as Rilke his feminine side. The unlikely gender reversal in the Ernest Hemingway and Martha Gellhorn marriage comes to mind. This may have proved an additional bond. After Rilke's death, she looks less serious in photos. The brow and the jaw are at peace with one another.

•

Reading Clara

How Clara takes Rilke's response to what was clearly an ultimatum is not hard to guess. She knows her Rainer Maria, and the balance of high-flown sentiments and 'conniving' charm is familiar. He does not expect to be loved, merely tolerated so he can get his own way, the managing director of his unique destiny. She knows as sure as eggs his next letter will drop the subject and continue with her education, for which she would be grateful. 'After all he's a brilliant art critic when he wants to be, and has a lady patron in every European city that has a major art gallery. He could make a good living as a freelance. But prefers not to.' The stoic sigh would have evaporated on second thoughts. She has reason to be angry. The bottom line of his fastidious roll in the mud that she's stuck in, is not that he is taking the road to Canossa, eating humble pie, but that nothing has changed.

She would remember from reading Kierkegaard together during their engagement that, 'God created the world out of nothing and everything that God uses he first reduces it to nothing.' 'My Rilke,' she thinks, 'is inclined to make nothing of what is happening, but knows it has to be faced, and so dons his protective blinkers. But it isn't that I'm being ceremoniously dumped. I'm being put on the long finger, and, given that I have mixed my labour with him, and loved him, though not in a fashion that he wanted, maintaining the status quo should be interesting. Not only as a *pis aller* (making the best of a bad lot). Everybody should have a Rilke in the background to see what is going to happen next, or not. And we do have interests in common, which means I can learn from him. He's generous with his ingenuity, on paper at least. I still cherish his translations of the letters of Kierkegaard to Regine that he presented me as a wedding present. Though I should have realised that when he quoted the Dane's 'Indirect communication is my natural qualification', he meant himself.

'At least Ruth will grow up knowing who her father is. He has already started sending her postcards, and the odd letter counselling her on reading (she was four this month. Did he remember her age or birthday? No.) and how to remain the angel he imagines her to be. Eventually he will send her one of his books for Christmas, and she will be able to show her friends at the crèche his signature. It could be worse... But I'm damned if he is going to be allowed with his pontifications from on high to prepare Ruth and me as a human sacrifice for his own purification.'

Clara has memorised the key paragraph, and repeats it to herself:

'I take out my heart and suspend it before your reproving words. Play with it from afar with a long stick if you must. I'm in your hands. But I won't give up my hazardous, even irresponsible, position in exchange for a compromise. Lou thinks that one hasn't the right to shirk the imperatives of art by bowing to the usual conventions... I had hoped that out of the driving necessity and purity of our union we would come to share all the immediate and natural difficulties that art in life, and life in art, present. Now you're back at home while I'm nowhere and everywhere. Shiftless and unshiftable, absorbing the realities around me as they come. But you and me will always have our solitude, our quiet moments. Consult yours, as I have mine. We must do nothing but listen to it, so the inner voices can be heard. And maybe one day when the last, ultimate, final voice has spoken to me... things will be different. I'll obey as absolutely as now I'm absolutely resisting.'

'And he will come back to me? That's the carrot,' thinks Clara. 'The stick is nothing's final until... St Glinglin's Day when the cows come home, and here goes!'

'A premature submission to "duty" would make things easier. I'd be less a prey to uncertainties and required to take evasive action. But the easy way out would betray the difficult path destiny has laid out for me...'

In sum, he has conjured up his 'spiritual presences' and Lou, and they tell him to do exactly what he wants. The mention of her is the last straw. Her name occurs twice in the first paragraph, five times in all in the letter, and now crucially as the spokeswoman on the pure poet's obligation to rise above lower things. His highfalutin' help-mate has the answer that suits him. And worse, here I am in wet and windy Worpswede, the boundless plains invisible with fog, stuck with my parents and it's Christmas. And in the postscript he's complaining about the weather in Capri. The pun capricious comes to mind.

Clara reads the letter again, and thinks: 'How white of Sunshine Rainer to give me full marks for effort as though it was a composition by an assiduous but untalented schoolgirl. But the presiding voice of Lou, introduced as though she is my friend too, is the limit? I know I'm stupid in comparison with her. But if he has a *ménage a trois* in mind, he's on his own. He admits (but without apology) to shirking his responsibilities towards Ruth and me, but cloaks and daggers it in the guise of 'duty' (with inverted commas) and 'convention', much mocked in Rodin's studio, even by the conventionally dutiful. He even likes the word 'responsibility', repeating it three times in the sentence, conceding supervised neglect. But it ends in a question mark. Rainer Maria prays for absolution for not sinning against his poet's purity.'

Clara has heard it all before. She could put the words to music and then bang down the piano lid on reaching what she now sees as the nub of his reply:

'I couldn't in good conscience take on a supplementary career' (as an art critic?). 'I'm working on my world-inner-space and that's a full-time obligation. I won't allow circumstantial matters, which are essentially minor in the larger scheme of things, to interfere with my poetry. I've always believed we could rely on one another for practical, mutual support. I'm sure it's still so, but I think it would be better that our life together remains as it is… I say this in the full knowledge that this is sacrificing happiness on the altar of art. Not merely mine. You too are an artist.

'Know, dear Clara, that only with you two did my life grow into something else, outwards from myself. It began to happen in the little snowbound cottage where Ruth was born. Since then, it has been growing and growing out of the centre, tempting me to give up everything for it. But I can't as long as the circumference of my inner existence is expanding towards… God-knows. It is a trial by compassion you'll remember from Kierkegaard. The most dangerous obstacle on the road was what moved the heart. Ordinary people are distracted into a diversion by it. The exceptions resist it, and bear with the consequences, like Baudelaire. When the cask supposedly containing a love potion turns out to be a poisoned chalice, he does not flinch and drinks it and his nightmares are poetry. You and me are obliged to turn away from the ordinary-everyday difficulties for the sake of the universal Difficult. There is no easy way out.'

Clara would have laughed at the trial-by-compassion sally. But her anger can be imagined at his homily on being a father: 'The rolled-up hedgehog with his snout in the stars even claims that having a baby has changed him. How is not too clear. And in the next paragraph he has the audacity to poetise poor Ruth. "She is the star from whose position I could for the first time in my life determine the movements of my heaven. Before her I was lost in the constellations." And nice of him to say that Ruth and myself are "the one tree in the indescribable wide plain of my journeying to which I will always find my way back to." Welcome wandering Rainer Maria. My name is Penelope. Penny for short. Short of a penny. Only for my parents. Read on, it's rich:'

'I often look to locate in my mind where you two are to tell me where I am and where to go. Listen, isn't there always a house for us, real enough, though it lacks a material presence, as only we can envisage it. This dear house in which we are together and will only leave to step out into the garden…'

Clara hoots. 'My inveterate traveller, would leap the imaginary garden gate, but his volte-face is a two-faced double-take that backtracks. Listen to this.':

'True, Lou said that our ideal home would have to be policed in domestic matters, and I take her seriously, but haven't choirs of angels guarded us against all that with their profound ability to achieve the inevitable…?'

'Proud and all as I am of Ruth, I don't think she is one of them… My dear Superior Being, you are guilty of lowering yourself by way of false claims, though kindly meant.'

Rilke would have realised that his soft words buttered no parsnips with Clara. Having in the previous paragraph made it clear that the marriage had failed so as not to fail his art, he senses her likely rage, and with regret, if not shame, he concedes that he has failed her:

'As a boy I felt unable to attach myself to grown-ups in the family. I wasn't up to the triviality it involved. The small things I had to do to be with them. I wanted a profound relationship. It clearly wasn't possible. Not that they noticed. I was let be. Now it seems the tables have been turned, and it's the ordinary-everyday that wants to attach itself to me. The profound space which I have sought to inhabit has somehow become shop-soiled, dishonourable, thus trivialising my raison d'etre.

'I try not to be disheartened. Lou of course was the first to encourage me to brave it out, and still does. She taught me that the hostile thing is not within life but myself and, by extension, the things in my life that would drag me down. If in my childhood I had embraced the ordinary to gain the love and affection of others, I would have ended hating myself and them. But at least I have loved without expecting to be loved in return. It's the same with my work. Though Keats says if you love a poem sufficiently to make it come true, it will love you.

'As there is purity in the unselfish, there is purity too in the selfish. Its dumb focus continues to come into play in order to lift me over all the obstacles, immediate and, legendary. It gives me a larger purpose, and ripens, in extraordinary ways, into the great beyond of writing. Through my work I've learned to love life. Thus, my devotion to it. I have received from indescribably knowing hands a right to that devotion. Being bound below in the everyday world would have destroyed me, but above, where the art of life and the life in art meet, it becomes beautiful, grows within me, and can be relied on to give birth...I have Lou once again to thank for that. She helped me like no other.'

Clara smiles grimly, jaw slack with disbelief. *'Oublie, oublie Loulou'* is a music-hall ditty she picked up in her student years in Paris. 'Now for his glorious isolation':

'I persevere in the stratosphere which I have inhabited most of my life. Is it not as real a place, with its own difficulties and duties, as the conventional world? And, if I go as far as possible with it, is there not the prospect of a return journey, and a point reached when the above and the below meet one another? When then perhaps those who took the lower path, can ascend on wings strengthened and given span by honesty and loyalty, to share the same nest.'

'That's something to look forward to,' thinks Clara.

'I feel a little like the Russian people. Outsiders always say they should be more normal, more like other nations. They've just got to face reality and become like everybody else. And now it would seem they must. Ideas from Western Europe are invading and expressing themselves on the street, blooding a revolution that cries out for the death of the Russian Soul. Not that their melancholy genius needs much encouragement to disappear back into the Steppes. This 'poor thing but their own' longs to be left alone, cut off from the world. No Russian worth his samovar doesn't crave for it while, at the same time, denouncing himself as a hopeless Slavophile, a backward Mazappa.
'Now the chances to be themselves are running out for the

Russians. As they are for me. I've squandered some of mine, but now must take them as they come, sacred missions to attain. God willing there will be always one left, one more up His sleeve. Perhaps God will indulge me because in taking these chances I'm blessed in the knowledge that I'm getting closer than others to understanding Him. I'm making small advances. My books are proof of that and if God doubts me, I'll offer Him a copy, but I don't think that will be necessary...'

My poor Rainer Maria you were always mean with giving out complementary copies. But bringing God into this suggests you think I'd show this letter to my parents and, indeed, my brothers (who you continue to keep up with through letters they daren't show me). Your army training has taught you that you can't just depend on yourself alone. You muster the troops, needing all the help you can get to put Ruth and me back in our box. I'm tired of telling them what they know are white lies. That you are sorting out your business affairs and health problems and will coming back here the next time we have a summer. While we are on God, have you forgotten how differently we see Him? For you He is on the side of the angels, for me it's the Big Battalions. But don't worry, I don't want an all-out war, and you can have your angels. Still, God's 'Good Book' is a reference point we have in common. Unlike Russia, which is all Dostoyevsky to me. In calling you a prodigal husband and father I was only teasing. I know you prefer to see yourself as a latter-day Job. Like him, you want to lose everything so you can get it all back again. And those who suffer on your behalf, and make you feel punished, won't be benefiting. Your fortune restored doesn't bring back the dead. You'd do better to keep thinking about the parable of the Prodigal Son. It's all about families.

Note (to myself): and he did.

'You've often said that loving the everyday is not love, it's habit. Yet love for you is a puppet and you pull the strings. That you have elevated it on stilts is so you can flap its wings until it flies off for a frothy frolic with your choirs of angels, and Lou. And when you get weary of it, you'll let it fall to earth again, and far from sorting out what's waiting for you below, you'll be evasive and bury yourself in your books. Alas, it's true that your everyday loves, Ruth and myself, don't count for butter in your larger scheme. But beware, withholding love is not good for the poetry. Mark Lou's words. I give it to her. Although I know her idea of love is as different as ours on God, only the other way around. I'm on the side of the angels and she of the battalions, which makes you her batman. I like that, and hate it.'

•

Apologia

It is not easy to be fair to Rilke, particularly if you're Clara. His blanket excuse for what is conventionally considered disgraceful behaviour is his quest to become a pure poet. But is that an excuse? Creative work is not on a see-saw with a humane life. Mallarmé and James Joyce, as driven as him with their work, were more than dutiful family men. Consider Rilke's older contemporary Van Gogh, taking on responsibility for Sien Hoornik and her two babies to keep her off the street. No greater love. Of course, as a bread-earner Vincent could only buy yesterday's crusts, and it was his brother who paid for his kindness to others.

Note (to myself): although Theo was well recompensed. Not merely by the paintings. The mine of letters he received from Vincent are arguably the richest from an artist in epistolary history. Rilke was no mean correspondent. Other than the hair standing on one end (*horripiler*), it was what he had most in common with Van Gogh. But it's the mad painter not the *sensible* writer (all writers like to think they are sensible, said Jean de La Bruyère) that wins hands down. Rilke read them compulsively on his travels and it led to Vincent taking over from Cezanne as the main focus of his educational letters to Clara. In a way he wanted to be him.

The Russian poet Marina Tsvetayeva, unaware that Rilke was fatally ill, wrote to him, 'Love lives on words and dies in deeds… I know you, Rainer, as I know myself… And the word is all I want. Each line of poetry is the truth of the moment. But it never turns to wood – only ashes.' A few months later Pasternak wrote to her, 'Rilke's [early] death is not in the natural order.' Her reply was ambiguous: 'No. It was his life that was not in the natural order.'

'What do we know about people?' I say with Marlene Dietrich over the dead body of Orson Welles, the crooked cop with the heart of marshmallow who like Dickens's Sidney Carter did the decent thing for once and paid for it (*Touch of Evil*, 1958). Dietrich's concludes, 'He was some sort of man.' And so is Rilke. Clara, who knows what is not in the writing is best placed 'to get to the bottom' of his 'Sincerity'. But couples can spend a quarter a lifetime together without knowing what the other thinks, and it's the second-guessing that keeps the marriage alive. Rilke prides himself in being a master 'second-guesser', particularly with women, with the exception of Lou. He met his match with her. Any hint of hypocrisy was detected and not tolerated. In time they learned to know where one another stood. But in his two-faced response to Clara's stern letter, smiling with one, weeping with the other, he second-guessed wrong. And she was left feeling his Sincerity was a bottomless pit.

Note (to myself): reading the letter against my transcription, I realise that I elaborated hints, evasions and understatements in the original, which I'm emboldened to believe Clara would not have missed. Unlike Kappus, who I could identify with (I once was a boy poet), I have never been an abandoned wife. Yet in garnishing some of his excessive zeal in defending himself with telling additions, I admit that like Flaubert with Madame Bovary, and Rilke feeling like the Russian people, I'm Clara as she read him. I tried to be fair. Dear reader, be patient with me. I hope to make amends.

•

Redeeming Rilke?

Clara receives her Cézanne epistle as promised. It is Rilke at his sympathetic best. 'He could have made a good living with his art appreciations,' Clara sighs. 'Instead, he puts valuable time by to write it solely for me. A pity.'

Rilke sees the recently deceased Cézanne as the Patron Saint of creative dedication:

> 'Thanks to his friendship with Pissarro, Cézanne got the taste for work in his late twenties (my age). And did nothing else for thirty years except work, work, work. It was a rage rather than a pleasure, ever at odds with what he thought he knew. He called what he sought *La Réalisation*, the ultimate fulfilment, which was to be found in the Venetians at the Louvre. His paintings are votive offerings to them. He sees it in Bellini,

Titian, Guardia and Tiepolo, and Chardin with his demystification of blue. In short, the *Réalisation* is the incarnation of the world *as a thing carrying absolute conviction*, the transformation of things, whose reality the artist has experienced and exalts until it becomes imperishable…

'Cézanne couldn't afford models, but sanctifies the simple objects around him – empty wine bottle, apples – and *forces* them to be beautiful, to represent the whole world in all its splendour. But Cézanne didn't know if he had succeeded or not ('in painting something can present itself which is impossible to handle'). He sat in the yard of his studio in Aix-en-Provence before his easel like an old dog, the doubting dog of Master Work. His Master keeps calling him to run and fetch, beats him, lets him go hungry, and only allows him return to God, his original owner, on Sundays for short visits. Cezanne was so preoccupied with failing to achieve *La Réalisation* that he missed his mother's funeral. Meanwhile, in Paris the name 'Cézanne' was bandied about by art-lovers, pleased with themselves to be in the know…'

Clara would have been glad to receive news of this exciting new old painter, and there is more to come in a stream of letters:

'Local Aix artists came to see Cézanne to tell him he is 'famous'. Paul knows in his head he's not and lets them talk as they wince at the portrait of Marie Hortense that he's working on, finding it ugly. No doubt they think his apples should be edible and his wife everybody's fantasy. He sees her, like the apples, not to devour, but caught in a moment that time cannot rot. While painting her he was said to recite Baudelaire's '*Charogne*', wanting to capture her essence, dead *and* alive.'

Bitter-sweet thoughts surfaced for Clara as mention of Cézanne became as frequent as Lou in the stern letter reply: 'Poor Madame Cézanne, sitting free for endless unachieved portraits, while no doubt the housework was mounting up. And Paul yatters on about "fulfilment". His not hers. Likewise, I'm serving Rainer Maria's purposes, but in a smaller way. First giving him a child, and now as an opportunity to wax lyrical about art that could provide ingredients for his poetry. No doubt what he dishes up will be enjoyed by posterity like the apples and Marie Hortense. Meanwhile I'm in the kitchen doing the washing up. No doubt the leftovers will make an excellent *soup du jour* for Ruth and myself.'

'They also serve who only stand and wait.' Clara came to know that and the duties that brought her second-hand powers. Rilke called on her at crucial times and she provided the saddle and reins to permit him to gallop. It happened when finishing *The Notebooks* became an ontological (and financial) imperative. And she responded to his call by dropping everything, and coming down to Paris to look after his daily requirements. When his need was the greatest, they could live together.

But she never could be his downtrodden drudge. Two strong characters don't necessarily have to lock antlers. The strength shows in the restraint. And Clara's must have been heroic. For on the creative chase, Rilke was Emerson's 'immovably-centred Hero'. He stayed still and allowed others to rearrange the pedestal with flowers and inscription. If he made a virtue out of inconsistency, pragmatism was his necessary vice. His demands on Clara, given an epoch when paterfamilias still reigned supreme, would have been considered normal ('It's not the "mal" in animal that frightens me as much as the "mal" in normal,' Joab Comfort says, quoting me in *Heavy Years*. 'And the "sin" in "Sincerity",' I added).

As for love, where did the Rilke-Westhoffs stand or fall? 'Love,' according to Jorge Luis Borges, 'is a religion in which the god is fallible.' In this case both parties proved to be more or less mortals. Clara did her best to practise love, while Rainer Maria generalised it. A balance between the two could never be even. But both knew what to expect, and respected the difference as how things were.

•

A Literary Restitution

Self-knowledge did not particularly interest Rilke, but knowing women was his troubadour métier. His astounding passage in *The Notebooks* on strong women might not have pleased Ellen Key, Lou and Clara, but it's about them:

> 'The lot of women is double-edged. For centuries they have been obliged to perform the two sides of love: not only to love,

but to love themselves on behalf of the other. Men mostly play them along until they either lose interest and become neglectful, or become charged with jealousy (a nasty form of neglect, a neglect of respect). However, what doesn't destroy a woman makes her stronger. And strong women can hold their own despite the indifference or misery men can inflict. They hold out something more sustaining than pleasure, passion. These passionate women are stronger than the men that would try to escape or subjugate them. They put love on an altar and if the object doesn't kneel before it, he is the loser, for these women have outgrown their men, and what remains is renunciation. They have had enough. In ancient times they founded a convent and dedicated their lives to God. One way or another, they inhabit a paradise that men have been banished from. Torment is turned into a transcendental triumph of higher things, a bitter-sweet splendour that leaves men only with regrets.'

Rilke/Malte's conclusion is surprisingly realistic:

'Alas, such strong women are all too few. Most simply have been worn out by submitting to the double-edged expectations that make themselves indispensable as the better half. Such women even begin to resemble their husbands, and others see them as the perfect couple. Perhaps, hope lurks somewhere in the shadows. More likely it is a memory of hope. A woman who never wanted children dies giving birth to her eighth and is remembered as light and airy as a young girl looking forward to love. Hope lingers on the surface as varnish on an old boot. Wives who put up with tyrants and drunks, in company keep up appearances with their devil-man. Their brave face fools nobody. Still, they console themselves with the idea that deep down there is a part of them that can't be touched. What is called a rich interior life (though it's a poor place). But neither being a hypocrite with others or keeping yourself to yourself, isolates the condition. Life reduces your self-respect insidiously, and you either become an actor in your own tragic fantasy, or you suffer in silence and die inside. Who knows how many women are walk-on parts in bad marriages or are dead to life when they sit down? It takes time for your own predicament to register fully, and then it is too late to cross the threshold of anguish and voice the reality. I bite my tongue, swallow my words. I'm a man.'

I've left it to Rilke not to restore the balance but to tilt it the other way.

Chapter Nineteen

Silent on a Peak: Letter Ten

(20 December 1908, Paris)

•

Death as a muse

The next two years are largely given over to completing the second volume of 'thing-poems' while travelling widely in Western Europe. His itinerary includes a long stay in Capri, where he hopes to give *The Notebooks* undivided attention. A third lecture tour takes him to Prague and Vienna (where he meets Kassner and Hugo von Hofmannsthal) and it pays for a holiday in Venice, which inspires additional poems for *New Poems*. But his stay is interrupted late November, 1907, by the sudden death of Paula Modersohn-Becker shortly after giving birth to a healthy baby. He immediately returns to Worpswede and Clara. The shock unites them.

In the new year he is off to Capri again to stay with Alice, the Baroness. Kippenberg, eager to see the novel out, and worried that his hostess will distract him with more Pre-Raphaelite translations, offers him a generous retainer so he can return to Paris and concentrate on finishing it. Rilke lodges in the historically grand but now rather run-down Palais Hotel Biron. Clara once had her studio there, and joins him, occupying a room on a different floor. He procrastinates on the novel, and instead puts the finishing touches to *New Poems*, dedicating it to Rodin. His return to the hotbed inner circle is now immanent. Auguste is pleased with what he considers Clara's comeback.

On the anniversary of Paula's death, he composes 'Requiem for a Friend' and another requiem on the suicide of Wolf, Count of Kalckreuth, a young Munich poet who had sought his advice. The difference between a life taken for a life and a life that takes itself is as an abyss to a 'Little Ease' cell. Paula, 'untimely ripped' by the 'fateless gods', free-floats in bliss, while Rilke in the sorry world below begs her not to haunt him, for as a 'spiritual presence' in death she would be unbearable.

Rilke is gentler with his acolyte, trapped in a hole. Wolf's self-willed death is easier to understand and the ardent lover of tender unhappiness and high priest of the inexpressible' (Florien Illies, 2013) in him is to the fore:

> 'Had but a woman's light hand touched the still mild beginnings of your darkening, you would not have destroyed the life you loved and didn't know it.' But ruing having missed a choir of opportunities to dissuade the young poet, he says, 'Nobody is to blame. It simply had to be' and wishes him an afterlife. 'When, dear boy, you meet up with the other dead, those who held out to the end, although burdened by our grief, there's no need to be ashamed, but greet them as usual. The big words from the past when one could see what was happening are no more. Death is not a victory, nor life a loss. Enduring is all.'

His requiem for Paula couldn't be more different (See, Chapter Twenty).

•

Divagations

When he writes the last letter to the young poet (the day after Christmas, 1908), he has just seen off the second volume of *New Poems* and is planning a trip to the South of France. His novel needs it, he reassures Kippenberg who, though not convinced, pays his way.

'I had hoped this would reach you before Christmas, my dear Kappus, but I've been living in my work all winter. The festive season crept up on me, and I hardly had time to buy presents, much less write a letter.' Evidently seasonal greetings had kept them in contact over the silent years, but Kappus's announcement that he had completed his military training calls for more.

The tone is chipper. Not surprisingly: his life has organised itself so his only responsibility is to the writing; the epistolary friendships with Lou continue as a support service; Clara and Ruth remain his family by remote control (he is a rich source of education for both of them, not least the letters about Van Gogh, who at last is getting known in Paris). True, there is the novel that wouldn't finish itself. But the need to write a money-spinner is less pressing without the need to support a family, and the kindness of others could be depended on. Paula Modersohn-Becker's death, though, was something else. His 'Requiem' was a plea to her shade to stop making him miserable. It seemed to work. The poem, commensurate with the one Worpswede artist who has withstood the test of time, ended his mourning.

Moreover, his presence in Paris is not going unnoticed. The revised monograph on Rodin went well with art critics and buyers and a second edition is in the air. He remains staunchly the maître's champion. Although privately (to Clara) he begins to detect traces of symbolism in recent work, particularly the drawings. 'I miss the plain craftsmanship of an Aristide Maillol,' and his 'worm making its way in the dark from place to place.' Nonetheless, he sticks to his early evaluation. No point in meddling with the monograph's theoretical base, which also serves to give his 'Thing-poems' authority. The maître's inner circle would have noted the endorsement of *New Poems* from the German-speaking avant-garde in Paris as truly modernist (a word Rodin would never use himself, but nodded to).

However, with his poetry not being translated into French, the exclusively male literary elite is only vaguely aware of him as a 'spiritual' presence on the fringe of the Great God Pan's flutings, who appears and disappears into himself. Rilke might be *a la lune* but this was the dark side.

Still, his women admirers had good reason to see him as the coming poet. Polyglot princesses clamour to put him up in their hunting lodges. His travels have stabilised into *la ronde/das reigen* with some diverting side trips. Indeed, he is well on the way to becoming a new category of poet-Hero, one moveably-unfixed. His *sacrée* solitude was respected by his patronesses, and he feels secure in the knowledge that he could 'live in his work without interruption' or worrying about who paid the rent.

The death of his father two years before freed him from a self-appointed witness to his life. He could now 'live more carelessly', as Pliny the Younger dubbed the advantage of becoming a late-onset orphan (Rilke was only a half one. His mother, as always, an irritating rather than a spiritual presence, was living in Switzerland). Josef Rilke could take paternal concern for a son he didn't understand to insensitive extremes ('It isn't too late to resume your military career'). Probably the one true success in Josef's life, apart from keeping up his handsome appearance, was escaping his wife Phia and her family with their aristocratic pretensions (a pity about the boy).

Residual filial piety added spice to Rilke's guilt at neglecting him in his later years and his entry in the *Duino Elegies* is moving but more sympathetic than he probably felt, judging from the two dismissive late poems.

A poem he wrote in 1903, 'Photograph of My Father as Young Man', is kind to be cruel:

> The eyes dream. The brow as if it could feel
> something far off.
> Around the lips, a freshness to seduce.
> Though there is no smile
> ...The distance he sees into was first grasped,
> and let slip, by hands, folded, going nowhere.
> A vapid, vaporous horizon. How could I understand
> this figure in a uniform fading into the background?

Now in *The Notebooks* he is cruel to be kind:

> Malte burns all his dead father's papers in the hearth. The photographs take longer for the flames to consume...They were mostly of feather-hatted women whose full-blown beauty would have pleased Rubens. He wonders about his father, seeing him through their veiled eyes. A vagrant memory comes back to him. "Crossing the road, holding my father's hand, a carriage slowing to greet him, and the eyes of these women lingered over me and there was no escape. 'They were comparing me with my father, a weedy boy and the Master of the Hunt. We could not bear comparison. My father was oblivious and didn't let go of my hand.'

Guilt is relieved posthumously by portraying Josef as a loving father.

The same could not be said for his mother, a serious embarrassment that he was trying to live down by avoiding her. Dr Freud would have wanted to know more about his parents when Lou confided her friend's frustrations to him. When in the last of his *Duino Elegies* he is naming the stars above in the Land of Sorrow, the one that stands out is the clear-cut 'M', *das die Mutter...*' Mother, it could just as well have been dial 'M' for *Mord*, murder.

The odd poem appeased his loathing. Another one is less vicious than the 'stone by stone' demolishment of 'the shack' that was him:

I set her down inside a glass case
in which there were various mementoes,
or objects that were considered precious.
A stranger, there she stood as though on loan.
And she grew merely old and blind.
And was not precious and was never rare.

•

'*Art is only a way of living*': *The Last Wave*

The tenth and final letter to Kappus is not as peremptory in tone as the valedictory previous. He reverts, almost nostalgically, to themes from the halcyon days of the correspondence, reprising them with gusto. Unlike the ninth, valedictory, letter, the congratulation is not merely for his advice. Credit where credit is due is given to the young man (no longer a poet).

> 'Good news. You've got your commission. Very good news, the more I think about it. I have been imagining you in your solitary redoubt amid the barren mountains, with the great southern winds tearing them apart in chunks as though bent on devouring them. The silence all around you is immense enough to hear the slightest sound or tremor, not least the distant roar of the sea, perhaps the most intimate note in this primordial harmony. One can only hope that you are trustingly, patiently letting the solitude, always with you, work on you to prepare for what is in store. It's presence – persistent, gently assertive, unseen – is to our souls what the blood of our ancestors is to our bodies, and together they fortify us to create the unique inimitable beings that we are.
> 'Now you're ready to move on. I'm so glad it's in a solid, clearly defined profession with a language of its own and a grammar to go with it. Rank, uniform, regulations, duties all dedicated to tangible and self-contained objectives. You are silent on a peak amidst imperious surroundings that accord with the necessary seriousness of your calling. Gloriously isolated amidst a small company of comrades, likewise face-to-face with their destiny. Let the circumstances work on you. Vigilant application, above and beyond the frivolity of barracks

life, will permit you to profit from the seemingly endless waiting inherent in the military profession, and mine too. You mustn't merely kill time. Find a point of application to hoist your self-reliance and cultivate it with ever-growing force, armed with the strength gained from engaging solitude, and the work it has done for you – all you need to find inspiration in the grand things of nature when from time to time they come before you.

'Art also is only a way of living, and it is possible, no matter how you live, to prepare for it without knowing. Everything real you are in touch with is nearer and better neighbours than those quasi-artistic professions which pretend to be the friend of art, and in practice attack and deny it at the same time. For example, the whole of journalism, and almost all criticism, and three-quarters of what popularly passes as literature, the populist stuff. I rejoice, in a word, that you haven't fallen into such traps, and that you've landed on your feet, a man alone braving rugged reality. May the coming years support and strengthen you in this.

'Ever yours,
'R.M. Rilke.'

Thus, finally ended their correspondence.

Rilke's enthusiasm for Kappus's burgeoning army career is perhaps tinged with nostalgia for what might have been for himself. He had just commemorated his thirty-third birthday, the christic age, and, mindful of Sigbjorn Obstfelder, his erstwhile alter ego, wondered if he too was doomed to fail. Perhaps sometimes he wearied of living up to being his own poet Hero. The army – at least in peace time – is an easy enough life. Everything laid on and you lie around a lot. His father's suggestion appeared for a moment not totally absurd. A soldierly sinecure in the mountains would have met his resolve never to waver from the path of poetry by going out and earning a living. Of course, the army has occupational hazards, but with the state of Europe at present, what with the Bolsheviks and Anarchists, it would be safer to serve the Kaiser than to be a man in the street. And Clara couldn't complain, 'Rainer Maria, you've never done an honest day's work in your life. Sponging off your rich women and indulging yourself.'

She might have thought that in dark moments but would know it was wrong. 'Nobody ever worked as hard as Rilke to avoid being stuck with "the vain tumult and salary" of a job. Think of all those letters he writes to promote a sense of reader complicity with his poetry, and not merely to editors and patrons. Housekeepers and schoolgirls. He is, in effect, creating a community of like souls, a "Mystical Body" of Rilke.'

She wouldn't know about the human moves necessary to keep the sentiments of his lady admirers at a courtly-love distance. The neo-troubadour's real work is labour-intensive: appearing above (or below) suspicion to the husband but touching his lady's heart, pleasing but being considered harmless, composing songs for dusk and dawn but avoiding night, a chaste chase but not bloodless. Rilke's Malte knew a thing or two about hunting from his father, and keeping the hounds off your scent. Wild flowers, prayers to God and intimations of madness are the neo-troubadour's best deodorants.

Samuel Beckett, another ladies' man who liked to keep his distance for the most part, in letters to his amatory exception, Barbara Bray, was top-heavy with groaning intimacies about being 'too tired, stupid and sad' to hold a pen. Compromising, if a husband came across them and sneaked a read. Rilke's letters are the other way around. They couldn't be called billet-doux or Cupid's darts. Inexhaustibly long with excessive endearments, conspicuously crafted yet prone to joy and pain in the same sentence. They're telling the snooping spouse, 'Relax. It's not what you think. Just accept that I'm an overexcited poet who amuses your wife. You have more important things to worry about. For instance, your mistresses…'

Rilke was a friend of the rich, but never rich. By bartering platonic friendship for bed and board, he was continuing an honourable tradition for poets from Dante to Samuel Johnson. That is, until the Romantics raised the stakes (even sometimes offering themselves as *cavaliere servants*). Clara can't accuse him of being a sponger, unless in the sense of John Locke's *negative capability*. Rilke 'effaced' himself 'to soak up impressions', and make a good one. As a 'chameleon poet', he adapted to the circumstances as needs be. Rilke effectively lived on his wits, and therefore was obliged to regard consistency as less a virtue than a convention, and pragmatism as a necessary vice (I'm not quite repeating myself). But he didn't have to justify himself in the Higher Court of posterity. His poetry would be what was argued over, not his way of life and, as he told Kappus, 'No matter what happens, life is always right.'

Note (to myself): I can't help humming Lorenz Hart's lyric, 'I was reading Schopenhauer last night / and I think that Schopenhauer was……' (*Pal Joey*).

Chapter Twenty

'A Requiem for a Friend' (1909)

•

The rightness of life must have been challenged by Paula Mendelsohn-Becker's sudden death. She was the unrequited love of his life, and by far the most gifted. When she wedded the recently widowed Otto Mendelsohn, he proved a bad loser. Rilke, scorned, took the high ground, moderating their friendship:

> 'If your love (for me) had remained alert, things would be different. But now the centre of gravity has shifted. I occupy myself with a wife and child.'

Marrying Clara on the rebound meant he monopolised her best friend. He could be said to be punishing Paula, and at the time she was unhappy. Wanting a child, she married Otto, but he declined consummating their union, wishing to remain faithful to his first wife.

Rilke knew Paula's value as an artist and, no doubt, her flight from Otto in 1906 to study in Paris pleased him. But Otto followed her and obviously got over his 'widower's nerves'. By then, Rilke had transferred his unrequited love for Paula to a requited one with her paintings. He was one of the first to recognise her greatness. She was doing for early expressionism what Berthe Morisot did for impressionism, giving it a female perspective that 'lightened the heavy' (Rilke).

Paula and Rilke had one thing in common, being only truly happy when working. There they could take refuge from an unwieldy world. Rilke's 'to work is to live without dying' could have been a joint motto. Paula's self-portrait as the Mona Lisa, but with teeth, casts a cold eye on her vanity mirror. But she warms to her fate with several beautiful paintings of herself pregnant and modestly naked. 'The colour and simplicity of form of Gauguin vies with the textural richness of Van Gogh,' says Joab Comfort. I find wit and pathos in them that makes me want to laugh and cry. One nude self-portrait has a crushed-up flower near her heart which could have been the blood clot that killed her.

In the year of her death she did her best work, and its predominant motif chimes with its cause, childbirth. Montaigne, when weighing the relative merits of conceiving a child and a work of art, was thoughtful: 'I do not know whether I would rather produce a perfectly formed child by intercourse with the Muses than with my wife. Few poets would not be prouder to father the Aeneid than the handsomest son in Rome, and more stoically endure the loss of a son than a poem.' Rilke would have agreed with Montaigne.

Note (to myself): Rilke didn't lose Ruth, but he mislaid her on his quest for poetry. I always think of her as Madame Bovary's child Berthe, more or less disowned for not being pretty. Ruth isn't in the early Worpswede photographs. But later ones have become available and show a winning child, anxious-looking when alone but assuredly adorable in the arms of Clara.

When Paula's mother asked Rilke to edit her extensive journals, he refused, saying it would distract from her work. And he was right. Her reputation, on the back of this bestseller, was of tragically unfulfilled potential rather than a gloriously achieved artist. Rilke's last word on the journals was 'they don't reflect the freedom she attained in her last year, and the great beauty of her departure from us'. He might have wanted to rephrase the second clause. A cardiac-infarction is hardly a thing of beauty. But mourning her with three months in Capri wasn't as capricious as it seems. She had always wanted to visit the island and never did.

Note (to myself): after Paula's death, Otto remarried within a year or so to a singer and overcame 'widower's nerves' to father two fine sons. His painterly career continued to prosper while Paula's reputation languished in obscurity. That was to be reversed with time, but not before Otto received a Goethe medal from Hitler and Goebbels condemned as 'decadent' a gallery opened in Bremen to show Paula's paintings.

Rilke in the 'Requiem' channels his feelings on losing her twice. While death is treated as their ultimate consummation, suffering is dismissed as a convention that shouldn't be allowed to go on too long. It's his most human poem, not least because he frames it within her last intimate paintings, and allows her death rather than the disease. The sorrow is painfully real but its 'closure' reveals even more about himself than the unsparing poems about his parents. His self-controlling way of life cannot be unknotted. ('That's how it has to be').

Note (to myself): Rilke's traditional German pentameters makes its verse form impossible to replicate in English, and so I translated it as a prose poem. There are obscurities in it for those who don't know the circumstances of Modersohn-Becker's death, the nature of her paintings, Schopenhauer's 'The indestructibility of being…', Cezanne's *La Réalisation*, and, finally, *Weltinnenraum* (world-inner-space) but I have spelt out the meaning when I feel mystifications were not intended. Rilke has made this possible for me to do with some loose threads in the composition, and so I'm not calling it a transcription.

•

'Requiem for a Friend' (*'Requiem für eine Freundin'*)

'I have my dead and I let them go. They are contented, even cheerfully at home with their state. Only you. You have come back. A brush of air steals past, a clinking sound betrays your presence. Why do you spoil my hard-won peace of mind? I was just getting used to your death. If you are moved by homesickness, I fear you've lost your way. The things of this world are what we imagine them to be, reflected on the polished surface of our being.

'I thought you would be much further on. You who have transformed yourself more than any other woman I know. I thought you would have no trouble in grasping with your imagination the next world. News of your death frightened us. Or rather it broke in on us, with a peremptory wrench. And "What's next" became a "Has been". Putting it in its place was what we had to do.

'The tremble in the air is so unlike you. You don't seem to know where you are. You're bewildered, distraught. And there's no reason for it. Where you are fear is meaningless. By coming back, you are wasting precious moments of eternity, missing out on the splendour of infinite forces. You who missed nothing. What has dragged you back into present time? What unfinished business?

'You have startled me from a dreamless sleep like a thief in the night. Instead of reassuring me with your abundant kindness that you wander in the above like a child out playing without a care in the world, you are pleading for help, mutely but I hear it in my heart's core. Nothing in my dark-nights-of-the-soul could scream within me such a bitter rebuke. I shrink into my lungs, entrails, and the empty chamber of my heart. It cuts me in two like a saw. What do you want? Why you are stealing back. Did you leave something behind that couldn't bear your absence?

'Tell me, must I go out to look for it? It will be, I know, somewhere you never saw, but that felt near to you as your own senses. Another country. I must set out for it, and get to know its rivers and valleys, and acquire its customs. I'll spend hours talking to the women at the doorsteps, observe them calling the children home, and learn how they wrap the land around themselves to work the fields and meadows. I will go before their ruler, bowing low, bribe the priests to gain entry to their temple, and there alone amongst the formidable statues, the doors shut on me, I'll learn enough to be free to watch the animals out on the hill, and let their composure become mine. In their eyes I will see my existence, held for a while, then let go, serenely, without judgement.

'The gardeners will recite the names of all the flowers. Names with a ring that bring back their hundred fragrances. I will buy fruit in whose sweetness the country's earth and sky live again. You who so well understood ripe fruit, and set them in a white bowl before your canvas, giving them their due weight with your colours. Women too, you saw, are fruits, and children curled up inside them lend shape to their ripeness. And at last you see yourself as a fruit, stepping out of your clothes, bringing your naked body before the mirror and letting it enter your gaze. It stands before you, not saying 'That's me', but 'It is'. Your gaze, impassive, unassuming. The flesh, poor thing, without desire, even for yourself, wants nothing. *Sacré*. You are to be cherished, deep within the mirror where you put yourself, far away from all the world.

> 'Why steal back like this, denying yourself, making me think in the amber beads of your self-portrait there is a heaviness not known to the clear skies of painting? Why in your stance do you stand for a bad omen? Why read the lifelines of your body like a palm, upturned to show me your fate, what happened to you? Come into the candlelight. I'm not afraid to look the dead in the face. On their return they have as much right as anything to linger and refresh themselves in our eyes. Come, and let's share a quiet moment. Look at the rose on my desk.

Isn't the light around it is as timid as the light around you? It too should not be here. It should have bloomed and withered in the garden. Nothing to do with me. Now it's preserved in a little porcelain vase. But what does it profit from my awareness of it? Don't be alarmed. I get it now, it's rising in me, and I'm trying to grasp it, must grasp it, even if it kills me, that you are here. I feel your fate like a blind man grasps an object, though I couldn't name it. Let's lament together that you have been plucked like a flower out of your mirror's depths.

'I can see you're beyond tears. The drops bubble into the fullness of your gaze. All the humours within you have hardened into a reality that circulates blindly, stubbornly. And so, finally, chance came and pulled you back from your chosen path into a space where beings have their *will* forever. Not with a wrench, but a lingering on of the thread of your life, a shred suspended out of time, which is incessantly encroached upon by a world that isn't yours, burdening your sense of wholeness, until you can no longer contain yourself, and break out of its confines, tearing yourself to bits, painfully, because you must.

'Then from the night-warm soil-bed of your heart, you dug out seeds, still green, to sprout your own death, your perfect death, your life's consummation. And having swallowed the pips of your death, you were surprised at the aftertaste of sweetness, the sweetness on your lips, you who in your flesh and blood was all sweetness.

'Let us lament. Shyly, as reluctantly as your blood called back from universal circulation. How confused it is to be regurgitated back into the body's narrow system. Full of distrust from the last time, when it flowed into the placenta and was suddenly exhausted by the long journey home. But now you can't stop. You drive, push, drag it like a terrified beast to the sacrificial altar. You want it, after all it's been through, to be happy. And persistence pays off. It yields to happiness, and you think, conscious you've got the measure of it, just a little time now. Time, you're in time. The middle of time. Your time. Time that goes on, that grows out of proportion. Ah! time is like a relapse after a long illness.

'A Requiem for a Friend'

'How short your life seems if you compare it with the empty hours you passed in silence, bending the abundance in your hands to divert future abundances into the seeding child that was to be your fate. A painful task, too much for anyone. But you performed it, day after day, propping yourself up before it, weaving the fine thread of the loom into manifold patterns, and plucking up your courage to celebrate when the work was done. You wished to be rewarded. Like a child who took her medicine. You chose your own reward, being so remote from other people that they couldn't possibly know what would please you. You sat up in your child bed and in front of you was a mirror, which reflected back everything. And this everything was you, you there before you. But inside the mirror was deception, the sweet deception of every woman who smiles as she puts on her jewellery and combs her hair.

'And so, you died as women used to die, at home, in your own warm bedroom, the oldest of deaths, a woman in childbirth, who tries to close the wound of labour, but can't, because the ancient darkness, which they also gave birth to, returns for them, forcing its way in and taking them away. Once there would have been keening. Women paid to beat their breasts and break the silence of the night with their plaintive cries. No more. The custom has been let die, like so many others. Disowned, disappeared. Like you. Yes, that's what you have come back for: to claim what we withheld, your right to a wake. Can you hear me? I would like to throw my voice like a cloth over the wreckage of your death, and rent it until it's in pieces and my words walk around shivering in the tatters of that voice, lamenting the lament.

'Now I must accuse: not the man who took you from yourself (I can't find him. He looks like everyone), but in this one man, I accuse all men. Deep within me I sense the child that I once was, in essence pure and simple. I no longer know that child. But from this sense I want to conjure up an angel to hurl upwards into the ranks of angels, who cry out, reminding God… that this suffering has lasted far too long. It's unbearable, tangling the leaden heart-strings into knots, a false love drawing on convention like a habit, the good death, just so, while fattening on its injustice.

'Show me the man with the right to possess what cannot hold its own self, that which, now and then, in a moment of joy catches itself, like a child playing with a ball, only to throw it away as quickly as possible. As little a right of possession as a ship's captain in holding the carved sign of victory-over-death, the Nike, on the prow, when the goddess figurehead breasting the waves pitches itself up lightly into a blinding tempest. As hopeless as one of us calling back the woman who now no longer sees us, and walks along the tightrope of existence, and, by some miracle, is secure in her step. And as wrong too, if anything is wrong, as not to permit love free rein to universalise itself. One must summon up all our inner freedom to release it. In love the ultimate act is letting each other go. Holding on is easy. It has to be unlearned.

'Are you still there? Standing in some corner? You know as well as me of what I speak. You who passed through life open as the break of day, and did so much, everything. I know how women suffer. For love means being alone, and you, like all true artists, by instinct were constantly transforming things, fulfilling them so they carry imperishable conviction. You suffered and transformed. An existence that the intrusion of fame could only distort. You were beyond all that. Making yourself as small as possible, almost invisible, discreetly veiling your beauty, withdrawing it like the colourful flags on the grey morning after a festival. You had one desire: a year to work in order to finish what now will never be finished. If you're still there in the darkness, your spirit resonating with the lowly sound waves of my voice, hear and help me. How easy it is to slip back from what we struggle to achieve into a life we never wanted. Cut off abruptly in full flow, we are trapped in a bad dream in which we die without waking up. This can so easily happen. A year's work can go by the way, the blood in it drained, and weakened; the dull thud of gravity makes it fall to ground. Worthless. For somehow there is an ancient enmity between our daily lives and the Great Work. Help me, when all's said and done, to get to the bottom of that.

'A Requiem for a Friend'

'Do not return. If you can bear to, stay dead with the dead. The dead have their own work cut out. But help me, if you can without distraction, as what is furthest sometimes helps with me. Stay where you are.'

Chapter Twenty-One

A Princess Comes to the Rescue
•
The Nut

Closeted in his Palais redoubt, Rilke told Kippenberg that he couldn't extract 'the fruit within the nut' of *The Notebooks*. The end was not in sight. Anton has a word with Clara, groaning that he is taking Rodin's 'legitimisation of unfinished work' too far. On her insistence, Rilke moves to a room without windows. Faced by a blank wall, his troubled distinction between prose and poetry to Rodin haunted him: 'poems are carried along by the rhythm of external things... But for prose you must plunge into the profound depths of one's being...to build a cathedral, and its construction is a matter of scaffolding... But you are only conscious of planks. And yet... people take form... emerge almost like figures from your marble.' The optimistic twist at the tail to please the maître is ominous. The 'nut' is not for cracking.

His tergiversations over the next year or so are doubly painful for Kippenberg. Apart from Rilke two-timing with another publisher (who is also bringing out the two 'Requiems' in a limited edition), his generous advance was about to be frittered away on a holiday in the South of France. He was wrong. Travelling concentrates Rilke's mind, and Avignon offers him a section for the novel on Popes and mad kings. Van Gogh and Provence are next on his itinerary and the trip proves providential.

Arles was where Van Gogh completed his life's work. Rilke's reading of his letters had inspired him to search out the paintings in Paris and he described Vincent's fulfilment for Clara: 'He achieved what never before had been painted by refusing to give up going beyond the possible. Had he shared his vision with anyone else he might have hesitated. In the letters (to Theo) he touched on it, but only in relation to work that had been finished.' In the wheat fields of Arles ideas harvest for Rilke, but the notes he jots down are blown away in the mistral. He is well on the way to ignoring Clara's advice ('Give the poems a rest'). She had returned home to Worpswede having done her best to get him going by reading the manuscript with practical suggestions, for instance breaking the text up into titled chapters (advice he was to ignore. The manuscript is one long paragraph).

Rilke's agonising over how to finish the novel lacked the epic patience that Flaubert brought to *L'Education Sentimentale* (1869), another novel about a callow youth who comes to seek his fortune in Paris. Flaubert took almost a quarter of century to abandon it to publication (more than three times as long as *The Notebooks*' gestation. Though he completed *Madame Bovary* and *Salammbô* in between). Hitherto, Rilke regarded prose, like letter-writing, as something to be gotten off your chest as quickly as possible. But the planks of the novel's scaffolding as erected are designed to build castles in the air, rather than cathedrals, and Flaubert's perfectionism is too much on his mind.

He stalls on the novel between 1906 and 1908, working on other things, travelling and publishing several slim volumes of poems. However, Arles is to hold the key to unlock the ending. In Alychamps, the necropolis immortalised by Van Gogh, the caretaker points out to him the reputed tomb of the Prodigal Son. This reminds him of something Clara said about the parable being all about family love. When he faces the blank wall again in the Palais, her words come back to him, and he dashes off a long letter to her on the Prodigal Son as 'the man that didn't want to be loved', which he doesn't send but adds to what was to be the penultimate section.

Impasses with poetry were something else. Poetry can't be dashed off. The epic one is with what was to become the *Duino Elegies*. After four years of foreplay, the first elegy was written in 1912, and he took ten years to finish the other nine (eight hundred and fifty-six lines in all), half the time Flaubert took with as many pages for *L'Education*. Nevertheless, the prose of *The Notebooks*, at quarter the length of the Flaubert, preoccupied him for six long years, during which 'sharing his vision' for it in letters to Lou, Clara and Kippenberg, exhausted their patience, but what could he do? He is endeavouring to turn castles in the air into a cathedral. The foundations were on the soggy side and, moreover, he couldn't decide if the emerging edifice should be topped with a crucifix or a Virgin.

•

The Fruit

But the eventual cracking of the 'nut' was already sitting in his mind.

A Princess Comes to the Rescue

Cathedrals, like the famous one in Narbonne that inspired Rodin, didn't have to be finished, and so the solution is essentially the same as Flaubert's with *L'Education Sentimentale*. When reading Jules Michelet's imaginative history, Gustave was struck by the way each volume trailed off to be only partially brought to resolution by an epigram or anecdote that sounded true, 'Indeed, Flaubert considered, all the great works of genius were endless. Homer, Shakespeare and Goethe, all the sons of God, were happy to leave things suspended in mid-air, like Lorck's tortoise over the Venetian lagoon.' And so, he broke with the *roman classique* by leaving the ending open, with the shared nostalgia of two boyhood friends for the night they went to the local brothel and presented the madame with a bunch of flowers stolen from a garden. 'It was our finest hour,' they both agree. A canny publisher would conclude it was the beginning of a sequel, a French *Huckleberry Finn*, and pay an advance. The critics of the day scorned *L'Education*, and it took thirty years before it got a proper reading, thanks to Proust, Andre Gide and the Paris literati. Rilke would have taken note. Belatedly in the telling of Malte's story, it becomes evident that St Augustine's 'Not yet', rather than Archimedes' '*Eureka*' is going to win out. However, how to finish the novel by not finishing it is a conundrum.

Princess Marie's presence in town seems like another diversion, but their meeting (the first, other than in letters) proves fortuitous in supporting the Michelet/Flaubert flying tortoise. They discuss the Prodigal Son, the Book of Job and how to finish the novel. Her advice is, 'Since you can't make up your mind, end it up in the air for the readers to decide.' And so, after rewriting the parable of the Prodigal Son, Rilke riddles an ambiguous ending and, in a frenzy of relief, takes a train to the Kippenbergs in Leipzig and dictates the last sections to them. They celebrated Christmas together.

Princess Marie's advice ('stop dithering') had been taken where others failed, and he dedicated *The Notebooks* to her. Perhaps Clara and Lou might have wanted to dispute it, having put up with a lot during its prolonged gestation. Almost twenty years later, Kappus must have regretted it too. Since the Thurn und Taxis fortune came from pioneering postal services in the seventeenth century, the dedication to Princess Marie would have been more appropriate for Rilke's posthumous *Letters to a Young Poet*.

The Notebooks seemed doomed to failure. The review in Gide's *Nouvelle Revue Francaise* condescends with faint praise: 'A barely mastered trembling but heavy with the mystique of living things.' However, as the influence of Kierkegaard, through J. P. Jacobsen, got around, Rilke began to interest philosophers on the trail of Karl Jaspers's *'existenz-philosophie'* (See Guiding Note 8). And Gide, no less, shows an interest in translating it. Extensive sections appeared in the *Nouvelle Revue*, 1911. *The Notebooks'* mystique has worn well, and it's often cited as the first existentialist novel. Still in print in many languages, some readers find it difficult to finish. Rilke would have understood that.

Chapter Twenty-Two

What Happened to Franz Xaver Kappus?

•

The Low Bow and Bow Out

In his preface to *The Letters*, Kappus says, 'After nine letters in eighteen months, the correspondence little by little petered out because life forced me into domains that he, in his warm, tender solicitude, had wanted to protect me from.' I repeat it as the 'little by little' suggests there were further letters between 1904 and 1908, excluded, probably, because they were just friendly waves rather than advice *per se*. Kappus's final sentence – 'When the great speak, it is a unique event, and it is for us lesser mortals to fall silent' – was both a low bow and a bow out. Despite a promising start, all that remains of his poems is the sonnet, 'An obscure anguish within me', which Rilke copied out and sent back to him, saying, 'Read it as though it's by someone else' (seventh letter).

•

Rilke expatiates on juvenilia in The Notebooks:

Poems amount to so little when you write them too early in life. You ought to wait and gather sense and sweetness for a whole lifetime, and a long life if possible, and then at the very end you might be able to write ten good lines. For poems are not what people think: simple emotions (we are born with enough of them!). Poems are experiences. 'For the sake of one poem you must see many cities, many people, many things, you must understand animals, feel how a bird flies and know what it's like to be a flower opening to the sun... And all these things you must forget as you go along. Recollection, like photo albums, misrepresents the experience. You must be patient and wait for life to bring to the surface sensations that are in your blood, which can blush or bleed into poetry.

This is about himself, not Kappus. In the nineties, Stefan George had cautioned the precocious and prolific Rilke against disclosing poems prematurely (Schoenberg was no doubt listening). And, at the time of writing, he was in the process of editing a reissue of his early work.

Rilke's anatomisation of inspiration is probably a recipe for putting poetry off until it's too late. As did Kierkegaard, who confided to his journal, 'I lack the experience to go with the gifts that God gave me to be a poet. Nevertheless, by way of poetical ideas, I've reached an understanding *with* the truth. But it's not an understanding *of* the truth, and not being the real thing, I fear, it will die with me.' The experience Kierkegaard believed he lacked was a failure to live his own ideas, only to think them. He was wrong, but his life's work was ending in polemics and his mind was not at peace. He was to be a poet who never versified. A pity that he hadn't a Rodin to convince him that poetry is a craft to be practised, not an idea to be lived. But then of course we wouldn't have the Kierkegaard who changed the course of philosophy and psychology, only a better class of Shack 'Stofflet (once the Danish poet of poets, now remembered for two lines: 'What is the flattering voice of fame's quest, / compared to the sigh of love from a maiden's breast').

Rilke, on the other hand, wasn't satisfied with mere workmanship. The 'thing-poems' were an entrée, an appetiser for the main course when, so to speak, his *negative capability* would meet its *objective correlative*. Dreaming of banqueting on a recipe of mystical expressionism, what was to become the *Duino Elegies*, made him abstemious. Nevertheless, he continued to 'snack' on occasional poems, and didn't become a hunger-artist. Rodin had reinforced Tolstoy's advice 'Just work, work, work' by adding 'and be patient', which was something of a contradiction. As a taskmaster he wasn't consistent, which suited Rilke's contrary nature. Ezra Pound's advice to another young poet, 'Write seventy-five lines a day', was telling him to practise his craft every day. Rilke didn't need to be told. But his homily on composing poems contains a signal truth. Most poets in their fine frenzy fail to register that poetry which makes 'the leap from what is close to you into the furthest distance' is rare, and even achieving ten lines in a lifetime that survive into the next generation is remarkable. So many poets, famous in their time, are forgotten (except by the scholars of cultural history).

Kappus was 'never to linger in the rightful garden' of poetry (Hilaire Belloc's regret), and the question has to be asked if Rilke's advice to the young poet put him off? No doubt when Kappus eventually read the passage in *The Notebooks*, he wondered whether Rilke was thinking of him, and re-read the copied poem as instructed, realising how little it was 'his own'. He would also have picked up on a passage in which Malte dismissed a play he wrote called *Marriage*: 'It seeks to prove something false by way of mystification.' He knew it was a warning that Rilke was giving himself. A mystique that rang true was what had drawn him to Rilke as a young poet. Now he knew from an old review in a Berlin newspaper (1901) that Rilke's failed play, *Ordinary Everyday Life*, included a wedding, and would have noted with admiration that his 'immovably-centred' poet Hero could be so acutely self-aware. Even unfair to himself, like he had sometimes been when writing to him.

A decade after writing *The Letters*, and many others to aspirant poets, Rilke was well aware of the vagaries of advice: 'Sometimes a little piece of string offered at the right moment has more impact in transforming a life than any amount of persuasion.' Wisdom is hard-earned.

•

His Career

Letters to a Young Poet was published three years after Rilke's death. Even though the great man had 'spoken', Kappus didn't, as he said, 'fall silent', but found his voice elsewhere, taking to the journalism and literary criticism against which Rilke had warned him. He left the army after the Great War. His active service was short, having been shot in the lung in 1914. He married the nurse who took care of him, and continued working in the press office, for which he was awarded the Knight's Cross of the Order of Franz Josef (1918). During the war he published pacifist pieces under a pseudonym for the main newspaper in his hometown Timisoara.

Kappus's admiration for Richard Dehmel certainly survived Rilke's onslaught on a rival. Dehmel's anti-war poem '*Hymnus Barbaricus*' (1917) would probably have meant more to him than the *Duino Elegies*. It ends:

> Human intelligence is unrelentingly intent
> on destroying mankind and all his works,
> and – mankind rejoices.

What Happened to Franz Xaver Kappus?

Kappus diverged into writing film scripts (Germany had the most highly developed cinema industry in Europe). His speciality was Depression stories with a social message more in the sly style of Preston Sturges's *Sullivan's Travels* (1941) than John Ford's mawkish *Grapes of Wrath* (1940). He published popular novels, cliff-hangers with titles like *Red Rider* (*Der rote reiter*) and *Lena Spoken For* (*Brautfahrt um Lena*). Mihail Sebastian, the celebrated Romanian playwright and novelist, called them 'instructive entertainments'. He edited a daily newspaper in his hometown that resembles *Le Journal* here in French Catalan in its even-handedness. Timisoara was on the border between Germany and Romania and neither the Nazis nor the Iron Guard bothered much about it. But, by not taking sides, his editorials were quietly subversive.

Kappus lay low during the Second World War and afterwards published a novel, *Hiding in Love* (*Flucht in die Liebe*) about the anti-Nazi Resistance in Germany and Romania. It was a bestseller and made into a film. But, like all his literary works, it is long out of print, as are the films he scripted.

By all accounts, Kappus lived a publicly-spirited life in the town he was born, dying in his eighties as a respected and honoured citizen. A tantalising detail of his cinematic career: in 1925 (the year before Rilke's death) he wrote a film called *The Wife of an Artist*. If Clara had recognised the name of the troubled military cadet, she might well have gone to see it. A pity that the nitrate reel burnt up before anyone thought of copying it.

When he published *The Letters*, I like to think that D. H. Lawrence's *Classic Studies in American Literature* (1922) was in his sights: 'Never trust the artist. Trust the tale. The proper function of a critic is to save the tale from the artist who created it.' I'm being fanciful. It wasn't yet translated into German. But 'I believe it because I hope for it' (Leon Blum). *The Letters* tell a tale or two, sometimes despite their writer and recipient. Out of context, they comprise much more than their intended advice to two young poets (for he was counselling himself too). Rilke would have been pleased to think that the words appeared on the page without his agency; that his writerly apocalypse had been achieved posthumously by critical default ('Happy are those who know behind all language there stands that which is beyond words...').

Chapter Twenty-Three

What Happened to Rilke

•

The New Life: Dante and Petrarch

On seeing *The Notebooks* into print, Rilke's transformation into a pure poet becomes more urgent. He recuperates with Princess Marie at Duino Castle where he was very much at home. It is located in the no-man's land between the German, Slovenian and Italian borders. At the time it was nominally in Italy, which pleased her highly educated entourage. Their preference was to talk Italian. It proved another providential place for him. Drained after finishing his novel, he starts translating Dante Alighieri's *La Vita Nuova* with the help of the Princess and her friends.

Dante was something of a kindred spirit, displaced so often in his life while being an 'immovably-centred' poet (but no hero). Inspired by the troubadours to change from classical Latin to the vernacular, in effect he salvaged poetry from the folios of savants to revive the oral tradition for the general. Poems were how people spoke. Moreover, when written down, they changed the language. And so, people sometimes spoke in quotations. Thus, the vernacular was embellished. Dante was secularised by his less spiritual 'son', Petrarch, and modern European poetry as we know it came into being.

Dante didn't jettison completely the feudal conventions of the troubadour. He was faithful to courtly love, but beyond the moral dimension is a humane one hitherto unknown. Rilke was drawn to Dante's yearning/longing for the unobtainable Beatrice, but baulked at a *Sehnsucht* that needed the Holy Ghost to requite it. *Geschlech* is a matter of elective affinities ('Is not the secret purpose of this shy earth to urge a pair of lovers to make everything leap within them?' 'Duino Elegy 9'). He had broken with the Romantic notion that beauty is truth to find it in Baudelaire's purgatorial redemptions of the 'unpleasing' in *Les fleurs du mal*. This is scarcely evident in the 'thing-poems', but the *maudit* poet, rather than a virtuous Virgil, acts as Malte's guide in confronting the hell and heaven of city life. Dante has been superseded. 'His *Paradiso* is a helplessly piled blissful mish-mash of smiling angelic purity that perplexes, unlike his inferno which is an encyclopaedia of life' (letter to Karl van de Heydt). He abandons translating his *La Vita Nuova* to Princess Marie's regret.

The Princess is Rilke's ideal hostess. She knows how to leave him alone, sure that he wouldn't neglect to keep her informed on his afflatus, and join her when formal occasions call. A note to her after an unproductive spell of work is not untypical of his hermit billet-doux: 'I rooted around all day in the thicket of my life, screaming to the heavens like a savage, clapping my hands. You wouldn't believe what hair-raising beasts it startled.' Such bizarre confidences bring them closer. By all accounts, she not only entertained, but is entertained by her poet, all alone with his art which is going nowhere and everywhere. Her affection is assured.

A year later, on a subsequent stay in Duino Castle, the Princess read him Petrarch. 'On Mont Ventoux with the sun blazing down on the barren waste he is elsewhere, thinking of his fellow man.' But it was the Petrarchan prosody that inspired his poetry-to-come rather than the humanism. *The Sonnets to Orpheus* and to some extent the *Duino Elegies* had found their form. But still there was the mute question of what vernacular to use. As Dante and Petrarch were ill-at-ease with the strictures of Latin, he felt the same about German as a Bohemian born in Prague. He was inclined to idealise French, but it was too far from being a first language to express his *felt* thoughts (where 'going beyond words' nevertheless needed them). In his later years, though as good as fluent, he was still trying to resolve this problem. His late French poems suggest it was well he stuck to German. According to Stanley Burnshaw, the struggle to soften the heavy, almost goose-stepping, metre succeeded in giving the language new life with the *Duino Elegies* and *The Sonnets to Orpheus*, opening it up to realms of feeling hitherto unknown and giving it a lyric grace, particularly in the shorter poems, not seen 'since Goethe'. Large claims I wouldn't dispute as my knowledge of German poetry down the ages is autodidactic.

But in the first decade of the twentieth century, Rilke's move into modernist modes was hesitant. For instance, he was loath to accept that verse could be free. Like a traditional fiddler, he was congenitally disposed to tap his foot, and didn't relax into rubato until the *Duino Elegies* was out of the way. However, Rilke had already achieved something he set out to do. Five years in advance of his letters to Kappus, his little-known long poem 'Notes on the Melody of Things' formulated a plan for the trajectory of future work. Will Stone in translating its forty formal stanzas found it 'mysterious and enigmatic, tantalising and sometimes infuriating in the way it falls back like a wave from the sea wall of clarity' The metaphor could apply to more than one of Rilke's poems after The *Book of Hours*. He was accurately anticipating what became his pride and glory, 'a clear expression of ambiguity', something Kafka, his younger Prague contemporary, and subsequently Samuel Beckett, were to do in prose.

The 'Melody of Things' makes one thing clear. 'Work, work, work' will be the inspiration, and that includes making the reader work. Not necessarily to understand the poem. It won't have a formula, or a direct line of communication. All they need to do is feel their way in order to arrive somewhere they have never been to before. It's as far as you can get from Dante with his well-defined circles of sin and punishment. However, Rilke didn't give up on Dante's *Inferno*. Nearly twenty years on, he transformed the final *Duino* elegy into an Underworld, not with historical but symbolic figures, like the Lament family, and the wandering poet's Virgil are the temperamental 'Order of the Angels'.

•

Centring himself

Rilke wasn't shy of seeing himself as the 'immovably-centred Hero'. Baudelaire, having using Emerson's epithet to describe Delacroix, added that 'it could equally be applied to certain doyens in the domain of poetry'. I take it, he had himself in mind, as Rilke did when he used it as the epigraph to his Rodin monograph. Being your own hero, you need to be self-centred, and a man of stone to further your art. Easier for Rodin than Rilke, given his fame and materials.

Rilke, though 'centred', was anything but 'immovable'. Montaigne says only fools cannot change their minds, and Rainer Maria was far from one. And physically he was a mover, moveably-unfixed, capable of uppingsticks at the drop of a hat. One March evening – between the sixth and seventh letter to the young poet – he went out for a stroll and, following the pony trot of a phaeton, he arrived at Gare de Lyon, where a train was whistling and smoking –on hearing the last call for Pisa he leapt on and the next day he was in Tuscany. Beckett, who also saw

Paris as the axis of hell and heaven, claimed, 'The artist who stakes his whole being comes from nowhere, and hath no kin.' It was not literally true of course for Sam or Rainer Maria but that's how they centred themselves, and the stone was in the fruit rather than the shoes. They had itchy feet.

•

The Augustine Detour

He takes to the road again, this time North Africa. *The Notebooks* had ended with Malte asking if 'even God could love him?' The narrator answers that 'it's possible, but not yet'. And so, it is not surprising that he makes the pilgrimage to Augustine of Hippo's birthplace in Tunisia and embarks on a close reading of the famous procrastinator.

He starts translating *The Confessions*, abandoning it curiously enough when Augustine is thirty-six, his own age, the age Augustine finally gave up worldly ways and converted to Christianity. Up to then he was asking himself did he love God, the other way around to Malte. Augustine's eventual conversion was moralistic rather than mystical. 'Spiritual presences' wouldn't have entered into it. Rilke must have felt deceived. Augustine had the sort of mother he would have liked to have, but his father was 'inadequate' like his own, and that neutralised his spiritual side.

Augustine had meant something special to Rilke from his youth upwards. It shows in *Letters to a Young Poet*. His insistence that one's relationship with the Ineffables is primordial chimes with Augustine's dictum on a lesser one: 'The secret of happiness is that we already possess it.' Rilke in melancholy moments might be tempted to search out his own happiness, rather than writing poems and letters for the happiness of others. Particularly as the desired effect isn't a given with intimates such as Lou, Paula, and Clara. 'Essentially, I am unlovable,' he might think. 'My mother knew that. The consolation is, I can remain staunchly unselfish in not being loved.* But maybe my poems love me as Keats promised. Certainly, I can be happy with them.'

Note (to myself): *so 'being loved' makes you 'selfish'? Yes, if it's unilateral and then it can become all about possession, possessiveness... But 'being loved' has been known to change people. 'Indulging the other' can be 'unselfish'.

What Happened to Rilke

In a letter to an admirer, Lili Schalk, the wife of an eminent Austrian conductor, Rilke expresses his disenchantment with Augustine:

> 'Petrarch upon his famous humanist epiphany on Mont Ventoux, opened his copy of *The Confessions* at random and came across the passage where he reproaches himself for being distracted from the state of his soul by the wonders of nature, the mountains rolling down to the mighty waves of the ocean, fed by the rivers and the stars above.'

•

Rumblings in Europe

As the decade advances, something larger than happiness and love (Lesser Ineffables) is looming in Europe. The Ottoman Empire is dismantling bloodily in the south and west. Fighting in the Baltic is destabilising the north. The Hapsburgs are losing their grip on the east... In sum, Rilke's world is falling apart. He and Kappus, with their Austro-Hungarian army credentials, would have been alert to the inevitability of a great war. It was a time to be bought out, or face the marching music, at least for Kappus. He chose duty.

Rilke, still under forty, could be called up. But as a poet in exile he feels immune, and he summers in Venice sitting at the feet of Eleanora Duse and winters in Spain. The year before the Great War broke out, he rather daringly travels in Germany and Austria, meeting Stefan Zweig, Kassner and other celebrated writers, including Freud through Lou. She panics at Rilke's latest book, *The Life of Mary,* a baker's dozen of poems on what it was like to be the Blessed Virgin, and lures him to a conference of theosophists which Sigmund is attending to follow up a case of religious mania. Rilke seemed perfectly normal to him (a minus in Sigmund's book). At least for a poet. Lou noted the mutual dislike of her two friends with interest. Could it be jealousy? Being an intelligent woman, she perishes the thought: Rilke merely wanted a friend, and Freud, a society disciple.

Stefan Zweig noted that in company, unlike his letters, Rilke was conspicuously word-shy, even in German, but 'his few utterances come in a ripple of clarity'. He has learned how to be listened to. The gushy obsequiousness that embarrassed Rodin (an achievement in itself) is in the past. Kassner commented, 'He doesn't hobnob with the famous.

Deference is as far as he goes.' In short, he keeps to himself while going through the motions, and this impresses more than being frightfully witty or wise.

Rilke's single-mindedness has hardened when his own higher purposes are not served. Even when meeting important writers, he effectively absents himself. Transformation as a poet is his sole ambition. The formidable prolixity with poems slows down. Paradoxically, his fateful visit to Duino Castle, when the boring business letter and high winds gives him the first line of the *Elegies*, results in the nearest thing in his life to drying up, the Mary book being his only one in this fallow period (1911–1914). It prompted a recent critic to claim that Rilke 'faked [religious] belief in order to get over writer's block'. He continues composing occasional poems out of habit, and thinks of publishing them under the title *Poems of the Dark Night* but thinks better of it. Like the *Mary* poems, they seem paltry to his ambitions.

As did Goethe's *Italian Journey*, which accompanied him to Venice. His reading moves from Hölderlin and the Bible, to Cervantes's *Don Quixote* and back to Dante, and on to Leopardi's 'L'Infinito': the eighteenth-century Italian romantic sitting on a hill is unable to see beyond the skyline, but can imagine eternal space... He stops to translate it with the help of Princess Marie and friends. Meanwhile, there is Proust's *Swann's Way* to read (and he is to become addicted to *À la recherche du temps perdu* as the volumes appear), and, above all, a mature re-reading of a youthful favourite, Adalbert Stifter, the Bohemian writer and artist (1805–1868),

'Stifter gives me strength to continue,' he writes to Lou Salomé. His psychological landscapes in fiction and paint, sacred to the Worpswede commune, offers him a sense of place in an uncertain world. It is a return to the Bohemia of his childhood. But Lou would have wondered if the Calamity Jane of mid-nineteenth-century Austrian literature could be a steadying influence. Everything Stilter touched turned to dust and ashes, except when he had a pen or a paint brush in his hand. Then he expressed his harmony with the natural world with exquisite ease, though not without a suspicion of storms on the horizon. His characters pursue moral beauty, the evils of life are in abeyance. But when the storm broke *in vivo*, his demons were unleashed and, taking to drink, he cut his own throat.

Rilke is in his late-thirties, and getting nowhere where he wants to be. Hitherto, he reckons, he was merely pawing the ground. Now he is reaching for the sky, but lacks the arm-span and foothold. Trying too hard is tripping him up and he's grasping at air. He feels his glory days of solitude should have reaped a harvest that permits him a comfortable life, loving the God, or gods, he doesn't believe in. But he isn't comfortable. He feels fate-less, foot-loose.

Kassner alerts him to the stories of a fellow German-language writer born in Prague, Franz Kafka, eight years his junior, and in later years he was to be more than generous in his praise, declaring that *The Castle* 'is the most important novel of our age'. There is no hint of rivalry towards a fellow 'Bohemian', rather complicity: they both write about 'a world that hadn't yet arrived' (Hannah Arendt). Not what is rumbling in Europe. But, still, war has often proved a blessing in disguise for men whose ambitions in life have been frustrated. In *The Notebooks* he had written about Charles the Bold, and other troubled figures redeemed by war. He had been trained for it. Maybe he would become the son his father so much wanted to make up for his own failure... Cornet Christoph Rilke, mark two.

Chapter Twenty-four

A Boring War and its Aftermath

•

A decade after Rilke wrote his eighth letter to Kappus on gender and the future of love, the lightning fell on the dust-dry fields of Europe, and Rilke, lacking proofs, found himself due to his reckless journeying stranded in Germany. Full of patriotic fervour, he composed five hymns to the God of War, and enthused to Kassner that it was for him 'an opening of the universal heart'. They were published in a national newspaper. Rilke came to regret it almost immediately. A few weeks later, he refused a reprint.

If his 'secret shame' was to make the unhappiness of others into tender art, he was in the right place. When the horror of a country at war hit home, his avowed 'reverence for life' is challenged and he wants 'Any Where Out of This World'. Moreover, travel abroad is *verboten*. He must remain a cog in the war machine. France is the enemy, so his Paris boats are burnt. There is no going back. Kassner arranges the auction of his belongings. They are so meagre; he has to pay outstanding debts out of his own pocket. The poet lived light.

Rilke writes to Lou, 'War is a sad, man-made complication,' and to Helene von Nostitz (who no longer loves him, so they are friends), 'A break in humanity from itself.' He tells Clara that he wants to run out in the street and shout *'C'est terrible.* Like Cezanne when the work got too much.' But instead goes to a Klee exhibition and decides it isn't a good time for abstract art. He tries to translate Michelangelo's sonnets and gives up to finish with a whimper his 'Exposed on the mountain of the heart' poem instead:

> ...He who was beginning to know is now silent,
> aware of the beasts roaming the foothills with intent,
> and the almighty bird circling the summit.
> Exposed, he is at risk on the mountain of the heart'.

Not knowing what to make of it all, Rilke made contact with the Gnostic philosophers Ludwig Klages and Alfred Schuler. Their *mythische Mensch* politicised Nietzsche's Superman by focusing on the *ultima Thule*, the spring-source of the Aryan race, and made it part of the Nazis' folk philosophy. Schuler, since his student days, was one of Rilke's 'immovably-centred' Heroes ('He is a mountain and I am just a wretched mole-heap'). Schuler had introduced him to the basic tenant of Gnosticism, that each man has within him a mystery to explore – the God in them – and on finding it is his own salvation. Exploring ancient burial practices together, their guiding principle is the Schopenhauerian tenant that death is just a blip and our essential being continues on reincarnating regardless.

However, it's Schuler's ideas on Orphic cult religions that grips and eventually releases Rilke to write *The Sonnets to Orpheus*. He acknowledged Schuler's influence on transforming him from the Apollinarian aplomb of the 'Thing-poems' to the Dionysian managed panic of his 'orphic unravelling of the Earth' (Mallarmé was on his table to translate). When Alfred died in 1923, Rilke put a bunch of narcissi on the altar of an abandoned country church near where he was born. 'A simple homage that returns him to the gods… Nobody properly understood Schuler except me.' Alas, Goebbels would beg to differ.

That Rilke's mid-life crisis with his poetry coincided with the Great War had silver linings. Firstly, though cut off from his patrons, his money-worries were relieved by a staggeringly generous anonymous donation by the Wittgenstein Foundation (10,000 crowns, the current equivalent of 60,000 euros), and a reissue of *The Lay of the Love and Death of Cornet Christoph Rilke* becoming a backpack success with soldiers. This risqué romantic tale of youth going to war in gentler times was to be his only truly popular success. I can hear 'riding, riding, riding through the day, through the night… Only when it is dark, do we sometimes think we know the way' reverberating down the line of trenches. The Wittgenstein windfall was something of a mystery. Subsequently it was revealed to have come at the bequest of Ludwig, the philosopher who liked 'the tone of Rilke's poems' but is said by friends to have found his later work 'trying'.

Note (to myself): Wittgenstein on the death of his hated father renounced his heritage and redistributed it amongst poets and artists rather than the poor ('it would only go to their heads like bad wine'). Apart from Rilke, Georg Trakl and Else Lasker-Schuler were recipients. Wittgenstein considered Trakl a 'man of genius' but they never met. On visiting him in a psychiatric hospital, he arrived too late. The poet had just committed suicide.

Else Lasker-Schuler's poetry, he remarked, had the 'odour of crime and the brothel'. Rilke if he lived long enough to read Wittgenstein's *Tractatus* would have been pleased by Ludwig's introductory caution that a work of philosophy is 'a poetic creation or nothing', echoing Kierkegaard. Wittgenstein went further than the Dane in claiming that the aesthetic and ethical stages of thought development are one and the same.

Rilke responded to the meaningless slaughter with a draft of what was to become his fourth *Duino* elegy. It's his most heart-felt lament for the human condition. Men are as puppets in the face of death's machinery. He goes back to childhood and his father's failure to realise that life is more than a game. But he goes further. Nijinsky's dance of death in Petrushka (Paris, 1911) could be the inspiration (Lou would have seen it), but the final result strongly resembles James Ensor's painting *Skeletons Fighting for the Body of a Hanged Man*. In Patrick Bridgwater's resume (*Duino Elegies*, Menard Press, 1999), 'The self-contained, timeless world of childhood is contrasted with the *Angst*-ridden, destructively self-conscious adult existence. But the main theme is a return to the existentialist vein of the diary section of *The Notebooks*, the nature of man's ordinary existence: the dividedness of man's mind and purpose which makes him, unlike the puppet, only half-play his part. Unable to forget himself, he is unable to surrender to the present (war), and to love, let alone attain to Schopenhauerian heroism in adversity.'

> Behold the dying.
> Ought they not sense how full of pretext
> is all we accomplished here?
> All things are other than themselves.

The rhetorical imperative is explained elsewhere. 'Pretext is the tyranny (in war) that imposes death as the aim of life.' Although hardly a humanist, Rilke is living through terrible times and it politicises him. He appeases a deep depression by reading Dostoyevsky's *The Brothers Karamazov*, and sympathises with Ivan who believed 'nothing, but nothing, could justify the tears of a child'. Years after the Great War, Rilke, with his own death very much on the horizon, in concluding the fourth elegy, rages against, 'the death each child carries with them into life. Murderers are easier to understand, but this; to harbour death, the whole of death, before life has begun, to see it thus, and not be angry, is impossible.' It wasn't Paula that he was thinking about but of her child, Tili, who survived. There is concern for humanity and, without irony, or Schopenhauer, he is raging against everybody's demise.

Note (to myself): Yeats would have been less 'annoyed' by it. But, yet and yet, as I read the 'Tenth Elegy', I wonder again if Rilke really believed in death other than as a passing disease. His Underworld is more like life disguised as a Halloween puppet-show. Elsewhere in his writings, not least his letters, he casts a doubt. Suffice to say, if 'inconsistency is the surest sign of virtue' (as my mother said, misquoting Rousseau), Rilke was its patron saint.

Rilke stops reading the newspapers and, head down, pushing his pen around to no great purpose, determined 'not to understand it', waits for the blood-lust to sate itself. And so, the violent depression over Europe becomes his. 'One can express one's own suffering, and its conquest, better than somebody else's, and that gives it an enduring meaning' (letter to Lou). Its obverse, suffering on behalf of others, had been given enduring meaning by Holderlin, for instance. But Rilke didn't commit himself into solitary confinement to write poems. His 'fateless gods' did not have an infant innocence. Writing a courtly love poem to an artist that he meets, Lou Albert-Lesard, it has the desired effect... and he wonders if he ought to have an 'affair'.

•

Human Relief

In 1915, to distract him, Lou had sent him her sex primer, *Three Letters to a Little Boy*. Rilke, in thanking her was reminded that around the time he wrote 'Orpheus, Eurydice, Hermes', they had shared an interest in the display of male pudenda in ancient sculptures and discovered an Egyptian phallic deity: 'You opined that the creation of the world was essentially an act of onanism.'

Note (to myself): it's difficult to put the myth behind this deity delicately: in short, Geb, the world-god, doesn't have an available mate. His female counterpart, the sky-goddess, Nut, is a cow squirting milk at the heavens to create the Milky Way. Geb in frustration is lying on his back and ejaculates the earth.

And so, Rilke comes out of his drought to write the seven poems celebrating the phallus. And sends them to his publisher and Kassner, who chortled in a letter to Kippenberg that Rainer Maria was 'sublimating something or other' and wondered if 'our friend has ever grown up'. In his posthumous memoir, Kassner was less skittish, saying Rilke was 'a sexual innocent like Kierkegaard' (a riposte perhaps to Rainer Maria calling Rudolf 'the spiritual child' of his unmarried Uncle Søren). Whatever, the last words of the *Duino Elegies*, celebrating the felicity of being astonished at the 'rise and fall of a happy thing', suggest a priapic meaning to some.

Kassner links the seven poems with some of the 'Thing-poems' ('The Swan', 'Flamingo', 'The Panther'), but does not mention possible phallic symbolism with the happy '*rise* and *fall*'. On the other hand, Bridgwater sees Rilke's phalli-centricity as a self-conscious device. Grief for the dead was the strongest emotion he ever knew, and it's often associated with unrequited love. In order to deal with love and death, he needed to construct something more universal than a particular relationship with himself and another. Bridgwater suggests that the last lines of the *Elegies* 'exults life and death, respectively, as a happy thing *rising*, and a happy thing that *falls*. As life must ultimately surrender itself to death.' In short, Rilke in representing it as an elated swoon that '*almost* bewilders us', is making the 'lived death' meet the real thing?

'Almost' is perplexing. Various translations qualify it (bewildered, astonished or overcome by). However, it is in such approximations that reason and poetry must make a pact. And tacit knowledge is necessary in order to take the ending as it comes. Although Bridgwater's case is as good as one can get to almost explaining the unexplainable, I remain perplexed but I must respect the poet's secret and it will in time reveal itself. After all, Rilke repeatedly told the young poet that with death, or writing a poem, or preparing for love, you are alone, and this triad come together in what for me is his greatest poem, the 'Requiem for a Friend'. He doesn't say you're on your own with love, only that you must make yourself ready for it, gently working on moulding of yourself until you become a world in yourself for the loved one's sake. Then, if you get the world right, it can be shared. In preparing for Paula, he got it wrong in this life, and he aspires to make up for it in death by composing a poem that her presence pervades and that makes himself eternally felt.

Nevertheless, with the phallic poems, Joab is not alone in intimating onanism. Herbert Gunter in his essay 'Misunderstandings around the Glory of Rilke' (1952), says 'most of his love poems are to himself. That's how he sublimates love.' Kassner says more or less the same for his poems in praise of the phallus. The café gossip in Paris about his friendship with Rilke was that Rudolf was in love with him, and that it only lasted because Rainer Maria didn't notice. However, he would have noted the frequency with which 'lovers' as 'us' and 'we' are sensually evoked elsewhere in the *Duino Elegies*. Joab concludes with a rare smile, 'Kassner, scorned, got it right, as Rilke sublimates sex with another, he is sublimating sex with himself. 'Ironic logic is triumphant.

Note (to myself): I confess the phallic poems made me blush for Rilke, and I won't embarrass myself or him by quoting from them. But if at destitute times they served like Oliver North's Fawn Hall as 'an item of human relief', I don't tut-tut him. However, Fawn Hall was North's document shredder. Perhaps Rilke needed one.

•

Blessed Release

Although it was twenty-five years since he had been at military school, he is called up (November 1915). But it is evident after three weeks drilling that he isn't physically up it. Due to the intervention of Zweig and Hugo von Hofmannsthal, he is relocated to administration in Vienna, recording causalities. Not surprisingly given his job, Rilke looks closely at the distribution of casualties and notes the class inequities. It was the peasants and proles laying down their lives, not the nobs and the educated. Lou and his regular correspondents thought he had gone socialist. *Au contraire*, the familial blood was up. He had wanted an officer rather than office posting, and to see action to show what a Cornet Rilke could do.

Maurice Ravel had a similar fate in attempting to fight for his country. They were the same age and the composer, because of his height (five foot) and light weight, presented himself as ideal for the air-force but was rejected and, though exempted from service, persisted and was mobilised as a lorry driver. His blue helmet couldn't be seen behind the wheel of the enormous military truck as he drove down the Champs-Elysees. There was some glory in that. Poor Rilke, who was some inches taller and less skinny, is reduced to fiddling his thumbs on a high stool thinking bitterly of his heroic ancestors.

At least he is in Vienna and can meet up with Zweig and Kraus. Kassner introduces him to expressionist artists Oscar Kokoschka and Lou Albert-Lasard; the latter paints a portrait of Rilke looking his best. Kassner had influential contacts in high places who, on being made aware of the great poet's menial situation, intervened. Rilke was discharged from the army (summer 1916). The nature of Rilke's friendship with Kassner was ambiguous to others, particularly Lou. In a letter, he confided to her that, 'Rudolf is the only man with whom I can get anywhere, and perhaps best so, the only one with whom it occurs to me to make a little use of the feminine in me.' Rilke certainly noticed something. But if Rilke was the love of Kassner's life, he kept it to himself, and acted like a true friend.

When demobilised in the summer of 1916, Rilke moves in with Lou Albert-Lasard. But she declares love on him, and he moves to Munich. There, the endgame of the Great War catches up with him and he is to lose all faith in the future of mankind. 'A monstrous tumour of hate is growing everywhere… The return to barbarism with the surge of slaughter has excited the masses, and ruthless generals are the heroes… Subterranean trench warfare, submarines at sea… The leaders going underground too, fearing assassination by their own, but won't parley a proper peace. Unlike in ancient times, when great tribulations had the power to purify man in order to face the gods, now there are only killing machines in this abattoir for young men. The only counter faces are widows and orphans, and they have less power than worms.'

•

A Happy Thing

As the war comes to a tumultuous end with riots and revolutions (Lenin's in Russia particularly distressed him), it is all too much for Rilke: 'A new beginning. Nothing new to me. I've always felt like a beginner.' In 1919 he fled to Italy to recuperate in the cafés of Trieste while staying in Duino Castle with Princess Marie.

There he writes his *Letter from a Young Worker*. This fictional letter strikes out with a bracing note of realism, 'Here is the angel, who does not exist, and the devil, who doesn't exist; and man, who does exist, makes their unreality more real to me', and ends up as a tract on the failure of Christianity and the success of his own poems in helping a young worker to realise why. This Kierkegaardian pastiche, unpublished in Rilke's lifetime, is difficult to read with a straight face. However, it is evidence that the Great War politicised him sufficiently to make a statement on the redemptive powers of poetry, and how these Christians hate one another.

Despite his loss of faith in the future, far from despairing of his work, he experienced a rush to the brain that produced his most prolific period since his pre-modernist youth. The first symptoms of leukaemia appeared when in Munich. And it could be said to be a blessing in disguise. Subclinical suffering proved a more faithful muse than even travel, and when they went together, he was up and away. He is to embark on another lecture tour while working on the fifty-odd sonnets for the Orpheus sequence. However, the *Duino Elegies* had stalled after the fourth one ('Murderers are easier to understand…'). But four years ago, before his call-up, Hertha Konig, his Viennese patroness, had lent him an apartment and furnished it with a painting by Picasso, *The Acrobats*, which, according to Bridgwater, gives him 'a first stab at the fifth elegy'. It inspired him to move on from men 'as puppets of war' to a flying circus, thus redeeming Death from Gauguin's Grim Reaper. 'Madame Lamort' is the motherly ring-mistress.

The fifth elegy was the last to get finished ('in a hurricane of the spirit', circa 1921). Rilke posits death as the reverse side of life, without which our existence would be meaningless and incomplete. His current reading probably played a part. When asked about his philosophy During a rare interview to the press two years later, Schopenhauer was the only name mentioned. Strangely, Kierkegaard and Rilke were revisiting the same philosopher in their dying years.

The *Duino Elegies* and *The Sonnets to Orpheus* were not to appear until five years after the armistice in 1922, three years before his death. They divide readers into two exclusive categories. Those who prefer Brecht to Rilke and vice versa and ne'er the twain meet. In his New Year Letter (1940), W. H. Auden mocked Rilke's emergence from his speleological excavations in the eighth elegy to happily identify with a gnat ('o *Gluke der Mucke*'), who 'leaps within the womb even on its wedding day'. (Had Auden a crystal ball and seen into Himmler's proposed plan in 1944 to punish SS officers slack on pest control by putting them in a cell infested with insects, he might have wanted to add another stanza).

His writerly revival, in effect, put paid to his political distress. Gone is the Dehmel-style outrage. He had no patience with poets as 'unacknowledged legislators' ('Making a public spectacle of yourself only leads to political dilettantism'). Still, the cannon-fodder of the last of the old wars, and the hovering fighter planes of new ones to come, encouraged reformist tendencies, and, to his non-aristocrat correspondents' amusement no doubt, Rilke wasn't immune. Radical change was in the air, but his idea of revolution, like his quasi-feminist theory of universal love, was at base conservative, with inbuilt procrastination (it could be indefinitely put off).

The 'November Revolution' (1918), which replaced the Kaiser with the Weimar Republic, met with his favour and he wrote animated letters to friends, saying it was 'about overcoming fraudulent conditions in favour of the deepest traditions'. This would hardly endear him to either side if repeated publicly. When some months later the revolt is brutally crushed by right-winger forces, and the government in Berlin supports them, he finally turns his back on Germany (and France where his welcome is still uncertain). Disgust neuters his vestigial politics and, when invited to lecture in Switzerland, he doesn't return. Zurich, with its prospering cache of artistic refugees, seemed to him 'the most cosmopolitan place in Europe'. Dada is in its dizzy pomp there, making sense of nonsense, and nonsense of sense, and, though interested in passing, he heads for the mountains where well-off admirers would welcome him in their chalets. There his reunion with his last 'special' friend 'Merline' Klossowska lifts his depression and, now back writing poems by the *vrac*, he has another go at translating Mallarmé.

Rilke's Swiss retreat in Valais sees him to the end of his life. Baladine helped him to find a rundown castle in the Rhone Valley and made it habitable for him. Castle Muzot was to be the first and last home of his own (he likened it to 'a large animal' and took to 'stroking its walls'). Despite his wartime bestseller and the Wittgenstein bequest, it wasn't paid for out of his pocket. Werner Reinhart, a patron of the arts, owned the castle and, to honour German poetry, lent it to Rilke rent-free.

Falling back on rich patrons was by now second nature to him, and making them worry on his behalf a subsidiary talent. Rilke, to her alarm, keeps 'Merline' at a distance and writes the self-lacerating 'The Testament' expressing regret at the incompatibility between the life of a pure poet and reciprocating love. Depression has been replaced by a reasonable fear that the state of his health won't permit him finish his Great Work, and a paranoiac insecurity. When he throws doubt on the safety of even Switzerland in an unsettled Europe, Princess Marie's husband, who does business with US Postal, offers to arrange Rilke's safe-conduct to America. But he demurs, stubbornly reiterating that the entire Anglophone world is of no interest to him.

Chapter Twenty-Five

What's Wrong with America?

•

Rilke's blithe indifference to America (and England more aggressively) could be attributed to his resistance to learning English ('The most foreign of languages to me'). His bias is not particularly well-informed ('Their machines don't have silencers'). The main gripes are 'the absence of wine and nightingales... Americans have the souls of shopkeepers, and are as dead as mutton to the life of the mind... Due to mass-production, they lack the "Laric value", and therefore have no house-hold gods... Everything is ersatz, mere dummies of the handmade things that we (Europeans) have inherited from our forefathers and take for granted...That is, the lived and living objects *that share our thoughts*. We are perhaps the last to have known such things.'

Such views were expressed in letters ranging from the late 1890s to 1925. He only updates them with phrases like 'frightful Americans', and hearing the English in a posh hotel in Italy say 'lovely' and 'charming', he comments how the words lack 'inner warmth'. In his extensive travels, Rilke never visited English-speaking countries, let alone America, where his popularity from the 1930s has been arguably greater than in Germany. Since it's largely based on translation, it's hard to say which Rilke is taking the laurels. Writers as unlike one another as Wallace Stevens, Hemingway and Clifford Odets are only the pinnacle of the pyramid. And yet the second-generation German-English poet and translator, Michael Hofmann, can say, 'Rilke is the poet in whom the German language's persuasions, abstracts and music are most triumphantly effective.' If he fills a gap in Anglo-American poetry, it can't be this.

Charles Bukowski, another second-generation German, read him as a young man, and 'the honey-ness cheered me up for a while. Then it was just like mathematics or religion: it ran right off me. What I needed seemed to be absent everywhere.' It was left to Robert Duncan to be the John the Baptist for the Americanised Rilke. His neo-Romantically inspired baroque afflatus prepared the ground. Although a fellow-traveller with Black Mountain and the Objectivists, he saw poetry 'as the soul's search for fulfilment in life' through 'the primary instinctual authority of the imagination'. This quest was open 'to compose... a symposium of the whole, a totality, including all the old orders... All that has been outcast and vagabond in our consideration of the figure of Man must be returned to and admitted into the creation of what we are.' Duncan's penchant for overreaching himself has a panacea that sometimes is irresistible:

> Come let me free myself from all that I love.
> Let me free what I love from me, let it go free...
> For I stand in the way, my destiny stands in the way.

And the next step upwards can only be Rilke. Duncan didn't see him as an 'immovably-centred poet hero', but the next best thing, the torso of Apollo that Rilke celebrates in the 'Thing-poem', 'Archaic':

> No great head, eyes that grow, or bulging groin.
> More a chandelier whose light contains him,
> and his look. The obvious traits are not missed
> for otherwise, his proud breast wouldn't blind you,
> his gentle turning loins would make you smile...
> He'd be a shoulder shrug, mere stone deformed,
> that couldn't shimmer like a wild beast's skin,
> and between ribs spark stars, so you can't hide
> from his heaving chest, 'You must change your life.

The torso of Apollo is cajoling his half-brother Dionysius, and not humans. Yet the much-quoted final clause has become the touchstone of the cult of Rilke in America. He not only continues to influence young poet aspirants into turning the inner-self inside out and enjoying the contortions, but has become a life-change guru on social media. *The Letters* are avidly read. But the cult has been vulgarised into a brand. 'Rilke is the most popular German literary export since Goethe,' is repeatedly said by people who haven't read Goethe, but know the name. Karen Leeder, the cultural critic, says, 'Rilke has been reinvented as a high priest of narcissism, and taken his place along workout videos and gourmet cook books.' This has exploded exponentially, and includes self-help manuals, most bizarrely in the form of guides to love and its fulfilment. Given his less-than-exemplary sentimental life, and confused and confusing sexuality, this is stretching the snapped. At the turn of the millennium there even was a bestseller video on 'the joys and pains' of Rilke's love life. Such exploitation tends to come from fortune cookies mistranslated from the poems and his advice to the young poet on solitude and 'spiritual presences'. Leeder notes the irony of Rilke's poetry serving the mass-production machine of American capitalism that he so despised.

Rilke was also exploited by the Nazis in the 1930s, although he was neither a Nationalist or Socialist by a long stretch. His high jacking by the Third Reich distorted his poetry to suit their quasi-spiritual folksy purposes. True, some of his ideas, derived from Lou's second-best friend, Nietzsche, and Alfred Schuler, the Gnostic, open themselves to misunderstanding, but his name association with the Nazism unjustly damaged his post-war reputation in Germany, at least.

Hannah Arendt, after her youthful běguin with Rilke's poetry, put a further dampener on his European reputation. She placed him in 'the empty space' between the 'no longer' and the 'not yet' in a present dispossessed by the Great War. Proust represented the 'no longer' with his 'farewell' to the nineteenth century, and Kafka the 'not yet' with writings on a world that hadn't quite arrived. However, it was Hermann Broch whom she chose to bridge the temporal gap between the past and the future, a name that scarcely rings bells in America despite his emigrating there.

Rilke, for Arendt, was pre-Proust. In her youthful monograph, 'Rilke's *Duino Elegies*' (1930), she wrote that that he was bent on 'redeeming a past since destabilised by its abandonment by God. Rather than reverting to nostalgia or losing faith, he sought to experience the absence, suspended in mid-air, neither at home in the world nor with a means to enter it. His equilibrium could be sustained by expressing his despair in elegies which not so much lament the loss of communion with his Creator, but loss itself'. Arendt calls this *positive* nihilism and sees it as 'the last resort of religiousness'.

In later years Arendt can still engage with the timeless felicities of the *Duino Elegies* (what Heidegger called world-inner-space), but not with the historical no man's land inhabited by representative figures such as Madame Lamort and the Order of the Angels. So, she turns to Hermann Broch, who concerned himself with the claims of human compassion in bridging the gulf between the generation lost to war and the generation that needs to start anew.

Arendt saw Bertolt Brecht as the poet who solved 'the problem of compassion' for the 'lost generation'. 'He never collapsed the distance, established as a young poet, between himself and "Poor BB", and thereby avoided the slide into 'self-pity and private bitterness', or worse (Gottfried Benn, Celine and her beloved teacher, Heidegger). Brecht, she opined, was able through 'the pathos of self-distance' to evade propaganda in his poetry (though it's close) and, in his best work, humanised doctrinaire politics. For example, 'the defeated' of the past are not to be lost to memory, but exist as examples upon which to build the future. A proper understanding of what went wrong is registered, and the compassion is practical rather than emotional. In the 'Ballad of the Waterwheel', the neo-angel is in the detail:

> The waterwheel keeps on turning.
> Things come and go. You know the deal.
> Below the water keeps on churning.
> Its only task to drive the wheel....
>
> But when the wheel's smashed to smithers,
> the stream, not wanted anymore,
> can gaily re-join the river,
> freed at last from the load it bore.

Up the revolution!

Note (to myself): Brecht was too young to fight in the Great War, but made enemies all of his own. Most notably Carl Schmitt, the renegade philosopher who declared Hegel dead and joined the Nazi Party: 'Poor BB, a great man for the big occasion, is selling cut-price tickets for his latest play to the workers on the barricades. When the cavalry police charge, by shocking good luck he gets knocked down and killed and becomes the next Rosa Luxemburg. A hero of the Revolution. His epitaph will be: there at the right place and right time. However, as his memory becomes a lucrative business, and brings in enough money to support his widows and orphans, revisionist historians will say BB's salient characteristic was an ability to turn everything to his own advantage, even his death.' It wasn't something Brecht did with his poetry, except perhaps the sonnets he wrote to appease offended lady-friends (it didn't work).

Rilke was not of the 'lost generation'. He was thirty-nine when the Great War broke out and hadn't a youth to lose. Still, lacking a concrete historical basis, Arendt didn't apply the Brecht argument to him. But Rilke would never have accepted the difference between the poet Hero and the Rainer Maria who filed his fingernails. He kept himself to himself, and put compassion for people and things into a world closer to Kafka's 'not yet' than the present age, and left the poetry speak for itself, for better or worse.

It was for the better to Delmore Schwartz, who, according to John Berryman on his late, demented poet-friend, was reconciled with Socrates by reading Rilke. And for the worse to Berryman:

> Rilke was a jerk.
> I admit his griefs and music
> & titled spelled all-disappointed ladies
> A threshold worse than the circle
> Where the vile settle and lurk,
> Rilke's. As I said.

(*Dream Songs*, song 3, 'A stimulant for an old beast')

The rock singer, 'La Patti Smith', backed the wrong poet. I was in Florence in the late 1970s, and one torrid July evening I heard her boom out Rilke's opening line of the *Duino Elegies*: 'Twist and shout, but who will hear me up there'. Next day, the newspaper headings were dominated by three English words, 'The Generation Gap', and the editorial of *Il Giorno* lamented their beautiful young *fanciulla*'s abandonment of pizzo (lace) for denim. Reports of syringes scattered all over the dusty parks were not exaggerated. But who could doubt the 'Sincerity' of La Patti? Although, getting to 'the bottom of it' is something I believe the more 'high-minded' Rockers, like U2's Bono, are 'still in the process of clarification'. However, she moved on and 'found' Rimbaud, the first hippie genius, turned businessman.

Her last word on Rilke was that he was a loser. This is better than calling him a jerk. Though he wouldn't have taken offence. Losing for him was a form of winning. Something I can share in theory. For example, losing your sight means you can't lose yourself in books, and you can still see what you hear; losing your way is often more interesting. You discover things and places you otherwise wouldn't come across; losing a ball in the rough is to find a flower; losing your life isn't the end of the world; lost at sea like Shelley would have its appeal for a poet. In life we are too landlocked. Death is a floating off into the seven seas. Readers may be at sea in his work but they are lost in order to find themselves…

'You've been reading too much Rilke,' sighs Joab.

'No, I've been reading Bruce Springsteen's autobiography, in which he bemoans adulation taking the place of love in his life. Wanting to be loved by his fans is a bottomless pit. He took to reading Rilke's *Letters* and wrote, "I'm working to turn the ghosts that haunt me into ancestors. I want to be an ancestor".'

'Ah! *The Tunnel of Love*. "You've got to live with what you can't rise above." "Christ in Hell" would have done him good.'

'No. Can't you see he's offering himself a *repetition forward*?'

Chapter Twenty-Six

Rilke: The Inimitable Poet?

•

Imitations and Transgressions

Samuel Johnson might be shyly invoked in support of Rilke's realisation of poems. Although it might not do him any favours as he had a dud ear, preferring plodding Dryden to the metaphysical flightiness of Donne, Marvell and Herbert. Johnson claimed that the true poets 'imitate nature and life, paint the forms of matter, and represent the operation of the intellect.' That definition could be lightly applied to Rilke, ever so lightly. For instance, in 'The Panther', he inscapes into a caged beast, imitating its action as it's poised to have a thought. Or in 'Parting' he replicates what it's like to be a plumtree whose branch springs-back as a cuckoo takes its leave in hurried flight... Or in 'Blind Man: Paris' he is the whites of unseeing eyes on which the town reflects itself, and 'the frisson' of emotion is a flutter of lids. This, of course, owes something to Nietzsche's reversal.

But I would dub him an inimitable 'imitator', abiding more than most poets to Seneca's truism that a writer is 'a bee that gathers pollen from many flowers'..

Yet, as Herbert Gunther noted in his essay, 'Rilke is one of the poets most imitated by would-be poets, the unmerited destiny of appreciation. The subject matter, for instance the torments, imaginary and real, that he gives to Malte in *The Notebooks* are not absent from his poems, they are what attract incipient poets, not the writing itself.' I would add that bad imitations of Rilke are easy (*close your eyes and say the first thing that comes into your mind). He knew that himself. *Felt* thoughts are easy to fake. As his letters mulling over work in progress show, he laboured as self-consciously on his poems as Coleridge, who wrote pages of notes on even the shortest to clarify his intentions.

Note (to myself): *his reply to Ellen Key on where he stood with immortality, 'Nothing that is real can pass away. But many people are not real,' should give you a start.

However, Herbert's contention that the cult of Rilke in Germany was founded on 'the sum of misunderstandings that gather around a name' (quoting Rainer Maria) should be modified by removing the 'mis'. Willed intentions are not sacred. Poems can mean more than one thing, and Rilke's are a well-laid tabula rasa. Readers can make what they will of what the young Joab dubbed 'metaphysical puns in a hall of mirrors' (*Museletter*, 1972). Poet-translators, having a hidden agenda (to make the poem their own), can be Jules Renard's criminal types, not just substituting one language for another, but one poem for another, an infraction because it's not a misunderstanding but deliberate. The list is long amongst anglophone poet-translators. Robert Lowell is the 'master criminal'.

Then again, Rilke knew the risk of (mis)understandings, knowing that even original poems are approximations (that stand in for what is beyond words).

•

Approximations

Early in *The Notebooks*, Malte sits in the Public Library reading about poets' deaths. He buries himself in a monograph on Felix Arvers, the nineteenth-century poet (whose poem, *L'Amour caché*, about not being understood by women, every French schoolboy knows).

'Felix Arvers was dying in hospital. Nobody suspected it except himself. The nurses busied themselves noisily sorting out other patients. The nun in charge, an ignorant country woman, was writing instructions for the cleaners using Felix's bed as a writing-pad. Felix saw the word '*corridor*' was misspelled as '*collidor*'. He raised himself up and corrected it. The effort killed him.'

Malte sees Felix Arvers's pedantry as the mark of a pure poet, faithful to the word to the end. 'Approximations are the enemy of poetry. Felix thought and simply couldn't have his last impression on earth collide with a misnomer. The *mot juste* was more important to him than life itself.

And the intervention wasn't self-serving, like John of God's 'last good deed'. On his deathbed, sighting a man about to hang himself from an apple tree in the garden, John of God dragged himself up and cut him down. Saving a sinner from death and damnation might seem to be a righteous way to end your life. But John was plunged into doubt about his action. What right had he to judge someone else's behaviour when his own was in the balance? Was he acting on ethical grounds, or a superstition that this coincidence would somehow reflect poorly on his own demise and prejudice his chances of eternal salvation? So, a martyr to ratiocination, John, plagued with doubts, dropped dead.

The devil's advocate saw it as the natural reflex of a trained soldier converted by God to pacifism, and he was made a saint. While Felix Arvers, his dignity as a poet restored, passed away peacefully and is forgotten, apart from *L'Amour caché*, the sonnet which ought to ring a bell for every divorced Frenchman.

Note (to myself): Welsh says that in France 'they change wives like dogs. The only difference is the dog is dead'.

Felix Arvers was a martyr to his art, and John of God merely to saving lives. Malte feels a holy joy envelope his being. Just reading about Arvers makes him a relic, though second-class. He asks himself, what aspiring young poet will be touched by touching his remains? And then remembers *Life-songs*, a pamphlet of poems he had published several years ago. The librarian searches through the index files and even descends to the reserve stock, before concluding sardonically that if it ever existed it would have been archived.

Malte remembers the poetry of their creation: burning the midnight oil on his school holidays in Jutland, inspired by stars falling from the heavens; convinced of his own genius, the rage for expression that make him oblivious of time and tide; the night sky stopped turning and bowed to him. Then he remembers the pride of thumbing the pages of the chapbook, and wants to forget the deadly silence of those he gave copies to. It is possible nobody had read his poems, except himself.

Malte wishes that he was as dead as his poems, but despair tells him it isn't in his gift. Since they hadn't an existence in the minds of others, his death wouldn't be a Romantic loss like Chatterton's. Though the marvellous boy and he had something in common. Chatterton pretended to be a medieval monk, and he pretends to be himself. But he is more himself now. The pretence is wearing off. Malte escapes the library like a dragonfly in a whirlwind: 'I'm not dead yet. It's not too late to be true to myself.' Out in the street he sees the pedestrians 'worming along the street, seemingly harmless caterpillars who will penetrate the bark of trees to rot the bole, or leach-leech like parasites who get under the skin of dogs, maddening them. Must bite someone. Yap, Yap.'

Malte is having the kind of manic release that is normal amongst aspirant young poets: wallowing in the gutter, ranting approximations. It could be fixed on the side of the road with a jump-start. Or a *petite gloire*: the electrical current of, say, a poem in a church newsletter about poor John of God will recharge his verbal batteries, and he is humming again, mounting the metaphors, cracking the rhymes, an exception to the rule, not concerned with knowing left from right, and right from wrong. In sum, akin to Rilke's 'Blind Man. Paris', 'interrupting the traffic like a black crack running through a china cup'.

Malte, akin to the 'Blind Man', only needs the whites of his eyes to register 'little waves of feeling which are his oasis, and a mirage for anybody else who happens to notice'. What he sees in himself is reflected in bystanders awe-struck by his festive, reckless air. 'If asked for my latest couplet, I'd scribble a few lines that would make me remembered forever.' A young poet may dream, but waking up to the dirty dawn of cold reality is the price. The crack in the teacup merely means that he'll have to buy a new one.

Note (to myself): I confess my transcription has transgressed 'trespass vision' by bringing another author into the text. I couldn't resist drawing from Raymond Queneau's *La Petite Gloire* (written in the 1930s, published posthumously in 1979), a parody of Malte, or perhaps a corrective, by an ever-playful novelist. Had Rilke lived he might well have borrowed from it for a new edition.

•

Absolutes

Louis Guillaume ('R. M. Rilke and Max Jacob', 1952) says, 'All writing is an approximation and the pure poem is impossible. Valéry, the most exacting of poets, said that all poems are essentially abandoned. Only the poet knows the point when his intention is past saving. It is the sum of these failures that nourishes the creative anguish that true poets have to live with.'

In short, the poet is carrying an embryo which is most likely to be stillborn, but if it sees the light of day, the poem must be left to fend for itself. Others will make of it what they will. For most readers it's all or nothing. The unfinished work is usually given only one chance. While the poet, one who dedicates his life to poetry, nothing is all: he starts again from it, aware that all he can truly accept is the judgement of posterity and he won't be there to share in it.

This bleak picture is hardly likely to ease the poet's creative anguish. And he may decide 'all my life what I thought was poetry may turn out to be a waste of space on a page'. No wonder so many poets turn to prose, and relinquish the 'pure' poet moniker. If only briefly for Rilke with his novel (the fables are essentially prose poems). Abhorring criticism and art appreciation, he turned to letters which for the most part were footnotes or recitatives to composing poems. In *Letters to a Young Poet* he went further in foraging for his poetry-to-be. In sum, Rilke was loyal to the poem no matter what other forms beckoned. No greater love, and pain.

Max Jacob responded to a young poet seeking his advice, 'I can't open the doors that I design, because the doors exist beyond me… Maybe you can do better.' There is no false modesty in the Rilke of *The Letters*. A superior spirit of humility prevails. It's not a question of the Kappus 'doing better' but Rilke himself. He is preparing the ground for his own future. The irony of this would not have escaped the young poet, hoping for help with his work. But he would be relieved at the tables being turned. 'Could do better' was a school-report put-down. And he could even bask in the feeling that, one way or other, they were both in this together.

Rilke was less closeted than Jacob with his working aesthetic and work conditions. Although he believed in closed doors to exclude interruptions, be they domestic or the banal business of making a living, he always had a window, preferably a skylight, thrown open for the 'spiritual presences' to fly in. Indeed, three years after the last letter, when the voice in the wind proclaimed, 'Who would hear me…if I cried out', it was their benediction and The *Duino Elegies* took wing. It proved to be a long flight. Still, although waylaid and led astray by the Great War, he arrived at his destination in the end, fuelled by relentless industry and saintly patience. His homecoming, like Ulysses', wasn't all roses. *The*

Rilke: The Inimitable Poet?

Sonnets for Orpheus kept him human and the *Elegies* in 'the hurricane wrote themselves', leaving him exhausted ('Every fibre in me, every tissue, cracked'). His inner and outer wars with body and soul collide in the late poem 'Christ in Hell'. It is to be a last wave to spiritual suffering, before physical pain finally took over.

Kappus's preface to *The Letters* has a sweet wistfulness. As a young poet he had been taken aback that the great Rilke thought he could do better. But with the years he came to appreciate the letters as an object lesson 'for anyone engaging in growth and change'. Opening up horizons has its hazards, but keeping your feet on the ground prevents accidents, and Rilke's insights into the practical aspects of work, like securing peace and quiet, made great good sense to Kappus. But he had to confess that the altitude of Rilke's roving ideas made him feel breathless. 'Rilke was going beyond German idealism into the outer space of absolutes, a place my own poems didn't have the oxygen for, and, instead of reaching out, they reach in. I'm stuck in a German groove, somewhere between Stefan George's grace and Richard Dehmel's disgrace'. And so, having had enough of morbid introspection without finding the words to 'give praise', he completed his military training, and became a friend of poetry rather than a poet.

But Kappus was wrong about absolutes. Rilke lacked them despite himself. He was not a mystic, preferring 'the noise of words' (Thomas a Kempis) to going beyond them, and less an intellectual than an opportunist of ideas. If he had lived to hear about Einstein's theory of relativity, his mind would have gone into a roundabout! The unkind critic who accused him of faking belief in supernatural things to get over writer's block missed the point. Belief for Rilke was a poetical kind of knowing: 'Any more than life, God and death are not just ideas. They were from the beginning of time part and parcel of nature. If a tree blossoms, death blossoms in it.'

'What Rilke couldn't understand,' said Robert Graves, led him to deploy 'supra-logical thought-processes'. Yet Rilke, echoing Nietzsche's 'the world is only justified as an aesthetic phenomenon', is perfectly rational with his dictate (which I repeat again as it's his aesthetic in a nutshell): 'Happy are those who know behind all language there stands that which is beyond words'. This clear expression of a belief becomes ambiguous, however, when considering its practical application for a poet. Not least because it was inscribed on a complimentary copy of the *Duino Elegies* in 1924, the twilight of his career. Rimbaud may have taken early retirement. But not Rilke, even though he had completed his Great Work. The question has to be asked whether this is a new ambition or, rather resigned acknowledgment that words would always be a receding wave.

Like Kierkegaard, Rilke had the Great Ineffables (death, God, (im)mortality) in his sights. But while their unreachability was the tragedy of the human condition for the Dane, for Rilke it was a challenge. Kierkegaard came to hope that poetry might break the impasse, but when words did not obey his call, he subsided into a 'quiet despair'. Rilke took a quasi-mystical route. He told Kappus that as a child he understood God but had lost the knowledge when he grew up. He hoped poems would be a Kierkegaardian *repetition forward* of his childhood conviction, and outreached himself by creating figurations, mounting metaphors on metaphors, melding metonyms with similes. But these were less *felt* thoughts than streams of *self*-consciousness, and they did not arrive at an absolute. Far from leading to 'a sickness unto death', like Kierkegaard, it left a vacuum that imploded happily enough, allowing in 'relatives', namely the Lesser Ineffables (love, happiness, sorrow, and pain). The last *Duino* elegy is the apotheosis of this tendency. The *felt* thoughts became less forced. In living (with) them, he was not grasping at straws but at the unique inner beauty of things. Abstract speculations on 'the meaning of life' could be put aside. The particular became the seed-bed of his mature work, from the objectivism of the 'thing-poems' to the symbolic expressionism of the *Duino Elegies*, with the *The Sonnets to Orpheus* somewhere in between. 'The rose does not ask' (Angelus Silesius) was to be his swan song.

In the long run, it was Cézanne rather than Rodin who his true maître. Like him, he developed a rage for solitary work in his late twenties, a lifelong quest to attain *La Réalisation*. That is, the exaltation of things that he was in touch with until they became imperishable in order to represent the world in all its beauteous splendour. Rilke went further, seeking through *felt* thoughts to put in words and associate images, not only what it is to be alive, but to be dead. In effect, he was a pure poet in the sense that Malte recognised in Felix Arvers: 'Faithful to the word to the end'. But couldn't avoid approximations. Particularly when it came to the Great Ineffables where metaphorical or symbolic tropes are all we have got. The Lesser Ineffables at least have experience and visible support to narrow the gap between absolutes and relatives.

As for the man, Rainer Maria, he was like no other, and defies judgement by the Blue Laws of Connecticut or any conventional moral standards. Marina Tsvetayeva got close to the bottom of his Sincerity in her famous response to Pasternak's 'Rilke's (early) death is not in the natural order': 'No. It was his life that was not in the natural order.' It is easy to agree, but to what? Napoleon remarked, 'everything that is unnatural is imperfect'; and since the Fall (or the vagaries of evolution), we have been in conflict with our nature. Human imperfection is the norm. However, Napoleon added, 'except Aventurine glass'. And, indeed, we are all seen through a glass darkly, beautiful but opaque…I raise a less than perfect glass to Rilke, and will drink from it with a clink to Spinoza's 'perfection is reality. Reality is imperfect. The imperfect is the summit.'

.

Chapter Twenty-Seven

The Author with a Glass in his Hand

•

Spinoza Out of Control

If only Rilke could have read Roland Barthes's *Le Grain de la Void* (1985), the *Duino Elegies* wouldn't have taken half his adult life to complete. He would have felt justified in giving himself fully to the light and airy naturalism of Adalbert Stifter. As it was, he was burdening himself with the wash from the 'magical idealism' of Novalis, the emotional extremism of *Sturm und Drang*, and, unavoidably, Goethe's 'joyous and trusting fatalism' (Nietzsche's phrase for his faith in that only the whole can justify the parts). No wonder he had a writer's-block.

A Stifter eagle could have been a triumphant ascension on the wing, and not a tortuous crawl back on all-fours after a depressing Great War. Roland Barthes, on the back of Merleau-Ponty, floats the body as the 'nature's instrument of desire' with 'a mind of its own capable of becoming the vessel that unifies everything."

Stifter pipped Merleau-Ponty (and Barthes) by almost a century in maintaining that when the body leads the mind to create art (rather than the other way around), something new can be made that overrides the obvious. Barthes says the same, only more viscerally: 'The bodily desire to create brings to the surface a natural substratum that provides a solid base for the ever-changing socio-cultural resources the mind depends upon for abstract thought.' Rilke could have sung with that, looking to the subsoil for his seed-bed rather than the sky for 'spiritual presences'. His championing of Jacobsen for Kappus was a Stifter substitute, and a poor one that lead nowhere except back to ritual solitude with its self-imposed strictures. He found himself crying out to the temperamental 'Order of the Angels' to hear him out. However, in his final poems, when he was released from the *Duino Elegies*, his childhood love of Stifter resurfaced, and his body, though racked with suffering, led the mind.

Note (to myself): Barthes even raised the possibility of establishing 'a corporal common denominator for the creative urge'. But two years later in *Roland Barthes par Roland Barthes*, Barthes rejected his own thesis as it 'encourages the avant garde to initiate its own mystifications… "Body" is a "mana-word", ardent, complex, ineffable, and somehow sacred, and thereby gives the illusion of holding the answer to everything.' Barthes, with his chameleon capriciousness, was not shy to embrace what my mother dubbed 'the eighth virtue', and changed his mind, sometimes in mid-discourse. Maybe it was when an idea began to bore his body, and he back-tracked to entertain it with an anti-thesis. Later he reverted to the original idea when listening to a harpsichordist, and attributed its thrill to what came from her bodily senses and not her education in the rudiments of music. Still, Rilke might have taken Barthes's switchback as an approval, a Hegelian synthesis that licensed his body, as the 'instrument of desire', to unify everything, and so do what he wanted in the *Elegies*: to rise above the obvious. But it wasn't to be. Perhaps because he had been reading Spinoza – 'The mind and the body are one and the same. The mind can think but cannot move. The body can move but cannot think, but together they can do both' – and his hand had disappointed him as an instrument of a writerly apocalypse.

•

'Little things said with big words' (*Pascal*)

The anachronistic Barthes connection is, of course, wishful thinking. But it helps to explain Heidegger's *Weltinnenraum* claim that Rilke sought his place in the external world in order to internalise it and thus create a *repetition forwards* in his 'inner-space'. Being a man of place rather than time, this is possibly true. For instance, history passes Malte by in the street-names, and he only notices if the honoured are immortal writers or artists. Rilke's alter ego is living in the poems of Baudelaire composed fifty years before, and ever present in the disease and death that they invoke all around him. His Paris resides in the timeless past: 'Creeping nature: the gardens, sanctuaries from the agitated traces of alleyways; cracked cobbles sprouting weeds; potholes after the rain filled with tadpoles, and above all, in its monuments of gothic art, cathedrals of the twelfth century, the patient industry of the Middle Ages which surpasses the power of words. These edifices are of the future as much as the past. Notre Dame may seem to stand and wait, but it grows some every day. Each time I see it, it seems larger.'

Note (to myself): even more so now with the scaffolding after the fire.

Rilke also feels the ever presence of Victor Hugo, Flaubert, Froissart, Verlaine, together with the living ones of Rodin and Cezanne. The writerly world, in which he sees his place, together with art and architecture, form a continuum that humbles ambition. His love/hate of Paris and its language shrunk his 'inner-space', the source of his *genie*. The solitude where the 'spiritual presences' spoke to him had been broken by 'the noise of words' (Thomas a Kempis), like it or not. He admitted to Betz that translating Gide and Valéry into German made his native tongue come out second best. The poems he wrote in French as a homage to the city towards the end of his life are some of his most touchingly personal but fall flat.

Regrettably, he overlooked the Paris of Pascal, Port-Royal, Racine and the Unities. He could have done with them for the 'Order of the Angels' as his poetical ideas moved more and more into futuristic pageants rather than the hoped-for *repetition forwards*. Conversely, in his later years Barthes's critical ideas retreated from his many 'isms' into what he called literary hedonism, indulging in the gazebo school of 'a good read, namely nineteenth-century realist novels. A *recollection backwards* he justified by claiming to want to write one himself. When at sixty-five he was knocked down by a laundry truck as he was coming out of the College de France, it was said he tripped over his briefcase because it was overloaded with Balzac.

Meanwhile, in the first decade of the twentieth century, Rilke is still torn between his 'spiritual presences' and the desire to know what it's like to be a lowly animal. Somewhere in the middle lurks Goethe's Primal Plant. Goethe claimed to have discovered the secret of the reproduction and organisation of plants. In a letter to Herder (1787), Goethe announced that he had 'found the hidden germ that would permit man to rule the plant world', and was busy conceptualising its blueprint. 'Nature herself will be envious of my idea, which is to construct a model for creating plants that, though they do not exist, might exist, not just as floral designs or poetic shadows, but possessing an Inner Truth and Necessity.' He had hopes of being able to apply this model 'to all other living things'.

The seeds of Goethe's idea fell on thorny scientific ground. But Rilke's essay, 'The Primal Sound' (1918), is perhaps a left-handed tribute to Goethe's unrealised ambition. He notes Edison's invention of the phonograph coincided with the year of his own birth: 'It preceded the disc-driven gramophone, and was designed to record as well as reproduce sounds. At school, I recall my classmates making a papier-mâché phonograph. A bristle on a waxed paper cylinder traced and retraced the rotations making a sound that no one had ever heard before, or since, but that still resonates within me. Tremulous, infinitely soft, hesitating, fading, and coming back again. It seemed like an appeal from elsewhere.' But it wasn't the sound that most impressed Rilke. 'The markings made on the cylinder resembled the indents of the cranial sutures of a skull. What if, like the wavering lines engraved by a needle on the cylinder,' he asks himself, 'these sutures were the mark of a transformation from one sense into another, from touch into sound? Would the skull then create a notional music which registers in the brain or, to be more precise, the inner ear? If so, would this tracing yield up the spectre of *techné*, the art and skill that haunts poetry? Why not,' he concludes with a Leap of Faith that strangely accords with modern science, 'accept that Orpheus, the poet singer, was the *prim*al phonographer?'

Give or take some scratches in the logic, I think, the four rhetorical questions conceptualise Rilke's ear for German prosody conditioned in childhood by the poems he learned by heart. In the second decade of the twentieth century, the dactylic rhythms of his return to the rather gravid tradition with the *Duino Elegies* are said to rival Goethe's. In sum, the verse in his head could be said to be spun from a 'bristle' applied to the vestige of the fusion of the bones of his skull. Words entered his brain and its inner ear tests their sound for metrical rightness. Now a decade after writing the letters to Kappus, his mind for poetry was no longer fragmented and 'frittering away good time trying to make it whole' (Byron). Fortified by expressionism, he had finally got the pieces in order, and was close to ending the *Duino Elegies* on a high note. The penultimate stanza '*Aber erweckten sie uns, die unendlich Toten, ein Gleichnis*', ('The immortal dead awaken within us a clash of symbols), heralds the slap-happy thought, '*Und wir, die a steigendes Gluck / denken, empfandem die Ruhrung / die uns beinah besturzt / wenn ein Gluckliches fallt*,' ('the emotion that almost overcomes us at the rise and fall of a happy thing'). The verse sounds a tocsin that is distinctly Teutonic.

Sometimes I have my doubts about the metaphysical reliability of Rainer Maria Rilke's thinking. It's like Goethe's science. Of course, they were primarily poets. But does that give them an antinomian dispensation to rationalise the irrational and say anything they like, lyrically? The question is from Blaise Pascal who made a cogent case against the public poets of his era. As his views are scattered through his *Pensées*, for coherence's sake my transcription puts them together as a continuum:

'A poet and not an honest man… If lightning fell on low places, poets, and those who can only reason about such things, would lack proof… People talk about poetical beauty. Why not mathematical beauty or even medical beauty? It would be reasonable to talk about a belle solution or beau surgery. They are disciplines with a logical basis, unlike poetry. In lieu of an apt epithet for it, we go all vague and ramble on about golden ages, wonders, fate. Fancy phrases. Most of what passes for poetry is little things said with big words… Imagine the Muse personifying it: you'll see a pretty girl adorned with tinsel and bangles, and smile at her, but go elsewhere to enjoy the charms of a mature woman. If you are an ignorant fool, and know no better, you will fall for her ridiculous dress, and crown her Queen of the May. Every village has one…

'Just by calling yourself a poet you are putting up a sign like a seamstress. "Skilled wordsmith" might convince the illiterate. Those that know would see little distinction between self-appointed poets and widows who take in washings. Those that have mastered their art or profession don't need such vulgar display. They come into society as themselves, and talk of matters that are on other people's minds. You don't say, "there goes a very clever surgeon or mathematician". He keeps that to himself.

'Peacock poets who indulge in displaying their plumage, ever thrusting their verse on the company, are best avoided. You have to lie to them with praise to shut them up. No self-respecting mathematician would ever recite numbers in your face or boggle you with a proof and expect lauds. But the poets in general are shameless, and want to be seen as someone exceptional. Even Racine, who cultivates the mien of a clerk of court after an all-night sitting, has an ever-so-subtle sidelong glance to check that he's been recognised. And if he hasn't, how he frets. Granted he's a poet that stands up to moral scrutiny, but he makes his three hundred words go a long way by exaggerating them. No proper mathematician would do that with numbers (though surgeons might be tempted to exaggerate the value of their limited procedures)... The educated man who makes art is content to be called just a learned gentleman. The generality is becoming. He leaves the work to speak for itself...

'The mantle of The Poet goes with a sweeping assumption. Here is a man who knows all that is to be known. Find me a poet who would demur at that and he probably is Shakespeare. But The Poet only knows one thing. It comes as a trinity:" I'm a poet, what I create is poetry, and that privileges me." Better to know a little about everything than all about one thing. It gives you a perspective beyond your own.

'Of course, if you can be both, so much the better. A little goes a long way, and everything comes from everything, and together they could theoretically make an immortal poet. But unless you are a Homer or a Solomon, you have to choose between the two. Lesser mortals are well advised to keep an open mind informed, and little by little you could appear to know more than you do. But you mustn't vaunt your knowingness, or you'll be found out. The world has a nose for fraudulence and, once caught in a scholastic babble by sceptics demanding more precise definitions, you won't be taken seriously ever again... However, lightning doesn't fall on low places and, unfortunately, self-anointed poets will always be with us. It may take the judgement of posterity to make their relative insignificance sink in.'

Thus, more or less, spoke Blaise Pascal, who said 'if you wish people to think good of you, don't speak'.

Alexander Pushkin is in accord (allow me an updated translation):

> Poet, so-called, let's call it off.
> Your much-hyped feelings are a sham

being made to measure and to scan.
The public never have enough.
Once readers went for locks of hair.
Now signing books in Waterstones
they want your pants and not your poems,
breathless to breathe your poet's air.

Your inner life's worn inside out.
You're hung like game until you're high.
Your body in the sun rots dry.
Admiring vultures kiss your mouth.
Posterity's the bottom line.
You're forced to count bones at the feast.
But you're no quick-change artiste.
Poetry must be given time.

Its secret is to play with fire
without being burnt on barbecues,
or swallowing whole the reviews.
You throw yourself on poetry's pyre.
Wearing braces as well as belts,
you must pretend to act your age.
Before the passion on the page
you learn to abdicate yourself.

•

The Poetry Not the Poet

When two great minds think the same, it only leaves fools to differ. My father who loved poetry, particularly the Romantics like Shelley and Keats, used to say, 'you don't have to be intelligent to be a poet.' It was one of the reasons I was emboldened to attempt poems, having been designated the 'fool of the family'. 'But fools can be right too,' my father said. 'Kings knew that.'

My mother, on the other hand, preferred light verse like Hilaire Belloc's cautionary tales, and said 'what's all this fuss about poetry. The mystique that surrounds it makes no sense. Verse is designed for economy of expression.' She blamed the Romantics. My father turned a deaf ear.

Her remark did not put me off Shelley, but my early reading of Rilke met with her put down.

Emerson's 'immovably-centred' Hero is a pretention that romantics covet and the Lake Poets glamourised. But it has lingered on into the twenty-first century. Not that the reading public generally notice. But still poets assert it. Both in desperation and in glory. When the Polish poet Czeslaw Milosz won the Nobel Prize in 1980 he declared that one verse of poetry is worth a thousand pages of prose. Zbigniew ('Mr Cogito') Herbert, who should have got it, was heard to remark, 'I doubt any verse of Milosz is worth Proust's *Remembrance of Things Past*.'

What is poetry is a question that remains open. The only indisputable definition is topographical. In any case, neither Pascal nor Pushkin were talking about poetry, only public poets and how they behave. Rilke learned a few lessons from Pascal without knowing it (not on his reading radar), but not enough for a heavenly Blaise to exclude him, though he would have admired the way he knew how to stay quietly in his room (reading Thomas à Kempis!). Rilke wouldn't have recognised himself in the Pushkin, and rightly so. But he could name a few who fitted the description. Poets who cut their spiritual losses and dumb-down performances for publicity. Rilke certainly didn't, and was a pure poet even in his way of life (though Alexander would have been tickled by his *rusè manigance*). Quite simply, the grail was to be found and Rilke took the 'divine risk' and undertook the quest, suffered on the way, but avoided distractions as much as humanly possible. Of course, death was a distraction he couldn't avoid even if he didn't believe in it. If he couldn't quite get to the poet's banana or whatever the grail turns out to be, almost a hundred years after his demise, he is still arriving in the mind of readers. 'The journey is what matters,' says T. S. Eliot and as a man and a poet Rilke would agree.

Note (to myself): two hundred years after Pascal, the 'exceptionalism' of poets was in full romantic flower. They had some surprising champions. 'Poets are strange fellows. They are made that way, and one must let them follow their bent. One cannot judge them by the standards that apply to ordinary or even extraordinary peopled'. Karl Marx, no less.

Epilogue

Lap of Honour (1925–)

•

Russian Poet Hero

As the years bore down on him, it can't have been easy being Rilke, his own 'immovably-centred' poet-Hero and neo-troubadour of European high society. His enemies couldn't keep up with his industry, but I wonder if he made a mistake of leaving his reputation to Russian friends who communicated with him in French and read him in translation.

The extraordinary letters from Marina Tsvetayeva, exiled in Paris at the height of Stalin's show trials, give him a better reason to feel 'like the Russian people' (response to Clara's stern letter). But the 'ardent lover of tender unhappiness' is overwhelmed by her inspired delight in his *Elegies* and *Orpheus*. She had not read (or received) them yet. But Boris had told her all about them in such detail that she feels she has. Her 'reading' makes him feel that she has inhabited the poems by proxy, making them her own.

Rilke declares more than his usual courtliness and an urgent desire to meet her. The ageing troubadour is roused by the complicity to declare his love, presenting her with roses, also by proxy. While reading it in his castle dungeon, he kisses her letter, still smelling of pressed flowers.

Both of them resist an encounter. Marina, living in penury with a problem husband and two children, certainly doesn't want to be loved, in person, by anyone, except God. This they have in common, though Rilke is weakening in his resolve and, at least on paper, is in danger of breaking the troubadour code. The precariousness of her mental and his physical health made for an off-guardedness that is further unbuttoned by her insistence in writing in macaronic German. But she makes it crystal clear that she loves the poet, not the man. Relieved probably, he opens up like never before on his personal life, for example, regret at not keeping up with Ruth, missing attending her marriage, and not seeing his grandchild. Marina would have noted the slight French shrug with the rider, 'but, that's how it had to be.'

Reading the tripart correspondence (1923/4), I'm struck by the mad enthusiasm of all three. The two Russians are ages with the Rilke who wrote the letters to Kappus, and these are not the missives of acolytes to a mentor, but a fulsome exchange of thoughts and ideas among equals which demands mutual admiration and tacit knowledge (they are not on first language terms). You find a very different Rilke from *The Letters*. Gone is the mordant grandiosity, and in its place, although he's at death's door, unbridled *joie de vivre*. Nevertheless, the 'ardent lover of tender unhappiness' enters by the backdoor with Marina, in particular with regard to regrets that couldn't be helped. Even his self-doubts are upbeat. Clara would be more amused than offended.

For sure, Rilke had not made it easy for himself. The embrace of the Difficult meant sacrifices that suppressed normal behaviour, and the consequent (mis)understandings could wound his pride. One that would not heal is his reputation in literary circles as the favourite poet of rich 'vultures for culture'. Robert Musil, the Austrian novelist, while on leave from the Great War, visited him in Trieste in 1916. He came to pay his respects to Rilke's poetry and Princess Marie later reported to a friend that he talked all the time about meeting a certain Franz Kafka in Prague until he got distracted by the presence of James Joyce in the café. Rilke left to go to the toilet and didn't return.

•

Humiliations

Robert Musil was everything he couldn't be. He was a star pupil in the military academy that Rilke dropped out from, and besides the success of Musil's soldier novel, *The Confusions of Young Torless*, published in 1906 when Rilke was struggling with *The Notebooks*, he saw active service in the Great War, retrained himself as an engineer and a philosopher, organised the 'Austrian Year' to celebrate Franz Joseph's seventieth anniversary as emperor in 1918, and yet managed to sustain a settled family life while writing a trilogy, *The Man Without Qualities*, 1920-1942, a tripartite novel that made Thomas Mann feel inadequate and had the Nazi's snapping at his heels. He died in Switzerland in 1942 while perfecting his gymnastics at the age of sixty-two. During a memorial dinner for Rilke organised by literary Berlin, Musil remarked, not unkindly, to a friend that 'although making it possible to write poems in German, The Poet was undervalued for most of his life, and by the time of his death he had turned into a delicate, well-matured liqueur suitable for bourgeois ladies, despite the fact his work is too demanding to be considered relaxing.'

W. H. Auden said that nobody had ever superseded Baudelaire either as a 'poet exception', or the 'squint-essential city poet'. Both were territories that Rilke cherished for himself. But he didn't need to be told that his argument with the *semblable et frère* that haunted Malte could only be lost. For instance, Baudelaire's depiction of blind beggars as misfortunate losers was closer to reality than Rilke's designated seers diverting the traffic in Paris. Even Flaubert's glaucous blind harbinger of ill-omen in *Madame Bovary* is more convincing. Auden's final slating of Rilke in *The Dyer's Hand* is a head-butt: 'Despite his undoubted craft his work is false and unreal.' Rilke aficionados say that this is because Auden translated some of his poems without success. This is true but, like Hannah Arendt, he had moved on to the certainties of Brecht, the first in his list of modern European 'lyric poets'. Politics prevailing over aesthetics, some would say. But no doubt a sense of history (and humour) contributed to Bertolt's more obvious 'compassion'.

•

Dark Nights and the Light of Day

In the early twenties, Rilke wouldn't have been too lonely in his castle as the *Elegies* increasingly became a 'celestial pantomime'. He wants to make his masterwork one that no one could fail to read except on his terms. In other words, the readership he is aiming for is everybody and nobody. Posterity be blessed (the tripart correspondence anticipated it*). Fluctuating health makes him less confident in his modus operandi. He encourages admirers as never before. Letters lead to visits. But the dog of doubt barks in the small hours of the night.

Note (to myself): * Boris and Marina shared the belief that the subjectivity of a pure poet is undying and continues to exist after death – a rather elitist variant of Schopenhauer's *will*. Marina kept saying to Boris, 'Rilke isn't a poet, he's the embodiment of poetry.' She didn't realise how close to '(im)mortality' he was.

Mindful of Mallarmé's growing eminence as the consummation of what happens when neo-symbolism (chez Baudelaire) puts expressionism into words, he must have reflected on how things would have worked out if he had done the conventional, 'decent thing' by his wife and child (his unrepentant regrets to Marina were yet to come). Meanwhile he asks himself, would his poetry have been more of this world, thus gaining him the only love he really wanted, love of his work?

Rilke hadn't found, despite many sacrifices (others' as well as his own), the ultimate requital in art, Cézanne's *La Réalisation*. And, on dark nights of his (f)ailing body, he must have thought about the life he proscribed for himself: never, for the sake of his poetry, to take on the responsibilities that love brings with it. Sometimes he felt that the poet Rilke was someone else, a doppelganger. Despite reaching an understanding with this other-worldly other, it proved impossible to forget himself or not to think of everybody else as would-be readers. His ego had an ideal reader in mind, but they do not exist. Rodin might have been, only he couldn't read the originals. Gide seemed promising: translating some of *The Notebooks* gave him a unique ingress. But in the end, he admitted giving up on *The Lay of the Love* (to translate instead Josef Conrad's *The Shadow Line*, about a ship becalmed eternally) and rarely mentions the poems (his German wasn't up to them). Then there were the aspiring young poets, mostly young women, who, on failing, lost interest, or, on succeeding, grow out of him. Now his best readers are the few friends, like Lou and Princess Marie, who read him sympathetically, knowing what he's trying to do. That leaves the legion of poetry-lovers who read the poet not the poems.

Rilke is learning to be unfair to himself. As a 'world-turner' he had been consistent in turning the world around his pure-poet status but his conscience has become less clean-cut. He feels the need to explain and even accuse himself, though with qualifications that made Clara sad. She would have winced on reading Benjamin Constant's famous moral twister:

> I detest that fatuity of mind which believes that what is explained is also excused; I hate that vanity which finds it interesting to describe the harm that it has done, and asks to be pitied at the end of its recital, and, as it patrols with impunity among the ruins for which it is responsible, gives to self-analysis the time which should be given to repentance.

Hannah Arendt's 'To understand is not to forgive' would have driven the nail in. But it's not for me to hammer it home. He suffered on his self-made cross and his late poem 'Christ in Hell', a descent into the human, proved therapeutic rather than redemptive.

Samuel Beckett was more forgiving. After reading the entry in Kierkegaard's *Journals* wishing Regine dead so he could love her eternally, wrote:

> I would like my love to die
> and the rain to be raining on the graveyard
> and on me walking the street
> mourning her who thought she loved me.

Rilke on the back of Baudelaire might have felt like that but, as in the 'Thing-poems', the object of love or attention is internalised so that the poet finds himself in them. Likewise, in the 'Requiem', Paula is kept very much alive as a spirit inhabiting him. He can forgive himself for the (mis)use of objects. It's less easy with a person. But he can manage. Clara who, for the most part, is a 'necessary absence', his 'true Penelope', also serves as his 'gentle law', the living witness of his life, and conscience, for better or worse. The balance is precarious, but it has its moments, one of which he immortalised in *The Book of Images*, in a poem written when they'd first met. She is the artist at work: 'You slowly raised a black tree / and as you grasped its meaning / tenderly your eyes let it go.' And 'The Requiem' (1900), commemorating Gretel Kottmeyer is written in Clara's voice, while she weaves a wreath for her friend. The floral tribute, being art, will not wither and die, and so Gretel will always be remembered.

Rilke's relationship with Clara remained throughout their life in 'teleological suspension' ('To suppress something for the time being in order that the truth may become truer', Kierkegaard). Neither ever replaced the other. They had mixed their labour together for a quarter of a century, mostly by indirect communication, and that led to a form of love-by-association, not romantic, but sustaining at difficult times. The 'truth' of this 'became truer' in 1924 when the leukaemia began to gallop.

She visits him in a clinic in Switzerland, and nurses him back to a miraculous remission so that he can return to Paris. Rodin was long dead, but admirers as important as Gide and Valéry in literary Paris arranged to honour Rilke in the presence of a crowd of younger poets, amongst them Pierre Jean Jouve and Jules Supervielle, who read him in translation and were more than curious.

•

Fame and infame

And so, Rilke lives to enjoyed a lap of honour, meeting Gide at last in person; presenting Paul Valéry with his translation of '*Le cimetiére marin*', 'The Graveyard by the Sea'; giving his first and last interview to a newspaper, during which Rilke acknowledges the influence of Schopenhauer (who likewise experienced eleventh-hour celebrity) and, when asked about James Joyce, expresses regret at lacking the English to read him in the original. Needless to say, J. J. is too busy working on his own *Duino Elegy*, *Finnegans Wake*, to pay his compliments, a case of 'What is truly parallel, / though infinite, can never meet' (Marvell).

It isn't quite the completion of a circle. His hour of glory was tainted by a sense that those writers and artists present influenced him more than he them. If it was Rilke's light of day, there were dark nights. He shared his gripes with Betz. Most of the writers that he corresponded warmly with were rather off-hand in the flesh, not least Gide – 'I felt alone in their company'. Nobody said anything on the two hundred or so poems he wrote in French. In dismay he parted from Paris with his mixed feelings leaning towards disillusionment. Nothing had changed, except him. And so, 'Fame at last' washed over him 'leaving him in the potholes for the carriages to splash'. 'I wouldn't have wanted it otherwise,' he told Lou. 'My love of Paris was for a city that died before I was born and where I only knew ghosts.'

The absence of women may have darkened his mood. The lap of honour was an all-male affair. Women writers were not to be taken seriously (dilettante aristocrats or lowlife Colette). Clara had left him in the good hands of Betz and returned to Germany as Ruth was expecting a baby. Rilke's delicate sensibilities that Rodin had mocked made men tip-toe around him. Whereas women generally wanted to mother him. In his memoir, Kassner, his nearest and dearest male friend, said Rilke 'adored above all the company of sentimental women. He gave himself whole-heartedly to their swooning and mooning.' After his death, Clara sighed that 'they'll repay his attentiveness with gushy memoirs, humourless and of little value in understanding the man'. Indeed, there are several books about him that confirm this tendency.

The German critic, Herbert Gunther, was more incisively objective: 'Despite being loved by many women, Rilke loved them not... Only one of his poems could truly be considered a personal love poem, 'Requiem for a Friend'. Princess Marie, who, like Lou, was not a 'sentimental woman', said 'Rilke was worse than Don Juan. He was never satisfied with any one woman. He was in constant evasion from them.' Katherine Kipperberg noted that he wasn't at all sentimental himself. 'Not attending his daughter's wedding and never getting to know his grandchild was for him a sacrifice on the altar of his art.' Nevertheless, Rilke's courtly love of women was an endearing quality that endured in letters, poems and, possibly, in his epitaph:

> *Rose, oh reiner Widerspruce, Lust*
> *Niemandes schlaf zu sein uter sovial lidern*
>
> *Rose, oh pure contradiction, delight*
> *in being no one's sleep under so many lids*

Could he be flirting with Madame Death by presenting her with a rose?

Around the time Rilke composed his epitaph, in a letter to Countess Soglio he refers to 'a tangled rosebush as Venus in Venusberg'. Since 'Venusberg' in German folklore tells the same story as *The Lay of the Love*, a young man seduced by a faery countess, Joab thinks Rilke, the neo-troubadour, is sublimating for all eternity his *Geschlecht*, pointing out that '*reiner*' translates as 'pure', and '*Lust*' does not have the same connotations as in English (though 'lustiness' in Scots means 'desirability'). 'The "pure contradiction" is in the melancholy truce between not wanting to be loved and a declaration of love to all womankind, perhaps.'

•

Human Warmth

The endgame for Rilke is not unhappy. Like Kierkegaard, he loosened up in the final years. He has doubts about himself, but not of his poetry. Having completed his Great Work, the *Duino Elegies*, there is an inevitable lowering of the sights. The titles of his poems and books become less grand. His posthumous slim volume, *From Pocket Notebooks and Memory Pads*, is a surprise return to pre-Rodin subjectivity, fortified by Hölderlin's 'fateless gods'. In reconciling pain with joy, Clara might have thought that he has found an antidote to Malte's plea 'for strength to stand by my own awfulness'. She knew and grudgingly admired his strength of mind in living an idea. He wasn't going to change his life, only its emphasis. Beset by bad blood, both systemic and socio-literary, he had a pressing need for human warmth.

Note (to myself): Joab agrees: 'The epitaph's melancholy truce is telling posterity that in his dying days, Rilke could have done with a hug.'

When Rilke discovered Kafka, he sensed they shared the same landscape with a horizon in which they would never live. Their mutual reading of Schopenhauer's 'On the indestructibility of being' was some sort of consolation. But for both of them it would be a little like the surviving *will* arriving in the right aeroplane at the wrong destination: Kafka expressed the desire to be a sex tourist in the Land of the Dead, while Rilke wanted to be a unicorn amongst the angels. If it was the other way around it would be more than a literary paradox: Franz, finding the angels frustrating, would turn them into refused insurance claims. Rainer Maria, not knowing what to do with the fleshpots, would send a *billet-doux* to Madame Lamort (né Lament) offering to superannuate them with the Order of the Angels. Kafka was to die two years before Rilke. They never met.

Posterity has been kinder to Rilke's literary reputation than Musil could ever have anticipated. Almost a hundred years after his death, his star continues to shine. He lives 'an imaginary life in the minds of others' (Pascal). Readers flock. Not merely due to the more accessible 'Thing-poems'. The quasi-mysticism of *The Sonnets to Orpheus* and the dramatic mystifications of the *Duino Elegies* are part of the received canon. But above all for *Letters to a Young Poet*, which will never be out of print as long as there are aspirant poets with idealist leanings and enquiring minds. *The Notebooks* may puzzle them, but it is still read, and continues to be translated, into English especially, and more literally, I hasten to add, than my transcriptions. Betz's French translation, which had Rilke's seal of approval, remains the gold standard, and the version I prefer to consult. Joab says Rilke is 'best *found* in translation' (and the 'sum of the (mis)understandings' mount). All in all, Rilke achieved what he set out to do. As far as the body of work is concerned, he had nothing to reproach himself for. It had given him what he wanted in the end, and at the same time had shown him that this wasn't as much as he expected. But there is no doubt that it has been good to readers, particularly those of a transcendental disposition, or who like to be surprised. That would have pleased him, a nod from the Archangel of his Order bringing his 'spiritual presences' down to earth.

But solid ground can be soggy. Particularly when your blood is playing up. As an all-purpose poet, Rilke waded on. In a letter to Clara during the last year of his life he resolved to 'continue abiding by hard work patiently exercised', adding 'while not missing out on any opportunity for joy or pleasure'. This is often quoted out of context as hedonism. A man living with leukaemia, and constantly in pain, craves for respites. In a letter to Lou Salomé, he wrote, 'If God exists, death doesn't, as what God creates cannot be unmade.' Opportunist thinking creates a denial that is understandable in the circumstances.

Rilke wrote the poem 'Christ in Hell' in the divine persona. As an alter ego he couldn't go higher. I don't think he thought of himself as God redeeming the earth, but he needed an extreme analogy to sublimate the pain (having refused opiates):

> Freed from the body and terrible pain,
> in the darkness, not knowing where he is.
> Alone with white bats; fearfully flitting,
> Dead air fogs up where his corpse is dumped.
>
> The preying beasts of the night are dormant,
> and so, the world is almost peaceable,
> a place of repose to appease his anguish.
> Mourning mankind, reaches out his arms…
>
> But the earth, parched by the thirst of his wounds,
> opens under him, and he hears the pleas
> of tormented souls, crying out in hope
> that his sacrifice would end their torture.
>
> Weighed down in spirit, he leaps into hell,
> startling the shadows bemoaning their fate.
> Seeing Adam, their eyes meet and, moved,
> he's sucked into the depths, and lost to sight.

LAP OF HONOUR

Weary of the human, he holds his breath,
rebounds up the pit, higher and higher.
Transfigured above the surging cries, he,
possessed by pain, masters it, and is quiet.

Note (to myself): wishful thinking triumphs over felt thoughts. As pain relief it is not visceral enough to be more than a passing distraction, I fear. But he was a brave patient. Clara knew this.

Post-script:

The Last Word to Rilke: 'Rose Thou Art Sick'

'The immortal dead awaken within us a clash of symbols

•

At his best, Rilke was open-minded about what to think on most subjects. The lowest common denominator of his avowed philosophy would be: to experience our existence in space rather than time, stop feeling, stop thinking; just stay with it and it will make itself felt. If this is wisdom, I'm happy to be my father's Fool. It made for poetry of the highest order. But he remained pig-headed about his Nietzschean reversal that death belongs to the disease, not the person.

The idea was not just a young man's treatment of death as an abstract concern. He wasn't denying that death is an end product of corporal dysfunction, but remained staunch in the belief that it is the disease that dies. That is, until leukaemia in his late forties made him take disease and death personally. The hyperactive white blood corpuscles turning his blood to poison may have belonged to the disease, but his body's ownership of death was no longer in doubt. Although he confided the medical reality to Lou and Clara, with everyone else his reaction to backtracking on a lifelong idea was to dispute the diagnosis; dying in his doctor's arms, still insisting that it was the prick of a thorn that poisoned him while picking a rose for a beautiful Egyptian princess. Although the courtly gest and its consequences did not make his death certificate, he gave the rose a life of its own in the enigmatic epitaph on his tombstone:

Rose, oh reiner Widerspruce, Lust
Niemandes schlaf zu sein uter sovial
lidern

The literal translation commonly used is:

Rose, oh pure contradiction, delight
in being no-one's sleep under so many
lids

THE LAST WORD TO RILKE:

When I ask Gretchen what it means, she says, 'It's a *felt* thought. Rilke is speaking from the grave to a flower, symbolically.' As the symbols seem to clash in the above translation, I work on a transcription, seeking her help. She tells me that the words are a jungle of puns and multiple meanings. Only five of the twelve words have a single one... The poem ends with *lidern* (eyelids) in the dative plural, which implies subordination but, to what, is the question.

I'm between the deep blue sea of finding an answer and the devil of inventing one. One of the possible meanings of *Widerspruce* is 'answering back', and this gives me a lead. As the ballasting of the German syntax with the capitalisation of three key words (giraffing doesn't have an equivalent in English, of course), I take the liberty of switching the clauses around to qualify the subordinate:

> *O rose, your innocence answers back, delighting,*
> *under so many lids, to be no-one's*
> *sleep.*

Assuming, as it's an epitaph, that 'sleep' is a metaphor for 'death', I think I know what it signifies: Rilke is forgiving the rose for being the symbolic cause of his death.

True, it's still a thorny question. 'A rose is a rose is a rose'; Gertrude Stein wasn't having symbols where there are none. But they come in useful. At the turn of the century, Rilke's contemporary Paul Claudel wrote on the fan of his favourite lady, '*Seule le rose est assez fragile pour exprimer l'eternite*', '*Only the rose is fragile enough to express eternity*'. Rilke would have sung with that, for once upon a time in Worpswede, the young poet Rainer Maria had charmed and disarmed Paula and Clara by presenting each of them with a red rose. Considering the dark side of the consequences, the rose had a lot to answer for.

Note (to myself): poets as different as William Dunbar and William Blake knew that there was 'no rose without a thorn' (See Guiding Note 10).

The disputed diagnosis is usually put down to Rilke's deep need to be poetical. However, a coincidence suggests there is more to it. Two years ago, I was attending a performance in Lyon of the opera *Cornet*, based on *The Lay of the Love*, and while browsing in the Christmas bookfair, I spotted *Rainer Maria Rilke* (Librairie Les Lettres, Paris, 1952), a tribute volume from his French and German literary friends and admirers. The pages were uncut. It proved a treasure trove of undocumented information on the man and the poet. Apart from the 'less deceived' Herbert Gunter, I could read his secretary's account of his last few months of life. Genia Tchernosvitow was just out of college, young and pretty, and a Russian. The courtly Rilke played her like a balalaika, and they were happy days. Love and pity go together in the Russian soul, and he responded to both with a liveliness that belied his fatal condition. But his fabled gallantry had the pathos of a dying troubadour. Genia mentions that he cut himself while picking a rose from the castle garden. The wound didn't heal throughout his final illness.

But in the precious volume there was more to come in an essay by Georges Cattaui on Rilke's letter-love with the Circassian beauty, Princess Nimet Eloui Bey. She was infatuated by his poetry but only met him in the last year of his life, visiting his 'rundown castle'. The princess was touched by 'this magnetic little man who spoke in vatic ripples and presented her with a rose he cut from his garden'. It was to be his neo-troubadour apotheosis, and nemesis.

The melancholy truce between not wanting to be loved and loving all womankind had already been broken. Rilke was loved whether he liked it or not, and including by those that had reason to feel hurt at being sacrificed to his art. The flower, symbolic or not, was the contradictory agent in brokering this. But he would have found it easy to forgive a rose. Its beauty, which is dangerous to grasp, has a fragrance that lingers in the air. He is willing the love in his life and the cause of his death to be loved eternally, the difficulties of life fading into the flourish of an immortal rose. In the churchyard of his castle in Raron, Switzerland, relays of votive roses on his tombstone perpetuate his wish.

Note (to myself): nobody, not even Gretchen, has observed that *reiner* (pure) is almost Rilke's adopted first name, Rainer. As a bad speller, I said nothing. However, Rilke would have wanted to have an aural signature on his epitaph. The pure poet (*reiner Poet*) had the last word.

•

Coda

After his death in 1926, Clara named her studio Café Rilke. Ruth served coffee and cakes to pilgrims. Clara, though fiercely independent, couldn't do without her errant poet, alive or dead. Another reason for the loose but not unbroken bond is a gothic one: a 'spiritual presence' in their shared solitude had done its work, and they were in each other's blood, for better or worse, 'living an idea', his idea. But Kierkegaard's 'First the severity of the ideal, then the gentleness' was to be, alas, posthumous for his daughter.

Ruth Sieber-Rilke wrote in 1927 to Hugo von Hofmannsthal to contribute to a tribute book edited by Kippenberg. His reply is strangely not unlike that of Rilke on the defensive (*i.e.*, the stern letter to Clara):

'I have a daughter of your age and hope that I will be remembered with such filial piety when I'm no longer... You want my frank thoughts on your father? As I see it, the afterthoughts of my contemporaries add an additional terror to death. The insipid sentiments vie with indiscretions to belittle a life that hopefully continues in the work. I've burnt all my letters so only my writings can be remembered... Your father's poetry now faces the struggle with posterity and I expect it to triumph. But who knows? In my youth, Hölderlin was dismissed as a madman, and out of print. It wasn't until his *Poems in a Time of Destitution* was reissued that we discovered it was the world not him that was mad...But I wander. Anton Kippenberg can be trusted to produce a book with loving care. I'm happy to talk to him to answer questions but not about the past. I am too old for that. Rilke's future is in the work, as mine is. And so, with a heavy heart, for your letter moved me, I must say, no. Remember me to my old friend Anton,

Yours,
Hofmannsthal'

Ruth and her husband edited six volumes of Rilke's letters (1936–1939). And although she died three years before his *Collected Works* (1976) appeared in Germany, her contribution is generously acknowledged. A labour of love her father could not refuse.

Appendix

Guiding Notes:

A Short Lexicon of Literary and Philosophic Terms

•

1. Neo-romantic symbolism was a movement in German art in the late nineteenth century. It jettisoned realistic modes and renewed romantic idealism in a search for absolutes. Absolutes are ineffable (beyond words) and so a symbolic way of reaching it must be found in order to establish figurations to encapsulate it. The romanticism was secularised and less nature based than psychological.

2. *Negative capability* is an idea of Locke's which Coleridge polished up into a credo for poets (calling it 'negative faith') and John Keats made his own by giving it a name in a letter (1820). Locke floated that the mind of a true creative artist is 'a sponge soaking up impressions, and voided of personal identity, preconceptions or any of the certainties'. Coleridge grounded it by saying the poet's mind is that of a chameleon. Self-consistency is not part of its make-up. And so, the poet can change his mind as the impressions takes him.

Rilke's statement (1920) that 'Art can only emerge from a purely anonymous centre' echoes Keats's view that the true poet lacks 'character', and 'self-passion', and is therefore able to identify with 'anyone particular beauteous star'.

3. Objective correlative: the mechanism by which any form of art evokes emotion. The term was coined in the 1830s by the American painter Washington Allston, whose portraits of Coleridge are our image of the 'chameleon' poet. T. S. Eliot interpreted it as the work of art finding 'a set of objects, a situation, a chain of events which formulates the particular emotion, such that the reader, by jettisoning pre-existing ideas, rises above their immediate context to experience a universal high.' Thus, the emotion is released.

4. *Elective Affinities* is a novel by Goethe, but not a novel idea. Love is chemistry:

GUIDING NOTES:

We are substances that bond in favourable circumstances. Goethe had a formula for it. AB + CD = AD + BC. As he was neither a reliable scientist nor mathematician, some wags say it was an aborted rhyming system for a sonnet, a Shakespearian one, with a DEAF for the quatrain.

5. Recollection (or/Repetition, Backwards and Forwards (a précis of Kierkegaard). Recollection for the Ancient Greeks was the source of all knowledge, and so all life could be said to be a repetition mediated by it. Striking the balance between recollection and repetition is a secure basis for regulating our lives. Recollection has nothing to lose and repetition everything to gain. They share the same lifeline, but move in opposite directions. Recollection is a passive backwards look, receding into the cul-de-sac of memory lane. If it is activated into repetition it collects itself forward. The spirit of the past is carried into the future. It lives again, renewed.

Recollection (or *repetition*) *backwards* is more inclined to make you unhappy. Even if the memory was happy, Boethius's consolation – 'in misfortune remembering happy times' – is the ultimate misery. An unhappy memory causes less distress, and offers a perverse relief ('Thank God I'm not capable of that now'). But it is not a feeling to share and therefore is outside the realm of life and love, let alone happiness. You are warning yourself against what's past.

On the other hand, *repetition forwards*, being forwardly collected, is almost always happy. Not being a 'has been', it has the blessing of the present instant, and offers you a future without the baggage of regret and dread that *recollection backwards* carries with it. Neither does *repetition forwards* burden you with hope and its anxieties. You step back to go forwards with confidence. Even if it leads you over the edge of a cliff, you die happy.

6. The Ineffables: Great and Lesser. An ineffable is that which is considered inexpressible in words. Needless to say, humans, particularly theologians, philosophers and poets, are not deterred from trying. Explanations or evocations through revelation, precepts and figurations are myriad. The Ineffables are the unanswered questions that beg to be broached. In the twenty-two thousand or so languages of the world, billions of words are squandered on them every day. Self-expression

GUIDING NOTES:

abounds and rebounds. A coherent consensus across cultures does not exist. Each tribe has their own spectrum of Ineffables and received ideas on them, so people can get on with their lives.

The Ineffables in Western societies can be classified into the Great (eternal) Ineffables – death, God, (im)mortality – and the Lesser (temporal) Ineffables – love, happiness, music, grief, pain, individual existence and other states of being or events which defy rational understanding.

The majority of people nowadays only think of the Great Ineffables as a last resort, preferring to go along with the view that the more one ponders them, the greater the mystery. Fear is a factor, like looking into infinite space and hearing the eternal silence (Pascal). Theologians reason with the Great Ineffables, but invariably faith comes before and after it. Scientists deny their existence if they can, and when they can't, reduce them to the lowest common denominator (a heart-stop, a kick-start, an unknown). Classical philosophers have always reasoned with them, but lacking proofs, tend to conjure up figurations based on the speculation rather than observation. In the nineteenth century the new philosophers, Schopenhauer, Kierkegaard, Nietzsche, engaged them with *felt* thoughts and get closer to the bone, but fleshing them out requires imaginative thinking akin to poetry.

The Lesser Ineffables are something else. Opinions on them are part of everyday life. Each culture has their own. Take personal identity in the West. Locke claimed it is based on memory. We remember who we are! Kierkegaard, on the other hand, warned that 'abstractions can't explain the existential', and that psychotherapies and other methods of self-exploration 'fall back on figurations comparing one's self to others'. However, this is not personal but social identity, and so the self is representative. In the present age of Narcissus writ-large, to 'know oneself' (the Delphic Oracle's decree) has become commercialised. Self-help manuals standardise a socially acceptable norm. Pascal said, 'The self is hateful,' meaning self-love. Rilke wouldn't have agreed, nor would most self-help gurus of today. My own search for a personal self stopped with David Hume, who said 'the mind is a theatre, and each of us creates its own main character'.

As it is, all else failing, writers, particularly the poets, tend to have the last word on the Ineffables, Great and Lesser. They are the new mystics. Hitherto, the priests and prophets held court as monitors of the Ineffables, being free to express them to their soul's content. The rub is that the 'soul' is another ineffable, one that may or may not exist, and that is probably why so many wars are fought about religion. The poets as 'legislators' have proved impotent. Their 'last word' is usually 'I told you so'. Not all poets are happy with this prerogative ('Eff the Ineffables,' says Samuel Beckett).

7. Gnosticism: St Paul invented theology as a shortcut to endless philosophising. The extreme wing of scholasticism revolted and put their faith in learning and speculation as practised by the Greeks, updated by the revelation that each individual has within him a mystery to explore – the God in them – and on finding it are saved. Early Christianity was a time for opportunists of ideas, and inevitably the Gnostics fought amongst themselves. This allowed the Lollards to condemn learning as a quagmire of intellectual pride. They sided with the Montanists. Montanism was revivalist in tone and irrational in content, veering wildly from the Pauline dichotomy of the carnal and spiritual and back to Greek unity, depending on the mood of the moment. The Gnostics attempted to standardise their ideas, but it was too late. The anti-Pauline Church Father, Tertullian, became a Montanist, as he couldn't square the Gnostics combination of learning and revelation. Faced by his eloquent advocacy, the Gnostics lost their influence, and the Pauline dictates of the Apostolic Church became the Christian norm. Theology re-established itself through dogma, 'the military wing of unreason (James Hogan senior), and anything else was heresy. Thinking for yourself in order to discover the secret of your godliness meant ex-communication.

8. Existentialism for Beginners: Existentialism is a philosophy that addresses the gap between thought and feelings. Kierkegaard is its acknowledged unmarried grand-uncle (Rilke was an early grandnephew!). He maintained that ideas that don't emerge from one's immediate experience are meaningless: 'Traditional philosophers, who detach themselves by objectivising existence, close off ideas from their lives. Their chances of grasping their place in an uncertain world are forfeited, and with it a purpose in life. They might as well accept their lot, and wait to die.'

Apart from the slave Stoic Epictetus (who believed philosophy was a way of life, not a theoretical discipline), philosophers hitherto dealt in things that could be observed objectively, the 'knowns' that sit in judgement of the self. Kierkegaard called it 'philosophy for philoso-

Guiding Notes:

phy's sake'. His emphasis on subjective experience puts *felt* thoughts to the fore. Commitment to them was how to live as a free being. But he was thoughtful about unconditional belief in this commitment. In sum, the subjective self is a whirlpool of hopes, fears, wilfulness and prejudice. Ethics and logic will question the *felt* ideas, and 'right reason' links you to past philosophers who advance their ideas by comparing themselves with predecessors. Nevertheless, such concepts only exist because they began. And so, one ought to abandon all dependence on received ideas and commit to a leap into the unknown.

What was holding him back was his Father's God and his childlike need to believe in Him. He pursued theology and almost became a pastor. His edifying discourses (sermons) were more heart-felt than mind-felt, and led to disillusionment in the end. After his father's death the parallel commitment to the new philosophy took over his life. He made himself an instrument to investigate 'living an idea'. In doing so, he put the cart of ideas before the horse of subjectivity, testing their application against his experience in life, and writing them up as psychological experiments. He qualified Socrates's 'Ignorance is our salvation' with the more subtle 'We must learn to know the things we cannot understand'. Kant had taken up Socrates's dictum with his famous 'stand back'. Kierkegaard took it forward by acting on it. But with a humanist dimension ('First the severity of the ideal. Then the gentleness').

He wasn't gentle with himself. What to believe remained the stumbling block. 'The purpose in life has to come from within the self. There is nobody else you can trust.' And he didn't always trust himself. It wasn't enough to know the things that we cannot understand, the challenge was to make something of it. Kierkegaard knew a purpose in life cannot simply be thought through. 'Arguing the toss with the eternal questions would take all eternity. But we are in real time and it has its limits. More than that we do not know for certain.' And in despair went off and wrote one of the 'edifying discourses' on which his reputation as a religious thinker rests. When I arrive at a contradiction, says Aquinas, I make a distinction. In this case, I would distinguish between his religious thinking and his *felt* thoughts. The former was a *recollection backwards* and the latter a *repetition forwards*. (See Guiding Note 5).

Existential thinkers go it alone, and that divides them into as many schools as those who engage in it. What they have broadly in common is a radical individualism that treats existence not as an abstract entity, but as the *self* that's purpose-built by experience, a construct that we participate in designing, for better or worse. Our life, and how it is conducted, is an experiment and, if it doesn't work out to our subjective satisfaction, one can try again.

Felt thoughts are often an existentialist's fallback. But their recognition pre-dates the movement. For instance, the proto-feminist, Mary Wollstonecraft wrote in 1792, 'We reason deeply when we forcefully feel'. Poets and philosophers from Kierkegaard to Rilke would not disagree.

9. The Problem of Evil: Evil is the devil to define and categorise. Thus, Joab calls it 'an amateur concept'. If it is an Ineffable, whether it's a Greater of Lesser one is impossible to say. Theodicy, the theological study of evil, attempts to explain why God would allow evil in His world. Some say it is an existential test of the subjective self when faced by tempting circumstances. We think the unthinkable but, thanks to God's grace, think the better of acting on it.

This presupposes it's a benign universe. And the history of mankind tells otherwise. People are at war with themselves, or more obviously with others, and God's grace is suspended (sometimes in God's name). The suspension can be personal and related to Lesser Ineffables, such as love, hate and parking spaces, or universal and related to Great Ineffables, as in war, economic or military. Evil is a fact of life most people think, basing it on experience or hearsay. Sometimes it's even considered 'necessary'.

One way or another, being a by-blow of the Ineffables, Lesser and Great, evil's existence is parasitic. It cannot exist on its own. So, strictly speaking, it's not an Ineffable. It exists in practice not theory, and that is why it bears description in court reports and in popular culture. Therein, perhaps, resides Hannah Arendt's dictum 'The banality of evil'.

Rilke's belief, fostered by Byron, that the invisible is the source of all good and evil is hard to grasp. Both good and evil are seen to be 'done'. Maybe he is thinking of Manet's 'The creation of every work of art should have about it something of the secrecy of a crime'. But what about the good? The good deed that is not seen is the greater good. This may be true, but good example is more important in a moral world. Rilke certainly didn't care to be seen as a paragon of virtue or vice. But maybe, like Byron's 'secret shame', he was a closet

GUIDING NOTES:

Good Samaritan. And so good at it nobody noticed, except those that loved him (despite his wishes, undoubtably he was loved, even by those that suffered because of him) and they kept quiet about it. That the evidence is against it does not exclude the remote possibility.

10. Rose Poems: The cruelty of roses is well known to poetry. Blake's 'The Sick Rose', for example. My favourite is from William Dunbar, the 16th century Scottish poet:

> 'Sweet rose of virtue and of gentleness,
> Delightsome lily of every lustiness,
> Richest in bounty and beauty clear
> And every virtue that is held dear,
> Except only that ye are merciless'.

11: 'Intertextual glossing': Christoph Schrempt, Kierkegaard's German translator (1890 – 1922), admitted in old age that as the Dane was prone to 'confuse the issue' with 'mystifications', in order to render the original coherently it was necessary to incorporate into the text his own 'understandings'. It is possibly why thinking on him in Germany is very different from, say, in America, where eminent divines, like Reverend Walter Lowrie, were the driving force. Given Kierkegaard's prolixity, selective editing of texts in translation have been deemed necessary, and he has been presented as essentially a religious writer. This is a view French commentators dismiss as simplistic. Kierkegaard is seen as the philosopher of 'the lived idea', the first existentialist. The German reading through Karl Jaspers is in accord but dedifferentiates him to align with experimental psychology. Thus, his reputation as a precursor of Freud.

Chronology of Rilke's Life

Réne (Rainer) Maria Rilke

•

1875: born on the 4th December in Prague, Bohemia. An only child (a sister was still-born). Baptised a Roman Catholic.

1885: parents – Josef and Sophia – separate.

1886: boards at the Military Academy at St Polten, Lower Austria.

1891: transfers to the upper school at Marisch-Weisskirchen. Drops out to study trade and commerce in Linz. Starts writing poems.

1894: publishes poems *Life and Songs*. The first of thirteen slim-volumes in nine years. Starts writing plays inspired by Ibsen.

1895: matriculates in the Humanities at Prague University.

1896: studies art history in Munich.

1897: meets Lou Andreas-Salomé, fourteen years older than Rilke, born in St Petersburg, the daughter of a Russian general. They become lifelong friends. Changes his first name to Rainer.

1898: divides his time between Italy and Germany. Publishes his fourth book of poems, *Advent*.

1899: meets writer Hugo von Hofmannsthal in Vienna. First trip to Russia with Lou Salomé and husband. Visits Tolstoy. Publication of *Prague Stories* and a collection of poems, *To Celebrate Myself* (dedicated to Lou).

1900: learns Danish in order to read Kierkegaard and J. P. Jacobsen. Has second thoughts about Ibsen as his plays aren't going well. Intensive preparation in language acquisition for second trip to Russia with Lou (without husband) and visits Tolstoy again. Less happily. Invited to the artist colony in Worpswede, North Germany, by Heinrich Vogeler. There meets the painter Paula Becker and sculptor Clara Westhoff, a pupil of Rodin. Publishes first volume of *Tales of the Good Lord*.

1901: refused by Paula, he marries Clara in April. Daughter, Ruth, born on the 10th December. Temporary cooling in the friendship with Lou. His theatrical ambitions fail. The first performance of *Ordinary Everyday Life* (based on Chekhov's *The Seagull*) in Berlin is the last. Translates Kierkegaard's letters of rejection to his fiancée Regine Olsen.

1902: marriage on the rocks. Goes to Paris to write a book on Rodin. Clara follows him, leaving Ruth behind with her family. The reconciliation is short-lived. *Book of Images* published. Inspired by Rodin, composes 'The Panther', the first of his modernist 'Thing-poems' (*dinggedichte*). Commissioned by Worpswede to write a monograph, he returns briefly.

1903: friends again with Lou, but mainly by letter. Publishes the Rodin and Worpswede monographs. First letter to Franz Xaver Kappus, a young poet/military cadet. Nine more to follow over the next five years (*Letters to a Young Poet*, 1929). Letters to Clara and Lou about Paris get him started on a novel. Problems with Rodin lead to a 'silent quarrel'. Takes time out from Paris to travel in Italy. In September installs himself in Rome (briefly visited by Clara). Ellen Key, the Swedish proto-feminist, writes admiringly of *Tales of the Good Lord*. An extensive correspondence ensues.

1904: sojourn in Sweden and Denmark under the aegis of Ellen Key. Brief flirtation with her women's rights movement. Thanks to Ellen Key, he starts seriously on the novel *The Notebooks of Malte Laurids Brigge*. Publishes second volume of *Tales of the Good Lord* (dedicated to Ellen Key).

1905: a peripatetic pattern of living as a guest in friends' mansions is normalised. While staying with Lou in Castletown, receives an affectionate letter from Rodin. Returns to Paris after detour to see Clara over money problems. Karl von Heydt, banker and writer, solves them. Briefly Rodin's private secretary and, subsequently, 'advocate' on German lecture tours.

1906: death of his father interrupts his second lecture tour. Quarrels again with Rodin (more loudly). Voyages to Belgium. Moves to Capri for Christmas. Published *The Lay of the Love and Death of Cornet Christoph Rilke*, a fantasy tale. Reissues *The Book of Images* with additional poems including 'Loneliness is like rain...', a poem that might make Clara wince.

1907: still in Italy for the first half of the year (Capri, Naples, Venice and Rome). And passes the remainder between Paris, Prague and Vienna (where he met Kassner and Hugo von Hofmannsthal) before returning to Venice. Starts a correspondence with the brilliant Baroness Sidonie Nadherny, a lifelong one as with Lou but without the baggage. Published his *New* ('Thing') *Poems*, his modernist debut. Extraordinary letter to Clara about Cézanne exhibition in Paris. Revised monograph on Rodin re-issued. Despite their estrangement, his admiration remains staunch. Third lecture tour cut short in Vienna by the death of Paula Modersohn-Becker after childbirth. Returns to Germany to be with Clara.

1908: lives between Paris and Capri. Publishes the translation of Elizabeth Barrett Browning's *Faux Sonnets from the Portuguese*, made with Alice Faehndrich in Capri two years before, and a second volume of *New* ('Thing') *Poems*. Last letter to Kappus, the young poet. Writes 'Requiem for a Friend' on the anniversary of Paula Modersohn-Becker's death.

On Clara's initiative he moves into the attic room of the Hotel Biron (no longer Grand) to finish his novel. Rodin needs a larger studio, and on Rilke's instigation rents a floor. The hotel was to become the Rodin Museum.

1909: Rilke sidetracks from the novel to concentrate on reissues of early poems. Doubts about the earthy modernism of the 'thing-poems' leads to an aesthetic crisis. Hesitations with finishing the novel. Travels extensively in the South of France. Pilgrimage to the studio of Cezanne (recently deceased) in Aix-en-Provence. In Arles experiences an epiphany in Alyscamps, the necropolis painted by Van Gogh. It gives him a lead to the closing pages of the novel. On return to Paris meets Princess Marie von Thurn und Taxis, who is to become his most important patron and second-best friend.

1910: *The Notebooks of Malte Laurids Brigge* finally delivered to his publisher (Insel-Verlag). *The Notebooks* comes out in the summer. He celebrates it by visiting Princess Marie in Duino, Italy, and winters in North Africa, ending up in Egypt.

Later Years

1911–2: travels, including Spain (Toledo, Ronda). Translates almost half of St Augustine's *Confessions*, Gide's *Return of the Prodigal Son* and *D'amour de Madelaine* (a sermon believed to be by Abbe Bonnet). While staying in Duino Castle with Princess Marie during a storm (1912), hears the first line of the *Duino Elegies*.

1913: publishes T*he Life of the Virgin Mary*. Meets Freud at a conference with Lou. Spends summer in Venice, sitting at the feet of Eleanora Duse, the tragic actress (whose early days he wrote about in the novel).

1914: money worries relieved by an anonymous donation of 10,000 crowns from a fund for poets now known to be created by Ludwig Wittgenstein. Agrees a divorce in principle with Clara but by Austrian law it would require him to renounce his Catholicism. He is stranded back in Germany by the declaration of the Great War and can't go back to Paris. Publishes patriotic poems in the newspaper and immediately regrets it. Consults his student guru Alfred Schuler, the Gnostic philosopher, on ancient Teutonic burial practices.

1915: called up by the Austro-Hungarian army but fails the physical. Assigned to the Imperial Army Archives, a depressing job. Writes seven poems celebrating the phallus.

1916: discharged from the army in June. Liquidity problems due to the war. Artist Lou Albert-Lasard paints a flattering portrait (much used in the republication of his works). He lodges with her. Participates in cultural life in Vienna (Kassner, Zweig, Karl Kraus, Kokoschka).

1917: lives between Munich and Berlin. Translates the French Renaissance *Sonnets of Louise Labè* (La Belle Cordiére) The October Revolution in Russia coincides with the first signs of a blood condition (leukaemia).

1919: depressed by the vengeful aftermath of the Great War, leaves Germany for good. Morale restored by his intimate friendship with Baladine ('Merline') Klossowska, mother of the painter Balthus, Back writing poetry and translating Mallarmé.

1920: moves to the Valais region (and holidays in Italy).

1921 Werner Reinhart, a patron of the arts, buys the rundown Muzot Castle and has it fitted it out for Rilke rent-free. Translates Valéry's long poem 'Le cimetiére marin' ('Graveyard by the sea'). Writes 'The Testament', a text on why for his poetry's sake he must distance himself from 'Merline' Klossowski.

1922: completes *The Sonnets to Orpheu* in relative calm and the *Duino Elegies* in a creative 'hurricane' which leaves him exhausted ('Every fibre in me, every tissue, bent and cracked'). Writes the fictive 'Letter from a Young Worker'.

1923–6: attends various clinics for his blood condition. After a visit from Clara, he recovers sufficiently to return to Paris, where he is feted by Gide, Valéry and their friends. Disconsolate with what he perceives as their lack of sincerity, he returns to his castle, where he welcomes visits by young admirers. Still writing letters and poems, he dies of leukaemia on 29 December 1926, aged fifty-two. In the last year his correspondence with Boris Pasternak and Marina Tsvetayeva was a lifeline. 'A letter is like an otherworldly communication, less perfect than a dream, but subject to the same rules. Neither the one or the other can be produced on command. You neither write a letter, nor dream a dream when you want to, but when *it* wants to: the letter – to be written; the dream – to be dreamed,' Marina to Rainer Maria/Boris, 1926.

1929: Kappus edits and publishes *Letters to a Young Poet*.

1931: death of Rilke's mother, Sophia.

1936–9: Ruth Sieber-Rilke edits six volumes of Rilke's letters with her husband.

1954: death of Clara Rilke.

1972: death of Ruth

1976 German publication of Rilke's collected works (co-edited by Ruth).

First published in Great Britain by:

Ashgrove Publishing

an imprint of:

Hollydata Publishers Ltd
21 Ewen House
Caledonian Road
London N1 0SH

© James Hogan, 2023

The right of Augustus Young (James Hogan) to be identified as the author of this work has been asserted by him in accordance with the Copyright, Designs and Patents Act 1988.

No part of this publication may be reproduced, stored in a retrieval system or transmitted, in any form or by any means, electronic, mechanical, photo-copying, recording or otherwise, without the prior permission of the publisher.

ISBN 978 185398 205 7

First Edition

Book design by Brad Thompson

Printed and bound in England